The New Day Devotional

We must work the works of Him who sent Me, as long as it is day...
John 9:4

Every day is a gift of God to learn, love and serve!

BY DAVID E. GUNDRUM

(These daily devotions were given weekly over a period of years in "The Antiochan," a weekly newsletter written by David Gundrum, Director of Church Extension Ministries for the Bible Fellowship Church denomination.)

WESTBOW
PRESS®
A DIVISION OF THOMAS NELSON
& ZONDERVAN

WestBow Press books may be ordered through booksellers or by contacting:

WestBow Press
A Division of Thomas Nelson & Zondervan
1663 Liberty Drive
Bloomington, IN 47403
www.westbowpress.com
1 (866) 928-1240

ISBN: 978-1-5127-4717-1 (sc)
ISBN: 978-1-5127-4718-8 (hc)
ISBN: 978-1-5127-4716-4 (e)

Library of Congress Control Number: 2016910129

Print information available on the last page.

WestBow Press rev. date: 9/19/2016

Acknowledgments

I would like to give glory and praise to God for the way the Holy Spirt guided me through compiling this devotional and leading me to the scripture texts and thoughts that accompany each daily devotional. Without His guidance this devotional would not have become a reality, Soli Deo Gloria!

I want to thank my diligent Administrative Assistant, Ruth Richards and Special Project Coordinator, Carol Snyder for the hours of editing they did on the devotional.

I also want to thank the hundreds of supporters who receive my weekly Antiochan Report, where the devotionals were gleaned, and so faithfully read the report and pray for my ministry.

Last, but very importantly, I want thank my wife Donna for putting up with my crazy and busy schedule these past 30 years of ministry. She is always there to support me with her understanding of my service to the Lord.

The New Day Devotional *is a daily guide designed to challenge the reader to reflect on God's sovereignty, and on the application of His greatness and truth to all of life. Theologically motivated, the writings are focused on the biblical teaching of God's sovereign and redemptive grace. The Bible's revelation of God, Lord and Creator of all things, is our ultimate and absolute guide and authority for all of worship and life.*

This devotional seeks to assist Christians in their apprehension of God's majesty, which bends low to lift up sinners through salvation in Jesus Christ and His great sacrifice on Calvary. Children of God are responsible not only to grow in the grace and the knowledge of Christ, but also to be a reflection of Christ in the way they think, live and act. May this guide help readers to grow in humility and Christ-likeness.

This guide may also act as a witness to unbelievers as they read the many exhortations to repent and believe upon the Lord Jesus Christ for salvation.

The readings unashamedly declare the view of God and His salvation which is best expressed as a Reformed and Calvinistic vista of the greatness of God and the depravity of humans. God redeems lost sinners, secures their eternal salvation, and lifts them to sainthood. This high view of God and the salvation He provides charges the reader to live and act in thanksgiving and obedience to God for His great gift of mercy and grace.

Each daily devotion has four parts. Part one presents text along with remarks, observations and exhortations. Part two lists Scripture references for reading and meditation. Part three presents probing questions and suggests applications; and part four directs prayer and praise for the Word, and for personal changes in thinking and action.

May the New Day Devotional *lift your mind to a high and majestic view of God and provide a motivation for daily living the light of Christ in a world of growing darkness.*

> *Oh, the depth of the riches both of the wisdom and knowledge of God! How unsearchable are His judgments and unfathomable His ways! For who has known the mind of the Lord, or who became His counselor? Or who has first given to Him that it might be paid back to him again? For from Him and through Him and to Him are all things. To Him be the glory forever. Amen. (Romans 11: 33-36)*

LIFE RESOLUTIONS

Ephesians 4:7 But to each one of us grace was given according to the measure of Christ's gift.

A new year! A time to evaluate the past year and make resolutions for the year ahead! I am reminded of the extensive list of resolutions which Jonathan Edwards—theologian and preacher of the Great Awakening—constructed. They were not meant merely to be followed for a given year and evaluated at the end of that year before preparing another list for the following year. No! Instead, his dozens of resolutions were life resolutions to be evaluated at the end of each day, and if not met, to be corrected at the dawn of the new day! In all of these resolutions, a common theme is evident: the theme of God's grace. I believe Edwards realized that it was the measure of God's grace given to him which allowed him the ability to live out his resolutions. Christ gives to His children His grace to not only carry out the development of particular spiritual gifts, but also to daily live holy and obedient lives. If you, like I, have made some resolutions, let them be life resolutions, evaluated daily, and endorsed and empowered by the grace of Christ.

*Look it up – **Ecclesiastes 5:4; Psalm 119:15–16; Daniel 1:8***

*This truth for me – **What life resolutions need to be made in order for your heart to be more in line with Christ's holiness?***

_____

_____

_____

*Pray – **For God to give you His power to fulfill your life resolutions.***

GRACE OVERCOMES FATIGUE

2 Corinthians 12:9 ...*My grace is sufficient for you, for My power is made perfect in weakness... (NIV)*

Vince Lombardi, the former coach of the championship Green Bay football teams of the 1960s, once stated, "Fatigue makes cowards of us all." So often the work of the Lord can be physically, emotionally and spiritually fatiguing. Before a servant realizes it, he or she may be showing the signs of fatigue: short attitudes, the Elijah complex of desiring to quit, questioning whether Christian service is really worth all the aggravation, and hoping that people would just disappear.

You may be asking, "How does he know how I feel?" Most likely it is because I have been there, and have come across our brothers and sisters in ministry who are crying out for relief because of fatigue. May I remind those who are in a stage of fatigue that the Lord's work does not need to be so burdensome. With proper rest, exposure of your needs to those you know will care, special quiet times with the Lord in His Word and in prayer, and waiting for His refreshing Spirit to blow some new fervency into your ministry, God will revive those who are fatigued. In John 1, we are reminded that the same grace which saved us unto eternity also continues to abound to us. In 2 Corinthians 12, a fatigued yet revived apostle tells us that God's grace is always sufficient for us—at its greatest power when we are at our lowest valleys!

*Look it up – **John 1:16; 2 Corinthians 9:8; Hebrews 4:16***

*This truth for me – **Do you doubt God's ability to help you? Renew your trust in the Lord and write out your commitment to believe He is able.***

---

*Pray – **That God will reveal His power to you in His answer to your prayers.***

IN THE BATTLE

1 Samuel 17:47 ...*for the battle is the LORD'S...*

When people greet one another, someone will often ask, "How are you doing?" My response is simple, "I'm in the battle!" The Christian is called to be a warrior for Christ ... but what is the battle we fight? In many places, Christians face severe persecution, brutality, isolation, physical attacks and imprisonment. Yet, as tragic as these physical battles are, the enduring battle for the Christian, whether under persecution or living in a peaceful setting, is the battle the Apostle Paul referred to in Romans 7:14-25, *For we know that the Law is spiritual; but I am of flesh...* The supreme battle each Christian fights is this battle of flesh versus spirit, as Paul said, *...for I am not practicing what I would like to do, but I am doing the very thing I hate.* Every Christian struggles in this conflict between the remaining old sin nature and the victorious new nature in Christ . . . yes, the *victorious new nature.* Believer, the new nature is victorious! It is forged in you by the hand of God, through Christ, by the power of the Holy Spirit. We fight this sin-flesh battle but the war is won. Christ is the Victor and we are victorious in Him!

> *Wretched man that I am! Who will set me free...? Thanks be to God through Jesus Christ, our Lord!... (Romans 7:24-25); ...we overwhelmingly conquer through Him who loved us. (Romans 8:37); But thanks be to God, who gives us the victory through our Lord Jesus Christ. (1 Corinthians 15:57); And who is the one who overcomes the world, but he who believes that Jesus is the Son of God? (1 John 5:5)*

*Look it up – **1 Peter 5:9; Ephesians 6:10; Philippians 4:1***

*This truth for me – **What battles are you fighting at this time? List them.***

_____

_____

_____

*Pray – **For God to fight the battles in your life and give you the victory.***

SAVED BY GRACE ALONE

Romans 9:16 ...*it does not depend on the man who wills or the man who runs...*

This section of Scripture has always been one of my favorites. It is clear in its focus on God's sovereignty in salvation. I remember when I was going through our denomination's orientation seminar for credentials, the brother teaching this doctrine took us to Romans 9 and showed us that salvation is entirely of the Lord. It seems to me that Romans 9 is the commentary on Jonah's experiences with the Lord as recorded in the Old Testament. Jonah ran from God. He rebelled against the Lord's will and ended up distressed and even wanting death. But when he ended up in the stomach of the great fish, God got hold of Jonah. He then repented and prayed, and concluded his prayer by crying out, **"Salvation is from the Lord."** This is exactly what Romans 9 says - *salvation is completely from the Lord.* Man cannot be saved by his own power, he cannot receive salvation by his ability, he cannot run or work for salvation. Salvation must come from God! And when it does, the sinner is able to cry out, as Jonah did, and receive salvation. Salvation is from the Lord to sinners dead in their trespasses and sin. If you are not born again, cry out to the God of salvation, repent of your sins, and receive Jesus Christ as your Savior and Lord.

"'Oh,' saith one, 'are good works of no use?' God's works are of use when a man is saved, they are the evidences of his being saved; but good works do not save a man, good works do not influence the mind of God to save a man, for if so, salvation would be a matter of debt and not of grace." Charles Spurgeon

Look it up – **Romans 4:1-6; Ephesians 1:7; Ephesians 2:8–9**

This truth for me – **Write what Christ did for you and see that your works cannot compare to His work of salvation for you.**

_____

_____

_____

Pray – **For God to show you that your salvation is secure in Christ and confirm this great truth in your heart.**

LIVING DAY BY DAY IN FAITH

Romans 1:17 ...the righteous shall live by faith. (ESV)

This doctrinal truth and scriptural statement turned the first century upside down! It was taught and preached by Paul, Barnabas, Silas, Luke, Timothy and many others that glory will reveal. Some sixteen hundred years later the world again would be transformed by the efforts of Reformers like Wycliffe, Tyndale, Hus, Luther, Melancthon, Calvin and Zwingli. We often forget that for these men there were no alternative churches to the Church of Rome. They had to plant churches which would preach and teach biblical truth.

At times I find myself *knowing* this great truth—salvation by faith alone—but *forgetting* that faith alone not only accomplished my salvation, but also extends to all my Christian life. When I don't see the outcome of a decision to be made, *faith alone;* when I can't understand the purpose of difficult circumstances, *faith alone;* when I think I can do it, and then find that I lack wisdom and strength, *faith alone.* The God-given faith which enables a sinner to cry out for salvation is also the faith needed through all of life. *Faith alone* does not have its conclusion at the cross. No, it is demanded of us as we carry that cross through life until we see Him face to face. Then faith becomes sight!

*Look it up – **Luke 12:22–32; Galatians 2:16; Hebrews 11:1–3,6***

*This truth for me – **In what areas of your life do you exercise little faith, and why is your faith so little in these areas?***

_____

_____

_____

*Pray – **That God will help you see that the faith He gave you was powerful enough to save you for all eternity and is powerful enough for all your life.***

REMEMBERING THOSE CALLED TO SERVE

Deuteronomy 25:4 You shall not muzzle the ox while he is threshing.

The Apostle Paul applied these Old Testament words to the New Testament concept of supporting those who labor in preaching and teaching the Word (1 Corinthians 9; 1 Timothy 5). Our missionaries—on both foreign fields and here in America planting churches—can find themselves muzzled when they lack support for themselves and their families. The work of the Lord is hindered and can easily become stagnant when God's servant finds it necessary to spend his time in providing for his and his family's daily needs. The oxen mentioned in the Old Testament had the right to eat the grain left on the threshing floor because it worked to harvest the grain. Similarly, the Lord's workers have the right to be paid for their Kingdom services in the harvest of souls. Today, consider those who labor in the vineyard of missions here and abroad, and thank God for their sacrifice.

*Look it up – **Philippians 4:14-18; 1 Corinthians 9:11-14; Colossians 4:3***

*This truth for me – **Do you support the mission of the Kingdom? How can you be more supportive of these missionaries in prayer and financial giving?***

_____

_____

_____

*Pray – **For God to give you a Kingdom vision and open doors to serve in your part of the Kingdom and support those who serve around the world.***

GO AND TELL

Luke 8:39 ...describe what great things God has done for you...

When was the last time you told someone what great things God did for you when He saved you? Christians call this their testimony. For the man possessed by the legion of demons in Luke 8, the moment Jesus exorcised the evil spirits and saved the man, he asked Jesus if he could be part of the band of disciples. But Jesus told him to go home and tell people that Jesus saved him. Not many Christians get to take their testimonies on the road, sharing it at a crusade or on television, but all Christians are told to go and tell.

Wow! What a story this man had to tell ... once shackled to demons, then set free by the Lord. Actually, however, every Christian has a story to tell. It may not be as dramatic as this man's testimony, but every Christian's testimony is unique and powerful. You see, the power of our testimony does not rest on the drama, but rather, on the power of our salvation centered in God saving us ... sinners in need of mercy and grace. ***Go and tell!***

*Look it up – **Mark 16:20; Luke 9:6; Acts 11:20***

*This truth for me – **Are you shy or scared when it comes to sharing the Gospel? Write down what scares you about giving your testimony or witnessing.***

_____

_____

_____

*Pray – **For God to give you the boldness to share Jesus with others and the alertness and courage to go through the open doors to share with people.***

SEEKING JUSTICE

Psalm 83:13 *O my God, make them like the whirling dust...*

Should a Christian invoke evil or Imprecation (a spoken curse) on another person? Psalm 83, along with a number of other psalms, are labeled *imprecatory psalms*. The writers of these psalms looked at the evil things being done by evil people and called upon God to intervene and bring destruction to such evil people. In the book of Nehemiah, the writer prays for God to deal harshly with the two governors opposing the efforts to rebuild the wall around Jerusalem. On other occasions God is asked to deal with the enemies of His people and those doing evil.

It is not wrong for God's people to pray and ask God to bring justice upon those who are evil and seeking to do evil. Yet, we must weigh our motivations and attitudes when we pray in such a manner. Are our imprecatory prayers for God's glory or from a vengeful heart? Are such prayers and invocations for the purpose of desiring that such evil people come to a saving knowledge of Christ? Asaph, the writer of Psalm 83, after invoking God's wrath to fall upon the enemies of God, concludes with this statement, *...pursue them... terrify them...fill their faces with dishonor, that they may seek Your name...that they may know that You alone...are the Most High over all the earth.* **We should seek justice and always seek it for the glory of God!**

Look it up – **Deuteronomy 16:20; Amos 5:24; Luke 11:42**

This truth for me – **What injustice exists in my city, my state, my country and what can I do about the injustice around me?**

_____

_____

_____

Pray – **For God to open your eyes to the injustice around you. Pray for those affected by abuse, neglect, poverty, abortion and other attacks on humanity.**

WAITING UPON THE LORD

Exodus 14:13 ...Stand by and see the salvation of the LORD...

When I was a young boy, my mother used to say to me, "Please, Davy"—yeah, that was her pet name for me—"can't you ever stand still?" As I look back on my life, and even review times in my life now, I still have a problem with standing still. In a spiritual sense, it can be perplexing to stand still before the Lord and WAIT in order to see His hand move. At times, I would imagine you can be like I am. We want to see things done yesterday! We think, I must do something right now! It is difficult to wait upon the Lord.

How many times do we miss the power of God when we jump in and run instead of standing still? How often are we cut short the real blessing of God and receive only what we ourselves carved out by running ahead of Him? Christians are faced with many anxious moments and times of wanting to either run ahead or run away. As the nation of Israel faced the Red Sea and heard the approaching hoof beats of Pharaoh's chariots, they wanted to run. But knowing that the Lord would rescue them, Moses commanded them to stand still, *The Lord will fight for you while you keep silent.* (v. 14) If the Lord would fight for such a grumbling and thankless people like Israel, how much more will our Father in heaven fight for His precious children who have been bought by the blood of His Son.

Look it up – **Psalm 46:10; Psalm 131:2; Isaiah 40:31**

This truth for me – **What makes you anxious? List those places or people you lose patience with and why.**

_____

_____

_____

Pray – **For the Lord to help you stand still and be silent, so that you may see His mighty hand move in ways you never could have imagined!**

WILLING TO SERVE

Romans 12:1 ...by the mercies of God...which is your spiritual service...

I must or *I will?* Is there a difference between these terms? I believe there is, especially when it comes to serving the Lord. If I look at my service to the Lord through the *I must* lens, then I might have a tendency to become legalistic in my service to God. I must do this or that in order to either maintain or acquire God's grace. Also, if my service is motivated by *I must,* then I might be susceptible to the *give-to-get* mentality—"God, I did what you said I must do; now you must do thus and so for me." In ministry, I can find myself falling prey to these *I must* fallacies. Certainly there are things which are necessary to our Christian lives and ministries; yet what is necessary is not best accomplished by an *I must* attitude, but rather an *I will* attitude. "I will serve you, Lord, and obey you because you graced your mercy upon me."

The Apostle Paul, after explaining the mercies of God—reconciliation, justification and sanctification—exhorts Christians to consider their worthy response to such acts of sovereign mercy. Our response should be a willing life of service, not motivated by the heaviness of a legalistic *I must* mentality, but rather the worthy submissive response, *I will.* We serve because we were first served by the perfect willing Servant, our Lord Jesus Christ.

*Look it up – **Deuteronomy 10:12; Romans 7:6; 2 Corinthians 6:4***

*This truth for me – **Have you discovered your spiritual gift? List it below. Are you using it to serve the Lord and His Church? If not, list what is hindering you.***

_____

_____

_____

*Pray – **For God to reveal your spiritual gift(s) if you have not discovered your gift(s), and pray for the Spirit to give you the energy and open door to serve.***

BE REFRESHED

Mark 3:7 And Jesus withdrew...

I am so appreciative of God's selective revelation. In Scripture, He reveals all He wants us to know and all that will best nourish our souls. God selectively placed the words—*Jesus withdrew*—in His Word to reveal His humanity and tell us of His need for refreshment. With these words, He also reminds us, especially those of us in ministry, that there are times when we need to withdraw from the rigors of life and ministry. We need to be refreshed for the next encounters of our callings.

I was blessed in my recent withdrawal, better known as vacation. I withdrew with my family and found, as I usually do, a renewed sense of strength. After continual ministry and work, we tend to grow weary, anxious and testy. Withdrawal for a time often relieves the burdened body and spirit. May I also suggest that both good yearly vacations, as well as weekly times of withdrawal, are necessary? My wife and I call Friday our family day. Only funerals or dire—and I do say *dire*—emergencies interrupt this day. These times of withdrawal are necessary for ministers of grace and those who work in and out of the house. If you are not setting time aside to withdraw, please do so. I pray God will richly refresh you.

Look it up – **Genesis 2:2–3; Romans 15:32; Exodus 31:17**

This truth for me – **Write out what things or places refresh you. Do you take enough time for refreshment? If not, what must you do to gain proper rest?**

_____

_____

_____

Pray – **For God to give you the diligence to commit to taking time to withdraw and rest by yourself, and with your spouse and family, if married.**

LET GOD DEFEND YOU

Exodus 23:22 ...I will be an enemy to your enemies and an adversary to your adversaries.

This is the passage upon which A.W. Tozer based one of his vows in his fine pamphlet, *Five Vows for Spiritual Power* (available online). The vow was, "... never defend yourself." I have found that there is tremendous pressure upon Christian ministers to be successful and to hit a home run every time they step into the pulpit. But on the ball field, home runs are few and far between; batting over .300 (3 hits out of ten) is quite an accomplishment. Yet, when it comes to being a pastor, church planter or Christian leader, there are some high expectations. When those expectations are not met—either in the mind of others or in ourselves—we have the natural tendency to defend ourselves, to have a rationale for why we didn't meet expectations. Not only Christian leaders have this problem; we all fight this battle. And yet, seeking to defend oneself can further complicate the situation. We might have the tendency to hedge the truth, to find reasons for not succeeding, or to deceive ourselves and others into thinking our lack of success wasn't that bad.

When Ananias and Sapphira defended their holding back money from the church from the sale of their property, they ended up lying to the Holy Spirit. Their punishment was death! We are not going to hit a home run with everything we attempt, and when we fail, it's our failures that often become our greatest testaments to God's grace. Therefore, let God defend you and allow His grace to support you in times when things don't go as planned.

*Look it up – **Psalm 46:1-3; Psalm 91:1,2; Jude 24,25***

*This truth for me – **List a time you felt that you needed to defend yourself.***

_____

_____

_____

*Pray – **For God to give you the understanding of how big and powerful He is to help in times of need.***

INTIMACY WITH JESUS

Hebrews 4:15 For we do not have a high priest who cannot sympathize with our weaknesses...

Have you ever wondered how our all-powerful Savior could possibly know weakness or be able to sympathize with our low moments and times of exhaustion? I submit three reasons for such knowledge. First, our Savior who is all-powerful is also all-knowing. David nailed down this perfection of omniscience in Psalm 139:1-3: *...You know...You understand...You scrutinize... and are intimately acquainted...* Jesus, in His divine nature, has the perfect ability to know our weaknesses. In fact, He knows me better than I know myself because He is God. Second, knowing is one thing, but sympathizing is another. Yet He can sympathize with my weaknesses because, as John 1:14a says, *And the Word became flesh, and dwelt among us.* Jesus assumed real humanity, suffered fatigue and distress, and experienced the hatred and abuse of others. He suffered pain and sorrow; He died for you and me. Thirdly, He knows and sympathizes with our weaknesses because He loves us with an everlasting love. As a pastor, it took time and prayer for me to develop a love for the flock; it just didn't happen. But year after year, by God's grace, I learned what it meant to love those I was called to shepherd. The assurance that my love was sincere came when I would visit one of the suffering sheep and I could feel their pain. Our High Priest, Jesus Christ, perfectly knows our weaknesses. Beyond that, He can sympathize with us at our lowest moments because He loves us with an unbounded love! Praise His holy name!

*Look it up – **Matthew 20:28; 1 Timothy 2:5; Hebrews 4:14–16***

*This truth for me – **What weakness do you have that needs to be turned over to Jesus?***

_____

_____

_____

*Pray – **That you will know how close Jesus is to you at all times.***

THE RIGHTEOUSNESS OF CHRIST

Isaiah 61:10 ...He has wrapped me with a robe of righteousness...

What beautiful word pictures are revealed in the Scriptures! One such word picture is that of being *robed in righteousness.* The prophet sees God's people as a peculiar people who are wearing garments of salvation and robes of righteousness. However, the mystery that was veiled from the prophet is that this righteousness is Christ Himself. For the Christian, we are robed in Christ. His righteousness has been imputed to the elect by means of His atonement on the Cross: *...through one act of righteousness, there resulted justification...* (Romans 5:18); *...the new self...has been created in righteousness...* (Ephesians 4:24). I think back when Mom would bundle me up to face the chilling winds of winter. She wrapped me up with so many garments that I could hardly move. Yet, the longer I was out in the cold, the more thankful I became for her care and thoughtfulness in putting those layers of clothing on me. As we face the elements of the world—the fiery darts of Satan and the battle with the flesh—we should become more and more thankful for this robe of Christ's righteousness that bundles us and protects us from those harsh, worldly elements. This robe can transform into a breastplate of righteousness and provide us with the assurance that we are His and He is ours. With Christ's robe there comes a responsibility to *...pursue righteousness.* May our Lord's robe of righteousness be our protection, comfort and warmth. May we grow in *His grace and His righteousness.*

*Look it up – **Philippians 3:8-9; 2 Timothy 4:8; 1 Peter 2:24***

*This truth for me – **Meditate on the depth of the righteousness that has been imputed (given) to you in Christ. Write your thankfulness for His righteousness.***

---

*Pray – **That God will give you the power to live in the light of Christ's righteousness so that all will see that you wear His beautiful robe.***

ARE YOU SHARING CHRIST

Acts 26:17-18 ...I am sending you, to open their eyes so that they may turn from darkness to light...

The word for *turn* in the Bible is most commonly translated *convert*. Standing before Agrippa, Paul stated his Christ-given commission to convert sinners. "But wait a minute," some may say. "Doesn't the idea of Christians seeking to convert sinners tread on a high view of God's sovereignty?" Some condemn any Gospel presentation that uses ideas as: *YOU must accept the Gospel* or *YOU must believe*. When the great missionary, William Carey, declared that we are to take the Gospel to the world, he was told, *"...sit down, young man,.... when God is pleased to convert the heathen, He will do it without your aid, or mine!"*

Have we lost the initiative to take the Gospel to the unsaved? Are we failing because we don't understand that our sovereign God has purposed and planned to save His elect through the Gospel proclamation? Do we understand that He uses His people to witness to sinners and seek conversions? I praise God for my training at a seminary that upheld the great sovereignty of our God. I am thankful for mentors who demonstrated how to honor God's sovereignty by following His command to be His witnesses. Are you exercising our evangelistic commission in order to see people *turn* to Christ? Don't let today pass by without witnessing to an unbeliever.

Look it up – **Luke 14:23; Acts 1:8; 2 Corinthians 5:20**

This truth for me – **Name those to whom you have witnessed. If your list is small or non-existent, then list those who need to hear the Gospel message.**

_____

_____

_____

Pray – **For God to give you eyes to see those who are heading to an eternity of damnation, and a mouth to share Jesus.**

TRIAL LEADS TO A GREATER SENSE OF GOD

Lamentations 3:21 ...Therefore I have hope...

Affliction, wormwood, wandering and bitterness are what precede Jeremiah's confirmation of the faithfulness of God. Isn't this so often the case: that what precedes our greatest acknowledgments of God's faithfulness are circumstances that have brought us low? I recall a number of times of testing when I was distressed and worn out by the circumstances of those trials. But it was there in the flames of trial that I discovered the Spirit's kindling of a renewed sense of God's faithfulness. Our Lord entered Gethsemane *very distressed and troubled* and *deeply grieved* (Mark 14:33,34). He then goes on to pray, *Abba! Father! All things are possible for You; remove this cup from me; yet not what I will, but what You will* (v. 36). At this most agonizing point in our Lord's trek to the Cross, His obedient trust in the Father's faithfulness is revealed: *not my will but your will!* He is faithful and therefore I have hope even when I face seemingly hopeless circumstances.

> **The Lord's lovingkindnesses indeed never cease, For His compassions never fail. They are new every morning; Great is Thy faithfulness.**
> **(Lamentations 3:22, 23)**

"Perhaps, O tried soul, the Lord is doing this to develop thy graces. There are some of thy graces which would never be discovered if it were not for thy trials. Dost thou not know that thy faith never looks so grand in summer weather as it does in winter?" Charles Spurgeon – Morning by Morning – Feb. 18

Look it up – **Matthew 11:28–30; James 1:2; 1 Peter 1:6-7**

This truth for me – **What trials are you going through? List them. How would you like to see God settle these trials?**

Pray – **For God to give you His vision for your trials and to see that from your trials there will be growth and wisdom for the days ahead of you.**

GRACE IS GREATER THAN ALL OUR SIN

Romans 5:20 ...where sin increased, grace abounded...

Where was it that sin reached its pinnacle and grace was most powerful? Some might say that sin was at its greatest in the concentration camps of World War II, or at the savage murdering of thousands by the Communists in China and Cambodia. Others may say that sin is at its greatest point when a child or an innocent person is abused or murdered. The Apostle Paul, in his letter to the Christians in Rome, implies that there was another place where sin increased and grace abounded, as G. Campbell Morgan writes, *"...sin deepened into densest darkness [on the cross], and grace broke forth in brightest brilliance [on the cross]."* The cross is where we see sin at its worse—darkest and most heinous. The cross reminds us that sin called for the perfect, unblemished Son of God to come and be brutally murdered at Calvary. Yet, in this death of deaths, when sin reached its pinnacle, grace soared higher and broke through to cover sin, bringing an end to the reign of sin and death. Where sin increased, grace abounded beyond human comprehension. This same abounding grace that defeated sin and death is freely given to every believer. It is available to us when sin is most oppressive. If times are dark in your Christian life, call upon the Lord for a special portion and indwelling of His grace to overcome the darkness.

Look it up – ***Romans 5:20, 21; 2 Corinthians 9:8; Ephesians 1:6–8***

This truth for me – ***Note some situations in your life where God's grace defeated the sin you were fighting.***

_____

_____

_____

Pray – ***For God to show you how great His grace not only saves you but keeps you until that day when He calls you home.***

TRUE HUMILITY

Philippians 2:5 Let the same mind be in you...(NRSV)

What mind is the Apostle speaking about? It is the mind of Christ. How is the mind of Christ characterized? By humility! It sounds a little like we are going down the path of a catechetical exercise. What lies at the heart of these questions is the perfection of Christ we are told we can possess, namely, *His humility.* John Calvin wrote in his <u>*Golden Booklet of the True Christian Life*</u>, *"The most effective poison to lead us to ruin is to boast in ourselves, in our own wisdom and will power. The only escape to safety is simply to follow the guidance of the Lord."* The antidote for the poison of pride is to humble ourselves before God and give Him *all* the glory even when our yearnings only desire an ounce of *me-ism.* In that mere ounce there lies enough poison to kill the glory we should give to God. Take note that God is due *all* glory and we are due none. How ironic that in this selflessness we are lifted up. But if we lift ourselves up, even a millimeter, we bring ourselves and God down. The Apostle Paul epitomized humility by reminding us that God became a man, a servant, and then died His death, even death on a cross.

In that moment of divine humility, we were lifted up for eternity!
Hallelujah, what a Savior!

Look it up – **Romans 8:3; Isaiah 42:2-3; Zechariah 9:9**

This truth for me – **Write out your definition of humility. Are there areas in your life that call for you to exercise a more humble spirit?**

_____

_____

_____

Pray – **For God to help you see the humility of Christ and His perfect expression of humility – God dying on the Cross.**

THE WEAKNESS OF HUMAN EFFORT

John 6:60 ...This is a difficult statement; who can listen to it?

"Be all that you can be." The strong implication of this familiar statement is that we, in and of ourselves, can do anything we set our minds and hands to accomplish. While listening to the World Series, I heard the account of a player from the Dominican Republic. The announcer stated that when the professional ballplayer was a boy, he promised his mother that one day he would be a famous baseball player and buy his mother a house of her own. His vow to his mother came true when he signed his first major league contract with the Los Angeles Dodgers. Hearing a story like this motivates us to think that if we really want something to happen, all we have to do is throw into the mixing bowl of success some hard work, commitment and a little talent. And while we need to work hard and diligently to realize our earthy dreams and aspirations, this will never work with eternal matters. It was hard for those following Christ to hear that He alone was their salvation and that they needed to feed off Him and His sacrifice of body and blood. Jesus concluded, *...no one can come to Me, unless it has been granted him from the Father* (John 6:65). Praise God this day that the Father called you to Christ and that your salvation was not dependent upon your own will, or work, or commitment, but rather on the obedient work and commitment of Christ. He died for His sheep in order to provide the atoning work we cannot accomplish in and of ourselves!

Look it up – **Romans 11:33-36; 2 Corinthians 12:9; Ephesians 3:21**

This truth for me – **Are there areas in your life that you think you can go it on your own and not include God's help? List times when you forgot to include God.**

_____

_____

_____

Pray – **For a greater realization to include God in all that you do. First pray!**

GOD'S LEADERS FOR THE CHURCH

Ephesians 4:11 And He gave some as...pastors and teachers

Recently, I preached and shared our church-planting ministry at a former church plant which recently gained the status of a particular Bible Fellowship Church. The focus of the morning was a wrap-up to the church's pastor's appreciation celebration. During the time of sharing, one member after another shared how precious their pastor is to them. At the covered dish fellowship after the service, gifts were given to the pastor, and children sang some special music in his honor.

Observing this demonstration of love and joy reminded me that pastors are precious gifts from God to churches. Take note the Apostle says, *He gave.* Only God calls and only God gives His servants to the church. No pastor is self-appointed. If he thinks he is, he will fail the church and the Lord. Also, it should be noted how special the flock is in each church. May we, as pastors, remember always that God gave us to the churches we serve, and it was not by our own ability or personality by which we were called, but rather by God's giving and calling to serve in love and grace. And also, may churches know the precious gift they have from God in the form of a pastor who serves them and teaches the whole counsel of the Word of God. *Let love of the brethren continue* (Hebrews 13:1).

*Look it up – **Acts 20:28; 1 Thessalonians 5:12–13; 1 Timothy 5:17***

This truth for me – **List the things you appreciate about your elders and particularly the teaching preaching elder (pastor).**

Pray – **For the leaders of your church, especially the pastor and elders.**

PRAY AND SUBMIT TO LEADERS

Daniel 2:21 It is He who changes the times and the epochs; He removes kings and establishes kings...

Do you vote? If what Daniel says is true (and it is), then some might say, *why should I vote if God is going to put in place the leaders He wants to rule and govern?* We vote for somewhat the same reason we evangelize. Evangelism is the process by which God calls His elect, and the voting of Americans is the means by which God chooses the president and all leaders who serve us. The one who takes the reins of power is God's choice. Therefore, no matter who God establishes as our leaders, our personal duty remains the same—to stand for justice, promote righteousness, and pray without ceasing for our leaders. We must also remember that our leaders are to uphold righteousness and promote mercy and justice. When we see that these qualities are not being supported or practiced by our leaders, then we have the biblical right to challenge such leaders and use the rules of government to see them removed from their offices.

Look it up – **Daniel 4:27; Romans 13:1; 1 Peter 2:13–18**

This truth for me – **How would you react to someone who is an immoral, unjust and sinful leader in government?**

_____

_____

_____

Pray – **For your local, state and federal leaders and that God would lead them to love mercy and do justice.**

THE POWER OF THE BLOOD

Genesis 4:10 ...your brother's blood is crying to Me from the ground.

Blood of those created in God's image is precious to Him. Here in Genesis 4, blood is mentioned for the first time in the Bible. When Cain killed his brother in a fit of jealousy and anger, it was Abel's innocent blood that witnessed against Cain. When innocent blood is shed, God knows the circumstances. Abel did not warrant such an act against him; his blood was shed by wicked hands.

We must remember the innocent blood shed by the evil of abortion. Annually on the Sanctity of Human Life day, thousands gather in Washington, D.C. to stand up for life. Are you and your church remembering the innocent blood of aborted children that continues to cry out to God? In recent years I have sensed that churches may not be as proactive, as they once were, in their stance against abortion. Yet, God still hears the blood of the aborted unborn child and He still judges.

God also hears the blood of the innocent Christ cry out for those whom He saves. Are you saved by the blood? Maybe you are reading this and you have had an abortion, or you know of one who has and still struggles. Christ's pure and innocent blood was shed to save sinners. Come to Jesus, be forgiven and cleansed by the blood of Christ and be freed from the prison of sin and death.

Look it up – **Romans 3:24-25; 1 Peter 1:18-19; Revelation 5:6-14, 7:14**

This truth for me – **How have you stood up for the helpless: the unborn, orphans and widows? List several things you can do to help the helpless.**

_____

_____

_____

Pray – **For the helpless and those mothers and children in crisis.**

GOD KNOWS THE SECRETS OF OUR HEARTS

Psalm 7:9 ...the righteous God tries the hearts and minds.

The Bible states that we cannot really know the heart of anyone, not even those we know best. The Apostle Paul asks the rhetorical question ...*who among men knows the thoughts of a man...* (1 Corinthians 2:11)? Of course the answer is no one! Yet, God knows the condition of our hearts. He sees them either in the darkness of sin or the light of His Son, Jesus Christ—forgiven and cleansed by Him. Jesus said ...*he who is not with Me is against Me...when the Son of Man comes in His glory... He will sit on His glorious throne...and He will separate them one from another...*

When Jesus was hanging on the cross between two criminals, He saw in one a sinful heart that rejected Him, but in the heart of the other, Jesus saw one who believed in Him for salvation. That faith guaranteed eternal life in heaven.

What will God see in our hearts when we stand before Him? Will it be our own form of salvation, or religion, our own form of philosophy, or good works? God searches our hearts to see the work of Jesus—it is He who forgives and gives clean hearts.

> **Jesus said...I am the resurrection and the life; he who believes in Me shall live even if he dies, and everyone who lives and believes in Me shall never die. Do you believe this? (John 11:25-26)**

Look it up – **1 Samuel 16:7; Psalm 26:2; 1 John 3:20**

This truth for me – **What things are hidden in your heart that should be confessed or discussed with God?**

_____

_____

_____

Pray – **For God to reveal your heart and pray always for a clean heart.**

ALL THINGS ARE POSSIBLE

Philippians 3:3 ...we...put no confidence in the flesh...

I would like to believe that this boast of Paul is true in my own life, yet so often a different boast is evident. It is one that looks to my own efforts for results and accomplishment. And if it is not looking to my own strength, it is looking at someone else's success and adapting their model, believing that if they have success, so will I. In either case, the bottom line is a trust in the flesh.

A wrong dependence on the flesh can also be exercised by what we might call an incorrect view of weakness. This occurs when we are not trusting the Holy Spirit to work through us, but rather are making our weaknesses an excuse for not doing God's will. A good, balanced understanding of God's power and our fleshly weaknesses can be learned by joining together the truth of what Jesus stated and the declaration of the Apostle Paul. Jesus said, ...*for apart from Me you can do nothing* (John 15:5); and the Apostle Paul learned, *I can do all things through Him who strengthens me* (Philippians 4:13). All of our confidence, all of our self-esteem must be placed in the life and work of Jesus Christ. Without Him we are nothing, but in Him and by His power we can accomplish the will of God.

Look it up – **Romans 6:19; 2 Corinthians 13:9; 1 John 4:4**

This truth for me – **Are you balanced in your approach to things, doing what you can do and trusting God to accomplish the rest? List where you might be imbalanced and trusting too much in yourself or not doing what you should.**

_____

_____

_____

Pray – **For the energy to do what you need to do and the understanding to trust God to accomplish His results through your efforts.**

BEING USEFUL IN THE KINGDOM

2 Timothy 4:11 ...Pick up Mark...for he is useful to me for service.

What a statement from the Apostle Paul—acknowledging that Mark had become useful to him in the service of the Lord. If you remember, this was the same young man who departed from Paul and Barnabas on the first missionary journey and left a bad impression in the mind of Paul, so much so that Paul got into a heated argument with Barnabas, who wanted to give Mark a second opportunity and take him along on the following missionary journey. What occurred in Mark's life between the time when he left Paul, to this point when Paul says Mark was a useful servant? One thing is certain: the Holy Spirit got hold of Mark's life and matured him in the ministry.

A pastor had shared with me that a woman he baptized had become very active in the ministry at his church. (I had been present at that baptism.) In her testimony, the woman shared that she came to the church because her daughter was attending, and she wanted to make sure the church was not a cult. As she checked out the church, the Holy Spirit convicted her and she was saved. The pastor then shared that since her baptism she has been very useful in the Lord's service. May the Holy Spirit take hold of many more lives in our communities and churches, and may we see Him save and mature former darkened sinners into obedient and committed disciples for service.

*Look it up – **Proverbs 4:18; 2 Peter 3:18; Philippians 3:12***

*This truth for me – **Are you useful for the Lord? List ways in which you are serving the Lord, and if not serving, list where you would like to serve.***

_____

_____

_____

*Pray – **For the Lord to bless you in your service or to open up a door of service for you.***

ARISE AND DO HIS WILL

Matthew 1:20 ...appeared to him [Joseph] in a dream...

On three occasions, as recorded by Matthew, an angel appeared to instruct Joseph as to what he should do regarding Mary's pregnancy and eventually the care of his family. In each angelic revelation, Joseph's reaction is the same: *and he arose* (Matthew 1:24; 2:14, 21). In simple terms, Joseph obeyed each time the word of the Lord came to him. Allow me to apply this to those of us who are in ministry leadership, as well as to those of us, moms and dads, who lead in our families. The word of the Lord does not come to us via angels, but God's word for leaders of the church and families is broadcast very clearly through the pages of the Bible. With each divine message of instruction, there is the divine command to arise and do what the Lord instructs. As leaders in the church or in the home, do we obey in spite of the way we feel about a command of the Lord? Do we arise and go about doing the Lord's will, even when we can't rationalize the logic of a command? One Puritan writer emphasized obedience this way, "...I do because He is God and I am His." Arise and be doing!

Look it up – ***2 Samuel 10:12; Zechariah 1:6; Colossians 3:23***

This truth for me – **When have you disregarded the commands of God's word? What commands of God do you find most difficult to obey?**

_____

_____

_____

Pray – **For God to give you the will and strength to obey Him and His word even when you don't feel like obeying.**

CHRIST WITH US

Luke 2:12 ...lying in a manger.

I remember one Lord's Day when I left my house at 5:30 a.m., traveled through a series of heavy rain storms and tornado warnings in New Jersey, a mud slide on the New York Taconic Parkway, a washed out bridge on NY Rt. 9, past downed power lines, and finally arrived four hours later at a church in Poughquag, NY. Perhaps I can sum up the drive with one word: *adventurous.* A power outage had made it necessary for the church to hook up a gas generator and choose between having lights or heat, since the generator could only run one or the other. They chose lights. As I preached in that dimly lit and chilly country church, I sensed what church is all about. Church is centered in God's Spirit and truth and in Christ's love. In that building there was little light and no heat, but there was enough brightness of God's Spirit and warmth of Christ's love to heat and light a huge cathedral! So often we measure a church's success by its building projects and sprawling facilities. But as I drove home through snow showers, I reflected upon the places Christ chose to meet with His people: a manger, a barren hillside, a boat on a lake and at a place called The Skull. Christ will meet with you right where you are! May He give you His peace and joy!

*Look it up – **John 15:5; 1 Corinthians 6:19–20; Ephesians 2:19–22***

*This truth for me – **When you think of church, do you think of: building or body? Write a short definition of the Church.***

_____

_____

_____

*Pray – **For God to give you an understanding of His Church as the Body of Christ, a community of the saints.***

THE GOOD THINGS GOD SEES

2 Chronicles 12:12b Indeed, there was some good in Judah. (NIV)

Shishak and the Egyptians had invaded Judah as God's hand of judgment upon Rehoboam and Judah for their forsaking of God. As the Egyptian forces captured the fortified cities and began their march to Jerusalem, King Rehoboam and the princes humbled themselves before God, acknowledging Him as the righteous one. Therefore, God granted a *measure of deliverance*. God's decision to grant deliverance was based upon His mercy and that *there was some good [things] in Judah*. As you meditate upon this, think of how gracious God is toward sinners. One of God's incomprehensible perfections is His long-suffering grace toward His children who are prone to wander.

In this wonderful country we call *the land of the free and the home of the brave*, we should consider how many *good things* God sees in America, and even more specifically, in His church. There might be ample reasons for God to judge America: abortion, immorality, paganism, heresy and apostasy. Where will God see the *good things* in order to give us a continued measure of deliverance? He must see it in your life and mine, as those who comprise the body of Christ. May today and the future be a time of growing the good things God has placed in us as Christians!

*Look it up – **Luke 6:35; Galatians 5:17; Philippians 2:13***

*This truth for me – **What good things can you do today and what good things can you make a habit of doing?***

_____

_____

_____

*Pray – **That you will see what good you can do in the name of the Lord for your brothers and sisters, family, neighbors and others with whom you have contact.***

NEW LOVES

Philippians 1:8 ...with the affection of Christ...

The work of the Holy Spirit is nothing less than amazing! He regenerates sinners and gives them new life, causing them to exercise new faith to believe on the Lord Jesus Christ and be saved. Possibly the greatest transformation that takes place in the previously dead sinner has to do with the new love he possesses for God and for God's people, the Church. Before a sinner is born again, he or she is dead in sin and in hatred for God and the Church. When we read the first chapter of the Apostle Paul's letter to the church in Philippi and compare his love to the hatred he possessed before his salvation, we are overwhelmed with his change of heart. Saul—as he was first known—was described as *ravaging the church* and actually hating Christ and His people. Saul even had Christians tried, imprisoned and executed. One great sign indicating someone has been born again is the change a person exhibits from having hatred to loving God and His Church.

If you are born again, rejoice in the transformation God wrought in your life when He saved you, removed your hatred toward Him and His Church, and gave you a heart of love. If you are not born again, then repent of your sin, ask Christ to come into your life to change you and give you His new love.

Look it up – **Romans 6:4,5; 2 Corinthians 5:17; Colossians 3:5-11**

This truth for me – **Can you point to the changes that Christ made in your life when you were born again? List them.**

_____

_____

_____

Pray – **Thank God for changing your life.**

A HEART OF MERCY

Galatians 2:10 *They only asked us to remember the poor...*

Am I a merciful child of God? The question seems to be a contradiction of terms. If I am a child of God, there should be no question as to whether or not I am merciful. But so often I catch myself—like I am sure many of you do—not being the merciful child of God I should be. Accustomed to American comfort, we expect to be comfortable. When our comfortable world is disrupted, immediately we attempt to correct circumstances which caused the discomfort and get things back to normal. When we are convicted by the need we see, we tend to offer a token of mercy instead of going all the way, as illustrated by the merciful Samaritan.

The directive to show mercy and *remember the poor* came from the Jerusalem Council at the same time its doctrinal decision, regarding justification by faith, was sent to the churches. I believe my doctrinal thinking is in good shape, but I must admit that my heart of mercy must be enlarged. Maybe all of us must seriously consider seeking to enlarge our hearts of compassion, justice, giving, humility and mercy. God calls us to be merciful people!

*Look it up – **Matthew 5:7; Luke 10:30-37; James 3:17***

*This truth for me – **How have you shown mercy in recent weeks? List several ways you can be merciful.***

_____

_____

_____

*Pray – **That you will realize the depth of the mercy that God extended to you, and then pray for ways to show mercy to others.***

SET FREE UNTO RIGHTEOUSNESS

Jeremiah 23:6 ...The LORD our righteousness.

I once heard a theologian describe an unregenerate sinner as a "walking, rotting corpse." Spiritually speaking, the language is graphic and true. By nature sinners are dead in their sins and will face an eternal damnation. In contrast, when the Lord saves us, we are given new life and are dressed in the eternal righteousness of Christ Jesus. In Him we are presented perfect, and brought into fellowship with our prefect Father.

John Newton (the writer of the hymn, *Amazing Grace*) was reminded daily of the condition from which Christ's righteousness had freed him. A banner hanging above his desk stated, *you were once a slave in Egypt.* Newton constantly wrote about being freed from his former slavery to sin and now possessing *righteousness through Christ.* Herein lies the tender balance: to be humbled by the truth of Christ saving us from the pit of sin and lifting us up by the righteousness He freely gave us.

*Look it up – **Psalm 45:7; Jeremiah 23:5-6; Romans 5:18-19***

*This truth for me – **Do you remember your former life in sin? But do you also now know your freedom in Christ? Write from what Christ set you free.***

_____

_____

_____

*Pray – **And thank God for setting you free so that there is no longer any condemnation awaiting you.***

THE POWERFUL WORD OF GOD

John 3:3 ...unless one is born again...

When I first began preaching, a mentor suggested that I take familiar and dynamic passages like John 3:3 and preach from them. I did as he said and formulated a series of messages entitled, *Those Familiar Passages.* John 3:3 was the first one I chose. After delivering the message, a wife and another couple from the same family made professions of faith. This started the Gospel moving through their other family members. Eventually this family filled an entire pew of the church. Both directly and indirectly, God used the preaching of this very familiar passage to save His chosen ones from this family. In turn, these people also became witnesses of the Gospel to others who then came to Christ. As preachers, teachers and lay Christians, we might have the tendency to think that familiar passages of Scripture are too common to be preached or shared. We may think that people already know all there is to know about such *overworked* verses. I don't think so. Take some time to preach, teach and share the *familiar passages*, and wait upon the Lord to add His blessing. Remember, the Word is God's powerful tool to save His people and bring them to salvation—ALL the Word.

*Look it up – **Matthew 4:4; Hebrews 1:3; Acts 4:31***

*This truth for me – **Are you still excited about the Word of God? How powerful has it been in your life in recent days?***

_____

_____

_____

*Pray – **That you will keep growing in God's Word and sharing the Word with others, for it has the power to convict and save sinners.***

THE JOY OF GODLY CHILDREN

Proverbs 10:1 A wise son makes a father glad...

I remember some years ago spending time with a father of three sons. He began sharing with me about his children. I was waiting for him to tell me about their educational degrees, their employment or their families, but instead he began to tell me how they are serving the Lord. It was pleasant and refreshing to hear this father speak of how the Lord was working in his sons' lives. As parents, we so often tout our children's secular accomplishments. It is fine to be proud of our children and puff out our chests because of their accomplishments. We should legitimately desire that our children reach great academic or career heights. However, this father reminded me that I must not only pray for my children to gain credible career accomplishments, but also keep my prayers fixed on their spiritual condition and the movement of the Spirit in their lives. If you are a parent, may your children be saved and may they rise up and call you blessed. If you are not a parent, please pray for those parents you know, that God will bless them with wisdom and godly children.

Look it up – **Deuteronomy 6:6–7; Proverbs 4:11-13; Proverbs 6:20-23, 13:1**

This truth for me – **Are you a parent? List some needs your children may have. If you are not a parent, list several parents you know whose children have needs. Pray for them.**

_____

_____

_____

Pray – **For the children of our land, that the Gospel will take hold in their lives; and pray for parents to give godly instruction and protection for the children.**

WHO IS FOR US?

Romans 8:31 ...If God is for us, who is against us?

Who is the *WHO* of Romans 8:31? *WHO* is someone many preachers don't like to mention. *WHO* is someone Hollywood loves to define in either gory terms or false bravado. This WHO has been overlooked in the Church for many years because this character makes people feel uncomfortable, and many Christians even doubt the existence of *WHO*. However, in stark contrast to how preachers, the Church, and we think about this entity, WHO is a very powerful enemy to all of us.

By now you may have concluded that the *WHO* we are talking about is the Devil. The Devil is totally and emphatically against every preacher, every church and every Christian. The only thing that can deliver sinners from the power of the Devil is the power of the Gospel. When sinners are saved, the Gospel's power delivers us from the power and darkness of the Devil, and delivers us unto Christ where we will never again be overpowered by the Devil. This is why Paul writes what he does in Romans 8. When we are in Christ, the Devil may influence us but cannot touch us. Praise God for the overpowering power of Christ and the Gospel.

Look it up – **Psalm 56:9; Zechariah 3:1–7; Romans 8:1**

This truth for me – **Do others accuse and condemn you? So you feel disheartened? Write out the things God says about you: you are adopted, in Christ...**

_____

_____

_____

Pray – **That you will always have the confirmation of God's love for you and safety in Him.**

LET THE NATIONS HEAR ABOUT OUR LORD

Psalm 117:1 Praise the LORD, all nations; Laud Him, all peoples!

It seems clear that God desires to save a people from all tribes and nations, whether living in foreign lands or in the diverse cities and towns of America. I would like to share a portion from *Apostolic Passion,* by Floyd McClung. *"The greatest enemy of the ambition to see Jesus worshipped in the nations is lack of focus. You can run around expending energy on all sorts of good ministries and not get one step closer to the nations...Focus on what? I believe God wants a people for Himself. Activity without a desire that God have a people for Himself is just activity, not missions. You can have evangelism without missions. Short-term ministries are great, as long as they focus on raising up workers to plant churches...It's always the will of God to have a people who worship His Son in the nations. You'll never have to worry about making God mad if you try to plant a church. It seems crazy to me that people are under the delusion that they need a special calling to save souls, to disciple them, and to get them together to love Jesu... you must understand one thing: church planting is not for us, it's for God. We do it so God will have a people to worship Him!"* (from *Missions Frontiers,* the official publication of the U.S. Center for World Mission <www.uscwm. org>).

For a very good book on this subject, please read *Let the Nations Be Glad* by John Piper.

Look it up – **Psalm 67:1-6; Psalm 96:1-3; John 3:16**

This truth for me – **Do you have any contact with people from other cultures? Write how many people you know from various nations and countries.**

_____

_____

_____

Pray – **That God will open your heart and move your feet to intentionally go to these people and share the Gospel.**

OPPORTUNITIES FOR THE GOSPEL

Romans 15:23 but now, with no further place for me in these regions...

As the Apostle Paul looked about the regions of Macedonia and Achaia, he came to the conclusion that there were no more opportunities to preach the Gospel in those areas. Is this a conclusion we can afford to make as we look at our American cities? Can we say that because there are churches in American cities, towns and rural areas, there are no further opportunities to preach the Gospel?

All around us, we see people who need to hear the Gospel. The nations of the world have arrived in our cities, and more Bible-preaching, disciple-making churches are needed. If we think America is a Christian nation, then we are sadly blinded to the reality of the post-Christian, hedonistic and secular America which is more a mission field today than ever before. We are not the *Shining City upon a hill*, as John Winthrop was hoping America to be. Rather, America is in need of the *marvelous light* of Christ. In our communities, we must preach the Gospel and make disciples among our nation's people of diverse tongues, tribes and nations.

*Look it up – **Matthew 9:35-38; Matthew 28:18-20; Acts 1:8***

*This truth for me – **How many Bible preaching/teaching/disciple-making churches are around you? How many people where you live do not go to church?***

_____

_____

_____

*Pray – **For God to open your eyes to the many unchurched/unsaved people around you.***

ABOUNDING GRACE FOR TIRED SOULS

John 1:16 For of His fullness we have all received, and grace upon grace.

Christians can lose sight of God's grace. We can know we were saved by grace alone, but then we can be tempted to believe that our maturing in the faith is based upon our own work and strength. Such Christians grow tired in well-doing and soon exhaust themselves through striving in their own strength to *work out their salvation*. The same grace that provides all that is necessary for salvation is the grace which abounds to us throughout our Christian life. What I do for the Lord, I do by the grace given me. The good works I do and service I render, I do by the grace of the Lord that continues to abound to me until the Day of Christ.

Brothers and sisters, please don't grow weary or exhausted, but rather call upon the grace of the Lord Jesus Christ and be renewed and refreshed in His strength day by day, *...having been justified by faith, we have peace with God through our Lord Jesus Christ, through whom also we have obtained our introduction by faith into this grace in which we stand; and we exult in hope of the glory of God* (Romans 5:1,2).

Look it up – **Deuteronomy 28:11; Romans 10:12; 2 Corinthians 9:8**

This truth for me – **Are you tired? Maybe you are trying too hard on your own. What fatigues you and where do you need the Lord's grace?**

_____

_____

_____

Pray – **For God's grace to abound to you in an area that is tiring you out. Let go and let God.**

A GOOD NEIGHBOR

Luke 10:29 ...And who is my neighbor?

This was a very pointed question from the lawyer interrogating Jesus. The answer Jesus gave, by telling of the story of the Good Samaritan, is very pointed in defining a real neighbor and showing true mercy. The point is this: our neighbors are all those who are in need, who need our expressions of mercy, especially the merciful witness of the Gospel. When we come across needy people in our cities, towns, schools, families and work place, Jesus calls us to be neighbors who will go as far as necessary to meet the need of another.

I once heard a missionary speaker share about the wonderful movement of the Spirit in various parts of the world. What was glaringly missing in his reporting was the fact that in America and the rest of western civilization (west of Poland, across Europe and into North America and Canada) we can no longer claim the wonderful workings of the Spirit like we see in other parts of the world. Perhaps the Church in the west needs to show sacrificial and neighborly love to the lost all around us so that they will see and understand Jesus' love for them.

Look it up – **Leviticus 19:18; Matthew 22:39; Luke 10:29-37**

This truth for me – **To whom can I be a better neighbor? What things can I do to be a better neighbor?**

_____

_____

_____

Pray – **For God to further develop you into a Good Samaritan.**

WE STAND ALONE BEFORE GOD

2 Chronicles 24:2 And Joash did what was right in the sight of the LORD all the days of Jehoiada the priest.

I recently shared from this passage with the junior and senior high students in a Christian School. I challenged the young people: *What will you do when you face the crisis of faith?* Joash did what was right as long as Jehoiada was around, but when Jehoiada died (vs.17-18), Joash abandoned God and later died in dishonor and disgrace.

One of the truths of the doctrine of the perseverance of the saints is that those who are truly saved will continue in the faith God has given them, even when everything around them is falling apart. True believers persevere in Him, because their faith does not depend on others or how well associated they are with religion. Their faith has been given by God and instilled in them by the Holy Spirit, never again to be removed. Just as we are saved by grace through faith, it is also by grace through faith that we endure. To those who by perseverance (Romans 2:7) do good and withstand the darts of the Devil, God will give eternal life and glorious blessing. Those who belong to God will persevere in Christ. We cannot piggyback our way into a right relationship with God. Let us not be like Joash, who was held in check by Jehoiada. But rather, let us trust God, for He and He alone saves and forgives His people!

Look it up – Ezekiel 18:1-4; Luke 6:44; 2 Timothy 4:16–17

*This truth for me – **We cannot point fingers at other people in our lives and make excuses for our sins. Have you done this? If so, when?***

———————————————————————————

———————————————————————————

———————————————————————————

*Pray – **That you will be ready to face God having your sins forgiven in Christ.***

THE SAVIOR WHO CARRIES AWAY OUR SINS

Luke 22:54 ...they led Him away...

Into the night of terror, brutality, foolish trials, lies and false accusations, the Savior trekked with His antagonists surrounding Him. Cruelly, His enemies were seeking His death.

The picture draws us to the Old Testament imagery of the sin-bearing scapegoat of Israel. With the sins of Israel placed upon the head of the goat, it would be led out into the darkness carrying the burden of the people's sins.

As our Lord's night of infamy progressed into the next morning's rendezvous with the cross, the sins of many would be placed upon the head of Christ. He became our sin bearer. Christ *who knew no sin became sin for us*, his elect children, our sins imputed onto Him and His righteousness imputed onto us. This is an incomprehensible work of the cross and yet so precious to us who are saved by His blood. We are commissioned to preach the cross and resurrection of Christ, to call sinners to lay their sin on Christ and repent and believe unto salvation. May the children of God be filled with the Holy Spirit to preach the cross and unashamedly call sinners to be saved.

*Look it up – **Leviticus 16:10; Isaiah 53:6; 1 Peter 2:24***

*This truth for me – **How does this truth humble you before God? Think about what it means for Christ to have carried your sins away.***

_____

_____

_____

*Pray – **To the Father to fill us with His Spirit and save His people through our proclamation of the cross.***

BLESSED IS THE LAMB OF GOD

Revelation 5:9 ...Worthy art Thou to take the book, and to break its seals; for Thou wast slain...

It is a fitting response ... the creatures and elders are singing as they witness the Lamb taking the book and breaking open the seals. But what gave Christ the right and ability to open this book? It was the perfect virtue of our Lord, the Lamb, who was slain. He redeemed us. Only He and He alone could pay the perfect blood price to satisfy God's wrath. Only He could be the worthy sacrifice required to pay for sins. He alone takes humans—totally depraved, nasty, undeserving humans—and makes them priests. God sent His one and only Lamb, the Man Christ Jesus, to accomplish the work of atonement and salvation for sinful mankind! What a wonderful privilege we have, as children who have been sprinkled by that precious blood, to share this Good News.

This day, who will hear this Good News of the Lamb of God from your lips? Jesus Christ, the Lamb of God, died for sinners and paid the price required of God. ...*To Him who sits on the throne, and to the Lamb, be blessing and honor and glory and dominion forever and ever* (Revelation 5:13).

*Look it up – **John 1:29; 1 Peter 1:17-19; Revelation 5:6–13***

*This truth for me – **Have you ever thought there were more ways to be saved than through Christ alone? In a world where so many think that there are many roads leading to God, stand firm in Christ, the only way to be saved.***

---

*Pray – **For God to keep you steadfast in the truth that Christ, and Christ alone, is the only way to be saved. Thank Him today for His atonement.***

GOD DELIVERS HIS CHILDREN

Psalm 50:15 ...call upon Me in the day of trouble; I shall rescue you...

In Spurgeon's <u>Twelve Sermons on Prayer</u>, he states: *...here are God and the praying man taking shares...First, here is your share: "Call upon me in the day of trouble." Secondly, here is God's share: "I will deliver thee."* Notice how Spurgeon's comments on prayer take us through the lens of God's sovereignty. Prayer reminds us that God is the all-powerful, all-knowing, all-sufficient giver of grace, and we are wholly and totally dependent upon our Father in heaven for all things.

I have at times approached the throne of God with a degree of self-worth, thinking that *my* coming in prayer will be pleasing to God. This approach brings glory to me. Prayer should bring glory to God. Even the posture of being on our knees denotes the understanding that we are dependent creatures, and that the only worth we have is that which is Christ's. It is He, the all-worthy One, who gives us His robe of righteousness. When we kneel in prayer and speak with Him, there is nothing of us and everything of Christ upon which my Father gazes. Therefore, we call upon the Lord in the name of Jesus and wait upon His deliverance, that He may receive all the glory.

Look it up – **Psalm 18:4; Psalm 114:1-4; Daniel 9:16-17**

This truth for me – **How do you approach the Lord in prayer? What pride or self-worth might be hindering your prayers?**

_____

_____

_____

Pray – **That when you enter into prayer, you will have a selfless spirit and the faith to trust God to answer your prayers.**

GOD HAS HIS PEOPLE OUT THERE

Luke 10:6 And if a man of peace is there...

While pastoring a church in Pennsylvania and leading a group that was participating in a weekly visitation program, I walked up the steps to the front door of a house and knocked. The door opened, but the man standing at the doorway was anything but hospitable. It didn't take long to realize that he was not the man of peace that Christ described to the seventy being sent out. I used this test as a gauge when I was visiting people in a proposed target site for a church plant. Would the contacts in this prospective church planting area be people of peace? Would they invite me in and allow me to spend time with them? Four families I visited that day were all people of peace. I had some great visits and prayed that the Lord would use these visits to further our establishment of a new church.

Is there a lesson here for evangelism? Yes! Be encouraged, for there are those in your community whom Christ has set apart as people of peace. They will invite you in and allow you to share the Gospel. If the Lord wills, you could be a part of His calling some to be saved. It was good to sit in those homes and share the Lord's grace. Take note: people of peace are not discovered unless you go! Arise and be doing!

Look it up – 1 Kings 19:15-18; Luke 15:1-7; Acts 16:8

This truth for me – We never know how God is working in someone's heart and we need to be ready at all times to speak with whomever He wants us to approach. Is God speaking to someone you know?

_____

_____

_____

Pray – For people of peace to be led by your path and be ready to create a Gospel relationship.

VOWS FOR SPIRITUAL POWER

Psalm 56:12 *Thy vows are binding upon me...I will render thank offerings to Thee.*

Are you adverse to taking vows? The Psalmist wasn't. He wanted his vows to *render praise* to God. For this to happen, vows to be made need to be particular and they need to be kept. A.W. Tozer, in his booklet, <u>*Five Vows for Spiritual Power*</u> (available online), presents five vows that have been helpful for me to remember as I walk this Christian walk. Let me list his vows:

1) *Deal thoroughly with sin*
2) *Never own anything* (that is, never let anything own you)
3) *Never defend yourself*
4) *Never pass anything on about anybody else that will hurt (them)*
5) *Never accept any glory.*

Wow, what challenges are encompassed in these vows! Here is Tozer's accompanying exhortation: *There are many religious tramps in the world who will not be bound by anything. They have turned the grace of God into personal license. But the great souls are ones who have gone reverently to God with the understanding that in their flesh dwells no good thing. And they know that without God's enablement any vows taken would be broken before sundown. Nevertheless, believing in God, reverently they took certain sacred vows.*

*Look it up – **Isaiah 40:31; 1 Thessalonians 1:5; 2 Timothy 1:7***

*This truth for me – **Which of Tozer's vows do you struggle with the most? How will you work on any weaknesses in these areas?***

_____

_____

_____

*Pray – **That God will bless you with power in your Christian walk to honor Him in all you do.***

REJOICE IN THE CHURCH OF JESUS CHRIST

1 Corinthians 11:18 ...when you come together as a church...

How would you locate the church? Would you look for signs or buildings? Would you look for a certain size of a group, or perhaps people doing religious things? Martin Luther wrote, *"People call that the Christian Church which is not the church, and that which is the church is often not acknowledged as such..."* In today's church atmosphere, we tend to identify church by buildings, size, religion and a number of other misnomers. But these things don't necessarily identify the church. Where then is the church? Allow me to use Luther again to answer this question. *"Whenever you hear or see this Word preached, believed, professed, and lived, do not doubt that ... a Christian holy people, must be there, even though their number is very small."*

As I travel, I see small, medium and large groups of holy people meeting to hear the preaching of God's Word. They believe its message and profess it in life and practice. Whether numbering 20 or 2,000, they are the Church, called out to hear, believe and live God's Word. God will build His Church through little and large flocks. *I was glad when they said to me, "Let us go to the house of the LORD"* (Psalm 122:1).

Look it up – **Psalm 87:1-3; Acts 2:46-47; 1 Corinthians 14:26**

This truth for me – **Do you view the church according to size? If so, what are you missing about the Church as the Body of Christ?**

_____

_____

_____

Pray – **For your local church, and rejoice that the Lord does not honor a church's size but rather its holiness.**

THE INVITATION TO CHRIST

Matthew 11:28 Come to Me... Acts 2:36 ...let all the house of Israel know...
Acts 21:19 ...he began to relate one by one the things which God had done...

Some time ago, a brother gave me an interesting paper entitled, <u>16 ways to give</u> <u>an Invitation</u>. I believe the author was trying to say that God calls the elect in various ways to be saved. In the last church I pastored, I taught through one book of the Scriptures at a time. Part of my preparation included thinking about the conclusion of the message, using a summary, application and then invitation to respond to the truth of Scripture. However, there were some who thought I never gave an invitation because it was not in a familiar form. Were these invitations less effective than those which called for people to step out and come forward? No! It is not the *style* of the invitation which calls sinners to be saved, but rather it is *God* who calls the elect sinner to salvation through the preaching of the Word and the convicting work of the Holy Spirit. Let us not fail to invite the Christian to respond to the Word nor neglect commanding the unsaved to repent and believe upon the Lord Jesus Christ.

*Look it up – **Isaiah 1:18; Romans 10:17; 2 Corinthians 5:11***

*This truth for me – **Develop your style of inviting people to Christ through using the Bible as your guide.***

_____

_____

_____

*Pray – **For people to be edified and saved through the preaching and teaching of the Word in your church, your home and your contacts.***

KNOW THAT THE LORD IS GOD

2 Chronicles 33:13 ...*Then Manasseh knew that the LORD was God.*

"Oh, yeah," we'll often say if confronted by something we knew but had forgotten. Manasseh had been exposed to God and His dealings with His people by virtue of his father Hezekiah, but Manasseh forgot God to such an extent that he did *...more evil than the nations whom the Lord destroyed before the sons of Israel* (2 Chronicles 33:9). Manasseh's infamous exploits included: witchcraft, divination, human sacrifice (his own sons), sorcery, idolatry and the defamation of the Temple. What a guy!

Yet, what a God! Manasseh came to an *oh, yeah* moment when God brought great distress upon Manasseh. He then prayed, humbled himself and repented, and God forgave and restored him. What an incomprehensible demonstrative of grace and mercy! *Then Manasseh knew that the LORD was God.*

We Christians can easily fall into the *Manassah category* and forget God. Rather than us saying, "Oh, yeah, God," may we declare, "Oh, God, I need Thee every hour."

*Look it up – **Exodus 6:7; Psalm 116:5; Lamentations 3:32***

*This truth for me – **Think on those times God forgave you when you sinned. Claim your forgiveness and go and sin no more.***

_____

_____

_____

*Pray – **Thank God for His longsuffering mercy toward you and for His gracious forgiveness.***

SERVING TO THE GLORY OF GOD

Acts 12:23 ...because he (Herod) *did not give God the glory...*

To whom does your gratitude and praise go when you have accomplished something? For Herod, gratitude and appreciation for giving such an eloquent speech returned to him. Apparently Herod got caught up in the cheers of the people and their comparison of his speech being like the voice of a god. We might not be compared to a god, but there are times when God uses us in special ways to accomplish wonderful things for His Kingdom and our praise returns to ourselves. When I hear how my ministry has touched people's lives and then see those individuals growing and doing wonderful things for God, I must catch my thoughts from going down the path of self-praise. It is too easy to think we are the primary reason for another's spiritual growth. We easily can fall prey to self-acclamation. Yet, were it not entirely for the grace of God, we would never have even the slightest spiritual effect upon a person's Christian life. We are privileged to be God's ambassadors and we are blessed to be able to minister to those around us, *To God be the glory, great things He has done!*

Look it up – **Psalm 29:2; Romans 11:36; 1 Corinthians 10:31**

This truth for me – **Was there a time that you felt puffed up about something you accomplished and did not first give God the glory? How were you reminded that God gets the glory?**

_____

_____

_____

Pray – *That you will always put God first in all you do and all you accomplish.*

UNASHAMED OF GOD

Ezra 3:3 Despite their fear... (NIV)

The New International Version of the Bible uses the word *despite,* in reference to Israel reestablishing its worship, even though the nation was in fear of the surrounding pagan peoples who could have been irritated by such action. Many times the Christian—like the Israelites—is called to worship God in spite of what people may think or how they might react. In places like India, China and the Sudan, it can be very costly, even to the point of losing one's life, to live and worship as a Christian.

Did you ever find yourself feeling ashamed because you failed to speak a word or act in a way which would honor God; rather, you worried about what people around you would think? Christian husbands and wives need to do what is honoring to God in their marriages, despite what others may think. Christian young people need to honor God in their decisions and actions despite how their friends may react. By God's grace, we who are the children of God must work to honor the Lord with all our hearts, souls and minds, despite fears we may have.

*Look it up – **2 Timothy 1:8; 1 Corinthians 9:16; Ephesians 6:10***

*This truth for me – **Are you bold for Jesus? If not, what do you think will build your courage to stand up for truth?***

_____

_____

_____

*Pray – **For God to show how powerful He is and for Him to give you boldness.***

HE STANDS IN MY PLACE

1 Peter 3:18 For Christ also died for sins once for all, the just for the unjust...

When I played sports, I hated to have a substitute come and take my place. But when it comes to my entrance into the Kingdom of God, I praise the Father for sending His Son to be my substitute. Peter uses a wonderful word in this passage, and some translations of the Bible reinforce the impact of this word by using it three times. The word is *for* or in the original, *huper*, which means, *in place of.* Herein lies the impact of the great doctrine of the substitutionary atonement of Christ, that God would send His Son to take the death sentence for such a wretch as me. I find, both in the church and outside it, the teaching that we can save ourselves—in essence, we can be our own substitute. Such teaching is not merely wrong but it is an affront to the grace of God; it dishonors the cross. The Father delivered up His Son, the Son died for sins, and the Spirit convicts the sinner of sin. Only when we recognize the fullness of Christ's work in being our substitute on the cross can we really cry out, *For from Him and through Him and to Him are all things. To Him be the glory forever. Amen* (Romans 11:36).

*Look it up – **Mark 10:45; 2 Corinthians 5:17–21; Galatians 3:13***

*This truth for me – **Think about the God of the universe standing in your place and taking away the penalty you should receive. How do you respond to this truth?***

_____

_____

_____

*Pray – **Fall on your knees and thank God for sending Jesus to stand in your place and face the wrath that is yours.***

NOT WHAT I EXPECTED

Habakkuk 3:18 Yet I will exult the LORD...

When we pray for things we desire and then don't receive them, we become terribly disappointed. Such could have been the case for the prophet Habakkuk. He probably did not expect God to tell him that He was going to give Israel over to the Babylonians for judgment and destruction. When he heard God's proclamation of judgment, he certainly could have gone home and sulked till that day came. Instead, he reminded himself of God's power and might. He looked at God's faithfulness and finally remembered God's righteousness.

These are the things of which we must remind ourselves when things don't go our way and God's response is contrary to what we expected. We must remember that God is mighty! He is faithful! He is just! My expectations may not be met. I may experience the fire of trial; I may struggle with sin, failure and loss, *yet I will exult in the Lord!*

*Look it up – **Job 17:10-17; Psalm 39:7,8; 2 Corinthians 8:3-5***

*This truth for me – **Has something ever surprised you in a negative way? How did you react? Was your reaction one of trust in God?***

_____

_____

_____

*Pray – **For strength to trust God when your expectations are not met.***

THE GOD WITHIN

Romans 1:19 ...*that which is known about God is evident within them...*

John Calvin wrote, *"Every man has a sense of deity within him."* Theologian Cornelius Van Til states, *"To not know God, man would have to destroy himself."* On one occasion while approaching people on the Rehoboth, DE boardwalk, I handed a young woman a Gospel of John, explaining what it was and asking that she might take the time to read it. Her response was, "I am an atheist. I don't believe that God exists." At first I was surprised because she didn't appear to me like one who would claim to be an atheist. But, on the other hand, what do atheists look like? Yet, what really played on my mind was how she was lying to herself. This so-called atheist, like all humans who have ever lived, knows there is the true God and knows their responsibility before God. Granted, this knowledge is crusted over by a marred and depraved heart, yet every human being is *without excuse.*

Where do we fit into this dilemma? As Christians we are commanded to confront people with their need of salvation in Christ, proclaim the Good News and teach the Gospel, then let God do His work. I prayed for that atheist and for God to use the Word I shared with her, and then I trusted God to accomplish His will with her life.

*Look it up – **Psalm 19:1–6; Romans 1:19–20; Acts 14:16-17***

*This truth for me – **Do you realize that more and more people are denying the existence of God and turning to paganism? How can you help these people to understand that God exists?***

_____

_____

_____

*Pray – **Praise God that He made Himself known to you in a special way through His Son Jesus Christ, and then pray for those you know who deny God and Christ.***

GOD CLEANS UP THE MESS

Exodus 20:25 ...if you wield your tool on it, you will profane it.

Have you ever considered what your salvation would be like if you had a part in such a gracious and glorious sovereign work by God? The answer to this question is simple! Look around at what humans have done to themselves and their environment. In short, and in a form of street vernacular, *it would be messed up*. More precisely, salvation would not be salvation at all if we had a part in it, for no one can satisfy the demands of a holy God. Only the God-man, Christ Jesus, can do that. Just as man was told by God not to put his efforts into cutting the stones for the sacrificial altar, because doing so would profane it, so we cannot add merit or effort to the sacrificial atonement of Christ. Our salvation is **not messed up** because it is the workmanship of God alone on the altar of the cross through Christ alone. Therefore, we can truly cry out like the hymnist:

> **Now in Christ's righteousness alone I stand before God's awesome throne, and grasp what only God could do, be just and justifier too.**
> **(Heaven's Gift, J.M. Boice and P.S. Jones)**

Look it up – Ezekiel 20:3; Mark 7:20–23; Romans 5:10

This truth for me – **What things in your life did you mess up? How did God help you get out of the mess?**

_____

_____

_____

Pray – **For God's help if you have a mess that needs to be cleaned up. Pray for others, trying to clean up their messes on their own, that they will turn to God for help.**

I NEED HIM EVERY MINUTE

Galatians 3:3 ...are you now being perfected by the flesh?

The *I-must-do* mindset can lead a Christian to a dependency upon their own ability while neglecting the power of the Spirit. When faced with a task, I tend to fall prey to responding with the words, *I must do this or that.*

With this thinking, a Christian can become fatigued and frustrated. Christian living is a calling to exercise the energy required to live for Christ. However, the Christian life does not depend totally or ultimately on an individual's own strength, ability or energy. Those who seek to live for Christ do so with the same dependence they had at the moment God saved them—a *total* dependence on the power of God, and not depending on our own power and strength.

Maybe you are feeling a little fatigued and frustrated by thinking *I must do.* Remember this . . . you began your walk with the Lord by totally depending on the Spirit's power. Don't be like the foolish Galatians (Galatians 3:3) and think that you can do God's will on your own. Cast yourself into the hands of a comforting and powerful Holy Spirit.

Look it up – **Deuteronomy 33:27; Isaiah 64:6; Hebrews 13:6**

This truth for me – **When have you recently said, "I must do ...?" Did you go before the Lord and ask for His help or just try to do it yourself?**

_____

_____

_____

Pray – **Tell the Lord you need His help every day, all the day, in the little and the big things and ask for forgiveness for the times you failed to seek His help.**

THE INFLUENCE OF THE GOSPEL

Matthew 5:47 ...what do you do more...?

I recently read an article declaring that Christians have made significant inroads into American culture. The article illustrated this by saying that Christian publications topped the best seller's lists in the past, and recently Christian contemporary music has sold more than jazz, classical and new age music combined. The irony of this article is that it was wedged into a section of the newspaper and was followed by three pages of ongoing crime problems and governmental struggles. As I pondered this, I wondered, *Has the popularity of Christianity in American culture been influential on our culture or merely another patch in the mosaic of Americana?*

One day, Jesus told the gathered multitude on the mountain that dwellers in His Kingdom were to be *more* than the culture around them; they were to impact the world with a flavor of godliness. Those who were to follow Him were to be more shaped by the beatitudes of Matthew 5 than the belligerence of a selfish society. They should be more molded by humility than by pride and greed. And His followers should be driven by a love that is willing to give up rather than accumulate. Inroads, yes, but what about influence?

Look it up – Matthew 5:16; John 1:10, 17:15; James 4:4-6

This truth for me – In what ways do you need to be more influential with the Gospel? Think on whether your life reflects the culture of the world or the culture of Christ.

Pray – That God would help your life to be a Christian influence on the world around you.

WALKING IN HIS FOOTSTEPS

Ephesians 4:1 ...walk in a manner worthy of the calling...

While playing baseball and fast pitch softball, I can remember several players who literally got hit right between the eyes with the ball. Needless to say, such violent encounters with those cowhide projectiles left the players staggering and wondering what had just clobbered them. The Bible with its clear and powerful truths has its own dynamic way of hitting us right between the eyes. Ephesians 4:1 is such a passage—bonk, right between our eyes: *walk in a manner worthy of the calling.* How could we ever attempt to walk in such a manner? Our calling is in Christ. It is in His purity, in His humiliation and death, in the power of His resurrection, and in His glory at the right hand of the Father. In our earthly walk, we can only walk this way by the grace God gives us. That grace allows us to be as the Ephesians passage continues: *humble, gentle, forbearing in love, and diligent in preserving unity and peace.* May God help us to walk His walk.

*Look it up – **Philippians 1:27; Colossians 2:6,7; 1 John 2:4-6***

*This truth for me – **In what ways do you need to improve your walk in the Lord? Are there things that need to be put away?***

---

*Pray – **For the Holy Spirit to guide your steps as He comes alongside you to help you walk in a worthy manner.***

THE GOSPEL IN TRUTH

Philippians 1:18 ...*whether in pretense or in truth, Christ is proclaimed...*

I recoil at hearing preaching that is not doctrinally sound. It makes me uncomfortable to listen to a so-called preacher making his *name-it-and-claim-it* exhortations, or telling his listeners that because they are so good, God will bless them. Also, I am uncomfortable when I hear preaching that states a sinner has the ability within himself to do that which would satisfy a holy God.

Certainly the Apostle Paul must have faced many false teachers in his day. He speaks out on numerous occasions about false teachers who peddle lies. Yet here, in today's passage, he rejoices with this group of troublemakers in Philippi because, even though their motives were wrong in the preaching of the Gospel, Christ was being proclaimed. I will continue to feel uncomfortable when I hear wrongly motivated preachers presenting questionable doctrine. However, I will try to do as Paul did and trust God to accomplish His work in the hearts of the people who hear the Gospel presented. For those of us who have the privilege of sharing the good news of Christ, the lesson here is to present Christ clearly, boldly and in truth.

Look it up – **Isaiah 9:16; 1Timothy 4:1-3, 6:20-21; Titus 1:10-11**

This truth for me – **Have you been led astray by what you thought was good teaching but, in reality, was a lie? What lessons need to be learned about false teaching?**

Pray – **That God will give you a discerning spirit and to study the Word so that you will not be led astray.**

ONLY CHRIST IS WORTHY

Luke 7:4... He is worthy...

God is merciful and extends grace to the elect sinner, whereby he or she receives freedom from sin, death and condemnation. In Luke 7 we read of the Jewish elders who came to Jesus to plead with Him to save the centurion's servant. The elders argued that they believed the centurion was a worthy man. But Jesus knew that no matter how good this centurion was, he was not deserving of the grace and mercy of God.

The Jewish leaders were counting on their own worth to please God. It was natural for them to see this centurion as a worthy man, based upon the good he had done for them. But Jesus saw this centurion as a sinner, condemned and in need of grace. The centurion also saw himself as needy. When he saw Jesus, he did not say to the Lord, "Heal my servant, because I am a good man and I deserve it." But rather, he fell down before Jesus and said, "I am not worthy." His faith was great because his focus was on a great Savior and not on his own worth. None of us deserve the grace that we receive; we are unworthy. But when Jesus speaks, we are taken from unworthiness into an inheritance as a child of God.

Look it up – ***Romans 3:10-12,23; Ephesians 2:4-9; Revelation 5:11-14***

This truth for me – ***How often do you think about God's sustaining grace? What were some examples of the Lord's grace in your life this past week?***

_____

_____

_____

Pray – ***For more understanding of the Lord's grace in your life and praise Him for His worth now being your worth.***

A ONE-ANOTHERING COMMUNITY OF FAITH

1 Corinthians 12:25 *...have the same care for one another.*

One-anothering (the act of caring for others) is a key ingredient in the Church of Jesus Christ. This practice takes precedent over caring for those outside the faith. Paul writes in his letter to the Galatians that we are to *...do good to all men, and especially to those who are of the household of the faith* (Galatians 6:10). One-anothering has to do with being humble and sacrificial. In the preceding verse of this text, Paul exhorts the church in Corinth to honor the less honorable members of the body. One-anothering also has to do with entering emotionally into another person's distress with practical assistance. Lastly, one-anothering is centered in God's love on the cross. Our greatest motivation to respond to another's need is the example of the Lord emptying Himself toward sinners like us. When it seems difficult to come alongside a brother or sister with love and care, look to the cross and remember that the Lord came alongside you when you were a spiritually rotting sinner and covered you with His love.

Look it up – **Philippians 2:2; 1 Thessalonians 4:9–10; Philemon 7**

This truth for me – **Is there something keeping you from loving other Christians . . . all Christians, and not just those who are your friends?**

_____

_____

_____

Pray – **Praise God for your brothers and sisters. Pray for those who need your care, those to whom you need to be more one-anothering.**

WEEP FOR THE SINNER

Luke 23:28 ...weep for yourselves...

The movie, *The Passion of the Christ*, was a success in many ways. It grossed record box office receipts. Clearly depicting the suffering of the Lord, the film is gruesome and bloody. After viewing the Lord's beatings and death on the cross, the viewer walks away with tear-filled eyes. An evangelistic tool, the movie remains a way to introduce people to the death of Christ and Gospel.

The Lord struggled through the streets on the way to Golgotha, followed by loudly weeping women. Jesus turned to them and said, *Stop weeping for me, but weep for yourselves and your children.* Jesus was crushed and beaten, but His suffering was pleasing to Him and to the Father because such suffering was the will of the Father for the salvation of sinners. His condition was not to be lamented, but rather we should weep for our own corrupt condition. Being dead in sin is the most horrible state in which to find oneself! Christian, weep for those without Christ; sinner, weep for yourself in your walking death. Cry out to Jesus for forgiveness and eternal life.

Look it up – ***Job 24:19; Ephesians 2:1-4; Colossians 2:13***

This truth for me – ***How do you see unsaved sinners? Do you say, "They are ok, they will work it out." Or do you see them as dead, in need of the Savior? Who do you know that needs life in Jesus?***

_____

_____

_____

Pray – ***For those you know who are perishing. Praise God for taking your corruption away.***

SAFE AND SOUND IN CHRIST

Hebrews 13:8 Jesus Christ is the same yesterday and today, yes and forever.

Some of our greatest fears occur when we face life changes. Change can cause anxiety and fear, mainly because it usually brings about unfamiliar circumstances and takes us from our comfort zones. I once heard a sermon illustration from a pastor who spoke directly to this. He held up the local newspaper—with its mundane headlines—and then held up the Sept. 11, 2001 issue, with its full-page colored picture of the horror in New York. What a dramatic change in just 24 hours, and what a change in our sense of security! We went from feeling secure in our investments and jobs to fearing that the bottom could fall out at any moment. It was an excellent time to be reminded of the promises of the Bible concerning fear and change.

For those of us who are born again, security is not found in the things of this world. Our security is held firmly in the never-changing person of Jesus Christ. A Christian needs never to fear because Jesus promises, *Lo, I am with you always.* God walks with His children and it is in His unchanging power and nature that we are protected and firmly secure. *"Let not your heart be troubled..."* Christ is with us!

Look it up – **Isaiah 38:14; John 10:27-29; Philippians 1:6**

This truth for me – **What makes you worry? Do you worry about your salvation? List all that Christ has done for you. Know you are secure in Him.**

_____

_____

_____

Pray – **For the Lord to give you peace about your security in Him and for the knowledge of how powerful He is.**

HE IS COMING AGAIN

1 Thessalonians 1:10 ...to wait for His Son...

What are you waiting for? There is a heightened sense on the part of many that something cataclysmic is about to happen. People are saying the end of the world is near. Some Christians are still interested in trying to date the Lord's return. The world continues to be in a state of economic and diplomatic uncertainty and tension. Other forms of waiting can also be fruitless, like the millions who wait each day for 7:00 pm to roll around to see if they hit the lottery. There is one form of waiting that should never produce stress: *waiting upon the Lord.* God calls His children to wait upon Him. Think for a moment what it is to wait upon the Lord. It is to wait upon One who is always perfectly on time, perfect in what He brings, and faithful to those who wait upon Him. In terms of time and space, the children of God ultimately wait for the Lord to return to take them home. Waiting doesn't need to be filled with the stresses of the unknown. We can wait upon the Lord and know that our waiting is resting in God's faithfulness. He will never disappoint us!

Look it up – ***1 Thessalonians 4:13-18; 2 Peter 3:8-18; 1 Corinthians 15:52-58***

This truth for me – ***What encourages you about the return of the Lord? Are you prepared for His return?***

_____

_____

_____

Pray – ***For the Lord to come quickly and reveal His glory; pray to be ready for this meeting.***

THE ONE AND ONLY WAY

1 Kings 18:37 ...Thou, O LORD, art God...

How many true religions are there? I heard a pastor pose the question like this, "Whose god is the right God?" In this religiously-sensitive atmosphere that permeates our country, it might get confusing, even for Christians, to stand firm and distinguish whose god is the true God. In the standoff between Elijah and the Baal prophets in 1 Kings, Elijah had no confusion concerning who was the right God. The right and true God has been and will always be the God of Abraham, Isaac and Jacob, the God of promise who declared to Abraham that a Messiah would come and redeem His people from sin. That covenant promise has been fulfilled in the person and work of Jesus Christ when He came to earth and was crucified, died, buried and rose again from the tomb. Elijah prayed, *...answer me, that this people may know that Thou, O LORD, art God...* The only true God did answer in a mighty way, devouring the altar of testing in flames and giving Elijah the power to kill all the Baal priests. This true covenant God, Jesus Christ, will have no other god before Him; no Buddha, no Mohammed, no Tao, no . . . not any! Let us not blend into the religious setting of today, but in love, testify to the true God and His Son, Jesus Christ!

*Look it up – **Isaiah 44:6; John 3:33; Ephesians 4:5,6***

*This truth for me – **Are you tolerant of other people's religions? How can you share that Christ is the only way?***

---

*Pray – **That God will open doors for you to share that Christ is the only way to salvation.***

THE GOOD WORK OF JESUS

Matthew 19:16 ...what good thing shall I do that I may obtain eternal life?

For several days I have been commenting on the spiritual climate of our country, warning Christians to be careful with thinking that all roads lead to God. I would like to point out yet another concern . . . that of good works. It is easy to think that good works will be pleasing to a righteous God, who will then grant forgiveness. When Jesus was confronted by the individual who asked *...what good things shall I do?* Jesus told him to *keep the commandments.* Jesus' answer indicated that there is no one who can be perfect and keep all the commandments. No amount of good works can take away sin and satisfy God's wrath; only Jesus could keep the Law (the commandments) perfectly. Our own works are like *filthy rags* before God. Christ's work on the cross is the only good work that God recognizes on our behalf. When we, by faith, trust fully in Christ, we are justified not by works but by faith in Christ's perfect work. Good works then flow from us in thanksgiving to Him who saved us. Charles Hodge ends his work on justification by faith with the words from one of John Wesley's hymns: ***...In Him complete we shine, His death, His life is mine, fully I am justified; free from sin...since he died for me.*** Do good in the name of Christ!

*Look it up – **Ephesians 2:10; Galatians 2:16; Titus 3:5***

*This truth for me – **How do you battle with thinking your good deeds will add to your salvation?***

_____

_____

*Pray – **In thanksgiving for the truth that Jesus paid the price for all your sin through His great work at Calvary.***

MY HOPE IS IN THE LORD

2 Corinthians 1:10 ...And He will yet deliver us.

Webster's dictionary defines hope as *"desire with the expectation of getting what is desired."* Many people exercise hope in this manner: they hope that their child will be safe, they hope that their ship will arrive to bail them out of difficult circumstances, they hope they will win the lottery. But hope as described in the Bible has a different twist, and specifically here in the Apostle Paul's use of it as he talks about the afflictions he endured while serving the Lord. True and assuring hope is settled in God and in the eternal life in heaven that He has promised His children. When our hope is fixed on God and His promises, it embraces expectation, trust and patient waiting for the day when we will be taken home to be with Him for eternity. The Christian's hope towers over any hope of a secular nature, because our hope rests in Christ and the salvation He gives to those who put their trust in Him.

My hope is built on nothing less, than Jesus' blood and righteousness...

Look it up – **Psalm 38:15; Psalm 130:7; 1 Timothy 1:1**

This truth for me – **Where does your hope rest? List things in which you are placing your hope, yet will not last.**

_____

_____

_____

Pray – **For God to let you see that He is your hope and all you need for peace.**

THE NARROW ROAD OF SALVATION

Matthew 7:14 For the gate is small...that leads to life...

Charles Fillmore (1854-1948), founder of the Unity School of Christianity (Note: there is nothing Christian at all about Fillmore's teachings), states that "*God is absolute good*" and that "*every human being has a spark of divinity within them, their very essence is of God and therefore man is inherently good.*"

However, in contrast, the Apostle Paul teaches in Ephesians 2:1-3 that all humans are totally depraved and by nature *children of wrath*. Were we to believe Fillmore, the gate to eternal life is really not small, but is wide to receive all people. Fillmore and his followers do not believe in heaven; they hold to a form of reincarnation—becoming one with the universe.

Like the Unity School, most people believe in universalism, that everyone will be saved in some manner. This is not the teaching of Christ or the Bible. Only those who respond to God's work, who repent and receive Christ as Savior, are promised eternal life. This chosen and redeemed band is traveling on a narrow road, but it is the road unto righteousness.

*Look it up – **Matthew 7:21; Luke 13:23-24; John 10:9***

*This truth for me – **Do you believe that everyone is ok, and that in some way all will be saved? How wide is the gate to heaven in your thinking?***

_____

_____

_____

*Pray – **To have a mind to know the truth about the narrow road and the heart to go to those staggering off on the wide road of destruction.***

MISUNDERSTOOD

Luke 2:49 ...Did you not know that I had to be in My Father's house?

Have you ever been misunderstood? Our Lord was the most misunderstood person in history. In this passage, even His earthly father and mother misjudged Him.

Misunderstandings can lead to false assumptions that burden us, and cause gossip, complaining and division. I remember reading of a tragic misunderstanding. A police officer was called to a home because it was thought that there was a burglary in process. When the officer called out to the man, the man turned and a shiny object in his hand flashed in the street light. The officer, thinking it was a gun, pulled his pistol and fired, shooting the man in the leg. As it turned out, the man was the owner of the house trying to get into his own locked house using a garden tool.

If someone is misunderstanding you and causing you concerns, don't retaliate; put it in God's hands. A.W. Tozer writes, *"The Lord will be your defender, you'll never need to defend yourself."* It is best not to make assumptions, but rather let God clarify things before they fester into a misunderstanding. Tozer again writes in his booklet, <u>Five Vows for Spiritual Power</u>, *"...if you want God to be patient with you, you are going to have to be patient with His children."*

Look it up – **Psalm 32:7; Matthew 12:49-53; John 6:52-58**

This truth for me – **Has a misunderstanding resulted in a problem? How could the misunderstanding have been sidetracked?**

_____

_____

_____

Pray – **For wisdom when you are misunderstood by others and patience to trust God for your defense.**

THY WILL, NOT MINE

Philippians 1:19 ...through your prayers...

What is the use? After praying long and hard for the healing of a sick loved one and then seeing that person die, one might wonder what is the use of praying. But prayer is not having what we want, but rather it is asking for God to have what He wants.

In his letter to the Philippians, the Apostle Paul was imprisoned and awaiting the outcome of his trial. He writes that he is confident of deliverance and the means of deliverance would be through the prayers of the saints on his behalf. But what kind of deliverance was Paul expecting through prayer? If we had time to develop the text, we would learn that he expected to be delivered either by being released from prison or released through death. This is indicated in verse 20 when he says, *whether by life or by death.* Paul sought the will of God through the prayers of the saints and was at peace with God's will—death or release. He knew that in either case, as verse 20 also says, *Christ shall... be exalted.* Here are the keys to prayer: pray for God's will to be accomplished and expectantly desire that God be glorified no matter what the answer may be. The result will be peace and confident hope!

*Look it up – **Psalm 62:8; Matthew 6:10; Colossians 1:9***

*This truth for me – **Regarding prayer, what is your greatest struggle? How can you eliminate doubt in your prayer life?***

_____

_____

_____

*Pray – **For acceptance of the Lord's will to be done through all your prayers.***

A SEEKING GOD

Luke 19:10 ...has come to seek and to save...

This is amazing: that God the Father would send His Son to seek out chosen sinners and then save them from their sins based upon the sacrificial work of Christ's blood atonement. Christ seeks us with a *desire*. His desire is to present us spotless and blameless to His Father. He seeks us with a *determination*. He will save all that the Father has chosen to be saved. Not one of the elect will be lost. He seeks with a *devotion* to bring all glory to God as an obedient Son. He seeks with a *destination* in mind. All who He saves will be in glory and have eternal life. Finally and most importantly, He seeks with a *deep love* for those lost in sin. None of the redeemed can ever reasonably doubt the love of God which is in Christ Jesus. Yes, we can find ourselves in pits of depression and fear, and doubt God's love, but the antidote to such doubting is to cast our eyes back on the cross and remember that supreme and divine act which demonstrated the love of God toward us while we were dead in sin. He is still seeking and saving and we are still His means of saving, by way of witnessing the Gospel. ***Therefore, go and preach the Gospel!***

*Look it up – **Ezekiel 34:16; Matthew 18:12; John 4:23***

*This truth for me – **If we are the means for God seeking out His people, what does this mean to you and what is your responsibility?***

---

*Pray – **Praise God for His love toward sinners and pray that He will seek out those people in your life who need the Gospel.***

HEARING, LEARNING AND DOING

Deuteronomy 31:12 ...that they may hear and learn and fear...

God had instituted a sabbatical year for the nation of Israel. Every seven years there was to be forgiveness of debts incurred by the people. This was God's way of dealing with poverty and avoiding a society separated by rich and poor. In Deuteronomy 31, Moses adds the public reading of the Law, and describes the effect this was to have upon the people. They were to *hear, learn* and *fear.* Hearing God's Word is the first step toward reverence and worship of God. Learning God's Word is the next step in true worship; to learn would be to take God's Word to heart and put it into action. Lastly, when we hear the Word, digest it and live it, the end result will be a deep reverence or fear of God. This reverent fear not only honors God, but also blesses us with peace and a sense of nearness to our God.

Do you have a special time for the public reading of God's Word in your worship service? Many churches are moving away from significant readings of Scripture in worship. How sad! Having our people follow along in the reading of God's Word during worship is not a mere ritual, but rather it could very well help produce a people who *fear* the Lord.

*Look it up – **James 1:19-25; Hebrews 1:2; Colossians 3:16***

*This truth for me – **How well do you hear the Word and then act upon it in the fear of the Lord? List how you can better hear and do.***

_____

_____

_____

*Pray – **For the time to read the Word and carry it out in your life no matter what the cost.***

SAFE AND SECURE

Romans 8:1 *There is therefore now no condemnation for those who are in Christ Jesus.*

Charles Spurgeon, the gifted preacher of 19th century London, England, once commented on Solomon's Song in the Old Testament, 4:7. He said, *"Our precious Husband (God) knows our silly hearts too well to take any offense at our ill manners."* For a sinner to be in Christ is a glorious position. When Christ applies His righteousness to our condemned lives, all condemnation against us is removed and we no longer face an eternity of hell. Instead, we receive the glory of heaven forever. Yes, Christians sin and fall prey to temptation, but once the blood of Christ is applied, our sin no longer leads us to eternal condemnation. It may cause God to discipline us but sin will never again cry out and cast us into the fire of damnation. Thanks be to God alone for this grace of *...sending His own Son in the likeness of sinful flesh and as an offering for sin...* (Romans 8:3). The child born in Bethlehem, Jesus, God in the flesh, was sent to keep God's Law, which we could never keep. Those who are born again in Christ Jesus can sing from the mountain, "No condemnation, no condemnation; thanks be to God for sending His Son!"

*Look it up – **Isaiah 50:9; Romans 8:33, 34; 1 Corinthians 11:32***

*This truth for me – **Do you ever feel like God is going to cast you away? Look up the many promises of God's faithfulness regarding His promise to save you and keep you.***

_____

_____

_____

*Pray – **For God to give you the assurance of your salvation.***

INTO THE LIGHT OF CHRIST

Luke 4:18 ...recovery of sight to the blind...

From all of the Old Testament passages Jesus could have selected to read and preach in His hometown synagogue, He selected this Messianic passage from Isaiah 61. Isaiah foretells of Israel's deliverance from the Babylonian captivity, which would take place when Cyrus the Great, of the Persian Empire, set free those Jews held captive in Babylon. But when Jesus reads this passage some eight hundred years after Isaiah's recording, and after the Persian defeat of the Babylonians, Jesus refers to the deliverance that He will bring by virtue of His life, death and resurrection from the grave. It is not a temporal deliverance, but an eternal deliverance from the darkness of sin and death.

On one occasion, I had the privilege of speaking with a man who began losing his physical sight at age eighteen. Now in his thirties, he was totally blind. After talking for several hours, the man prayed, asking Christ for forgiveness and for salvation. This man who had no physical sight gained spiritual sight because Jesus Christ, the One who came to give sight to those blinded by sin, worked his salvation.

*Look it up – **Psalm 56:13; Romans 7:24, 25; Colossians 1:13***

*This truth for me – **From what darkness has Christ saved you?***

_____

_____

_____

*Pray – **Praise God for saving you from the darkness of sin and leading you into the light of Christ.***

HE WAS BORN TO BEAR

Luke 1:31,32 *And behold, you will conceive in your womb, and bear a son...*
He will be great, and will be called the Son of the Most High...

The uniqueness of the Christian faith is that biblical Christianity calls sinners to *come*. This was the cry of Jesus as He walked the earth, *Come unto me*. In contrast, the world's religions tell people to *go* and find a way to God, through their own contrivances or through the ritual of religiosity. The reason Christ, and we His ambassadors, call sinners to come, is that we know that a sinner cannot find a way to please a holy God by themselves. Mankind is lost and in need of a substitute who can stand before God and say, *I paid this sinner's debt and I now present him to you, Father, robed in my divine righteousness*. Only the God-man—Jesus the Son—can be man's substitute before a holy God.

As I read through the Old Testament and the Gospel accounts of the birth of the Messiah, I find one glaring theme. Jesus was unique. God came to earth and became a man in Jesus Christ. This child would march His way to the cross, and it is on the cross that we see God dying for the forgiveness of sins, the perfect man dying in our place. This is why we call His death a substitutionary atonement. He was born to live and die as the God-man, to forgive sins and take God's wrath from us as our perfect substitute. If you are born again, you stand in Jesus, the Son of God. Never forget your position!

Look it up – **Genesis 3:15; Romans 5:8; 2 Corinthians 5:21**

This truth for me – **How does Christ's substitutionary death for you affect your hope, your witness and your worship of the Lord?**

_____

_____

Pray – **For God to allow you to see your position in Christ: His love, His joy, His peace.**

AN ASTONISHING ASSURANCE

Judges 13:12 ...*Now when your words come to pass...*

The *gift of faith* is a spiritual gift which the Holy Spirit bestows on some Christians. I understand this gift to be as Dr. James Boice defined it: *"...to discern with extraordinary confidence the will and purposes of God for the future of His work."*

Manoah's words here in Judges are an exercise of faith and a very good illustration of the extraordinary gift of faith. Manoah's wife was told by the angel of the Lord that, although she had been barren, she would conceive a son. After she shared the news with her husband, Manoah prayed and asked God to have the man of God come and teach them how to raise this special child. God answered Manoah's prayer, and when the visitation occurred, Manoah's first declaration was, *Now when your words come true...* Manoah knew that what the angel of the Lord said was going to come true. He had extraordinary confidence that he would have a son. I am convinced that this angel of the Lord was God, Himself, and most likely, God the Son, the pre-incarnate Jesus Christ. May we be able to manifest this Manoah-type faith, to believe what Christ tells us through His word and live with confidence in our Lord. Do you need help to acquire such faith? Ask God, read His word, and look for His gift of faith.

*Look it up – **Matthew 9:29; Hebrews 11:6; James 2:17***

*This truth for me – **In what ways do you lack faith? What things hinder you from growing in faith?***

_____

_____

_____

*Pray – **For your faith to increase and to understand the bigness of God.***

CALLED A CHRISTIAN

Acts 11:26 ...the disciples were first called Christians in Antioch.

Luke records his account of the first-century Church in the book of Acts. After Stephen was martyred in Jerusalem (Acts 7), a persecution broke out against the Christians. Many of them fled Jerusalem and some ended up in cities north of Palestine, like Antioch. Luke's account tells us that as these Christians entered Antioch, they began proclaiming the Gospel of the Lord Jesus. As a result of these evangelistic efforts, *considerable numbers were brought to the Lord.* When the church in Jerusalem heard of this, they sent a trusted servant, Barnabas, to Antioch to investigate what was taking place.

When Barnabas arrived, he was overwhelmed by what he saw. He *witnessed the grace of God* saving Gentiles and Jews. Barnabas understood he had to disciple these new converts in the faith. He sent for Saul, later known as the Apostle Paul, and together they taught these new believers. It is in Antioch that the followers of Christ were first recognized as Christians (Greek, *christianos, follower of Christ* or *little Christ*). Antioch is the ideal model for church planting: proclamation of the Gospel, God saving through the witness of the Word, and discipleship—making converts into disciples. Are you zealous for Christ, so that those around you say, "There goes a little Jesus?"

*Look it up – **Psalm 42:1; Matthew 7:16; 1 Peter 3:14-17***

*This truth for me – **How would you rate your zeal for the Lord (scale of 1-10)?***

---

*Pray – **For the Holy Spirit to build His fire inside of you for the Kingdom of God.***

THE SNAKE THAT LIES CLOSE AT HAND

Romans 7:19 ...I practice the very evil that I do not wish.

At a men's seminar, the speaker said something I will never forget. In speaking on the heart of man, he said, *"I find that there are times in my life that I have to repent of the manner by which I repent."* The flesh and the Spirit is an ongoing struggle for the child of God. Like a snake ready to launch its fangs, the evil flesh is ready to rob us of even the good intentioned efforts of our lives.

At times I find my prayers tainted with selfishness, my counsel colored by bias or anger, and even my teaching and preaching stinking of pride or self-pity. At these times I can enter into the cry of the apostle, *wretched man that I am.* This battle of flesh and Spirit will persist, and only death will bring it to a final and ultimate defeat.

So what is the Christian to do? The same thing the apostle did—turn to Jesus Christ. *Thanks be to God through Jesus Christ, our Lord.* Let me emphasize *our* Lord. A Christian has the Lord on his side, and even though we are beset by the flesh, Christ has conquered the flesh, sin and death. Has the flesh been trying to rob you of your joy in Jesus? Turn it over to the Lord. He has defeated the deadly snake of flesh in you. Thanks be to God!

*Look it up – **Psalm 56:4; Romans 8:3-9; Galatians 6:7,8***

*This truth for me – **Does the flesh rob you of your desire to do good? What good do you want to do and can't seem to get it done?***

_____

_____

_____

*Pray – **For victory over the Devil and sin and for the power to do the good you know you want to do.***

A HEART HEAVY FOR SOULS

Psalm 96:2,3 ...Proclaim good tidings of His salvation...Tell of His glory among the nations...

Samuel Rutherford's first church was at Anwoth on the Solway. There he wrestled with God for his heart's desire. Like the Apostle Paul in Romans 10:1, his heart beat for the salvation of souls in Anwoth. He desired to be the instrument by which they would hear the Gospel and repent. Clarence Macartney characterized Rutherford's passion for evangelism in the words of Anne Cousin, *"O Anwoth, by the Solway, To me thou still art dear, E'en from the gate of heaven I'll drop for thee a tear. Oh, if one soul from Anwoth meet me at God's right hand, My heaven will be two heavens in Immanuel's Land."*

Like Rutherford, our Lord looked across His city and cried out for the salvation of the people in Jerusalem. He then put that precious evangelistic heart into action and matched His tears with His blood so that those He came to seek would be saved. My heart is beating for the salvation of souls. May this year be the year of salvation; may my heart's desire be matched by my feet in going and my mouth in proclaiming. Will you join me? Go like never before into the community and among the people with the goal of proclaiming Christ and winning souls. Let us pray that the Lord of the Harvest will be with us as we take the light to the lost.

Look it up – ***Psalm 51:10-13; Psalm 70:4; Romans 10:14-15***

This truth for me – ***List those you want to see saved and then, day by day, pray and seek ways to go to them and talk about their need for Christ.***

———————————————————————————

———————————————————————————

———————————————————————————

Pray – ***For the salvation of people with whom you live and work and socialize.***

GRACE, GRACE, GOD'S GRACE

Romans 9:20 ...O man, who answers back to God...

Although the letter of Romans was written primarily to Gentile Christians at Rome, if you were a Jew listening in or even a Jewish convert, Paul's abrupt and dogmatic statement would have set you back on your heels. The bottom line to the sovereignty of God in salvation is not debatable and therefore Paul does not debate the suspected questions he believes will arise (verse 19), but rather he challenges our innate desire to put ourself into the work of salvation.

In the church I serve, we firmly hold to the sovereign decrees of grace, grace alone (sola gratia). In my limited estimation of the American church, it seems that much of the church has drifted into the shallow waters of man-centered theological beliefs. The Bible over and over challenges us to confirm the theology of God's sovereignty and grace alone. Why bring this to our attention? Because by nature we are all self-centered. There could be a slipping back into the thinking which puts man and his efforts at the center of the church. It is incumbent upon each of us to stand firm on the Bible's teaching that God is sovereign and only by grace are we saved and not of ourselves. Churches must return to teaching and preaching God's grace and holiness, even if there are costly outcomes, ...so help us God!

*Look it up – **Ezra 9:8,9; Ephesians 2:8,9; Philippians 3:8,9***

*This truth for me – **Do you think you need to add something to the salvation God freely gave you? Is there anything that gets in the way of seeing that God's grace is free in Christ?***

_____

_____

_____

*Pray – **Thank God for His abounding grace that He extended in saving you.***

GODLINESS IN HEART NOT FORM

2 Timothy 3:2, 5 For men will be...holding to a form of godliness...

I have often thought of how wonderful it would be to be able to play the cello and sail a boat. The hindrances which stopped me from ever doing these things were the time and discipline needed to learn how to play and sail.

I have seen people who want to practice religion and do Christian things, but don't want to follow the disciplines set down in the Word of God. The liberal church, that denies the full inspiration of the Scriptures and takes a selective interpretation of the Bible, says it is following the teachings of Christ. Yet liberalism is unwilling to follow His commands when they contradict so-called personal freedoms. Others want to take the Bible and make it fit their own interpretations and predictions, even if it means treading on holy ground. In these last days, there will be great temptation to move away from living a biblical, disciplined life. We must not stray from the disciplines of the Christian faith as revealed in the Bible. We must also not be fooled by forms of godliness—those religious beliefs that look good on the surface but, when you begin scraping away, are false teaching. Let us hold on to what is true!

Look it up – 1 Timothy 6:11; Titus 2:11-13; 2 Peter 1:3,4

*This truth for me – **What is the difference between godliness and forms of godliness? List character traits that form godliness.***

_____

_____

_____

*Pray – **For God to help His Church be characterized by true godliness and not forms of godliness.***

WHEN GOD GIVES, HE REALLY GIVES

John 3:16 For God so loved the world, that He gave...

No matter what your view of the meaning of *world* in this passage, we all should agree that John 3:16 demonstrates to us that our God has a deep heart of mercy with regard to sinners. C. John Miller, who helped to start the New Life Presbyterian Churches in the Philadelphia area, is author of the book, *Evangelism & Your Church*. In it, he quotes R. B. Kuiper: *"John 3:16 makes the amazing...well-nigh unbelievable declaration that the holy God sovereignly loves hell-deserving sinners..."*

I teach in my theology classes the positives of the doctrines of grace, particularly the doctrine of justification by grace. I tell the class that the greatest motivation for missions is twofold: that God saved me unconditionally, a sinner destined for hell, and that because His grace saved such a hopeless, spiritual corpse from eternal damnation, I am compelled by *obedience* and *thanksgiving* to tell everyone about the Lord. I am to direct them to the cross where they need to repent and believe upon Jesus Christ. I praise God for His great salvation. Praise Him that He gave His Son.

Look it up – **John 4:10; 2 Corinthians 9:15; 1 John 4:9**

This truth for me – **In your mind, measure the depth of God's love for you and meditate upon that love. Now, how can you respond to that love today?**

_____

_____

_____

Pray – **Giving thanks to God for the gift of Jesus and for God to lead you to what your response is to such a love.**

THE POWERFUL DUO OF THE WORD AND THE SPIRIT

1 Thessalonians 2:13 ...the word of God, which also performs its work in you who believe.

The Thessalonians were intimately related to the Word of God. They received the Word and they sounded forth the Word. They also had the Word of God performing its work in them. Recently I took a moment to listen to a Christian TV show. While listening to the host and his advertisement for an upcoming fundraiser, he said something to this effect, *"Be prepared to have God work in your life. The more you give, the more Christ-like you will become."* If there is any spark of truth in this statement (which is doubtful), it gets buried in the intent of prompting people to give money so the network can stay on the air. God saved us so He would have a people shaped in the likeness of His Son, Jesus Christ. As is always the case, not only has God designed this plan for His children to bear the image of His Son, He has also provided the means by which we are conformed to Christ. That means is through the mighty truth of the Bible. The Word of God performs its work in those who believe. We are made to be more like Christ, as we read, study and obey the teachings of the Bible. A gift to a TV ministry might help them stay on the air but it won't make you more Christ-like. Only the Holy Spirit and the Word will perform that transformation.

*Look it up – **Proverbs 1:23; Isaiah 40:7; Ephesians 6:17***

*This truth for me – **How much time do you spend in God's Word? Would you say you are growing in the Lord? How do we grow more like Jesus?***

---

*Pray – **Thanking God for His Word as revealed to us by the Spirit through His Word.***

HOW BEAUTIFUL IS OUR DELIVERER

2 Corinthians 1:10 who delivered us...will deliver us...will yet deliver us.

In this passage, the emphasis is clear, God delivers His people. He has delivered us from the death of sin, He is delivering us from the attacks and perils of this world, and He will deliver us unto His heavenly glory when the appointed time arrives. Each aspect of His deliverance is meaningful to our lives. The Christian knows that the curse of sin and its condemnation has been lifted by the work of Christ on the Cross. What assurance and peace we now can have in knowing that no matter how terrible the circumstance, He is delivering me by the promises of His Word and the testimony of His faithfulness. Finally, the crescendo to His deliverance is that He will one day give me my inheritance in Christ. Oh, how great a salvation! How great a response of thanksgiving we should sing forth to our great God and Deliverer...

> *No condemnation now I dread; Jesus, and all in Him, is mine!*
> *Alive in Him, my living head, and clothed in righteousness divine,*
> *Bold I approach the eternal throne,*
> *And claim the crown, thru Christ my own.*
> *Amazing Love! How can it be, that Thou my God, shouldst die for me!*
> (C. Wesley)

*Look it up – **Psalm 32:7; Psalm 68:20; 2 Corinthians 1:10***

*This truth for me – **From what has God delivered you? List what He will deliver you onto when Christ returns.** _____*

_____

_____

*Pray – **For the eyes to see those around you who need God's deliverance.***

THE HEAVY BURDEN OF GOD'S WRATH

Romans 1:18 For the wrath of God is revealed from heaven against...

O sinner! consider the fearful danger you are in: it is...a wide and bottomless pit, full of the fire of wrath, that you are held over in the hand of that God, whose wrath is provoked and incensed...against you... You hang by a slender thread... (Jonathan Edwards, <u>Sinners in the Hand of an Angry God</u>)

No hot drops have as yet fallen, but a shower of fire is coming. No terrible winds howl around you, but God's tempest is gathering... the water floods are dammed up by mercy, but the flood gates shall soon be opened;... how awful shall that moment be when God... shall march forth in fury! (Charles Spurgeon, <u>Devotional Classics of C. H. Spurgeon</u>)

The coming wrath of God upon the sinner is not a popular subject in American Christianity. In former times, sermons on wrath were not proclaimed by the ignorant or unlearned trying scare tactics on their hearers. Rather, Jonathan Edwards is considered to be one of the most brilliant men who ever lived in America, and Spurgeon was recognized by British contemporaries as a most accomplished intellect. Question: could our lack of conversion growth in the United States be a result of a lack of preaching and teaching on God's impending wrath? Don't ignore the wrath of God!

*Look it up – **Psalm 2:5-12; Romans 1:21-32; 2 Thessalonians 1:9***

*This truth for me – **Do you ever think about God's wrath? No worry for the Christian regarding His wrath but what will the unbeliever face? What is God's wrath?***

_____

_____

_____

*Pray – **For those you know facing the wrath of God if they were to die today.***

FALLING, FALLING... GONE

Luke 10:11 Even the dust of your city...we wipe off...

When sharing the Gospel with the unsaved, it is very difficult to know when enough is enough and move on. Many of us have faced individuals who strained our patience and we finally had to wipe the dust of their insincerity off our Gospel feet.

Thomas Hooker, a 17th century Puritan preacher, wrote a sermon, *The Danger of Desertion*. It was a typical prophetic Puritan "Jeremiad," a confrontation of England's sinful way like Jeremiah the prophet condemned Israel. Hooker attacks the falling away of England from the Gospel and states, *"God is going from England...He is packing up His Gospel and moving to a white harvest."* In looking at England now, Hooker's words were truly prophetic. If it hasn't already, England is very close to being an Islamic country. At some point, this country of Spurgeon and Wesley, Whitfield and Wilberforce turned its back on the Gospel, and we might say that God gave them over to their trampling of the beautiful Gospel. There are signs that America is slipping down the same slope as our friends across the Atlantic. Pray and work hard for the sake of the Gospel here in America.

Look it up – **Mark 4:16-19; 2 Peter 2:1-3; Hebrews 6:1-8**

This truth for me – **What does falling away from the faith mean to you? How would you approach someone who you see drifting away from the Lord?**

_____

_____

_____

Pray – **For America to be revived and for those you know who need revival in their hearts.**

INTO THE HIGHWAYS AND BYWAYS

Luke 1:68 ...For He has visited us and accomplished redemption for His people.

Richard Baxter, in his book, *The Reformed Pastor,* speaks of the necessity for ministers and elders to be visiting their people. A special dynamic of intimacy occurs when you sit in people's homes, see their surroundings, and learn of their interests and hobbies. Sometimes visiting brings surprises.

I remember visiting a man who lost his wife to sickness and was on his own. After a time, he asked me if I wanted to stay for dinner and I said "yes," hoping to learn more about the man. He went into the kitchen and began to put the stew he had been cooking onto plates for the two of us. As we ate, I commented that the stew was very good. His response was, "Yes, I was fortunate. I got to the pheasant right after it was hit along the road and it was still warm when I brought it home to prepare for the stew."

On that afternoon, visitation meant eating road kill! But the climax to this story is that as we talked, this man shared with me that he had never been baptized and wanted to learn more about it. This visitation led to this man giving his public testimony in the waters of baptism. Let's get out and visit and find the jewels God has hidden for us.

*Look it up – **Acts 20:28; Colossians 3:16; James 1:27***

*This truth for me – **Make a list of four people you could visit in the next four weeks and then go and encourage them.***

_____

_____

_____

*Pray – **For the energy and courage to intentionally visit.***

IN DUE TIME HE WILL

Mark 4:28 *The soil produces crops by itself...*

A pastor shared with me how God was growing his ministry. I asked what he had been doing? His statement was, "I don't think that I have been doing anything other than the normal ministry and outreach activities that I do regularly." Many pastors have observed the same wonder when they have gone through growth periods. They preach, evangelize and do outreach, and in God's providence, there are times when they see growth. In the parable of Mark 4, the lesson is clear as to what we should do. We should sow the Word and harvest the fruit. We should also rest and get up to do our ministry all over again on a new day. But we should not think we can bring forth the fruit. Whether planting new churches or attempting to grow established churches, we are responsible for what the Lord has entrusted to us: sowing, harvesting and waiting upon Him to bless our efforts. We can do all the sowing and do it very well, but growth is in the hands of the Lord. In our own Christian life, we must also follow the same pattern. We sow the Word into our minds, pray, obey and live for Christ, and then watch as the Lord does His transforming power in our lives.

*Look it up – **Psalm 27:14; Isaiah 40:31; Galatians 5:5***

*This truth for me – **What hinders you from being patient? How can you be more trusting in God's faithfulness?***

_____

_____

_____

*Pray – **For a greater understanding of God's faithfulness to produce His results in your life.***

YEAH, WAY TO GO

Romans 15:5 ...God who gives perseverance and encouragement...

At the end of World War II, our soldiers arrived home to the thanks and praise of every American for defending our country against the tyranny of Nazi Germany and Imperial Japan. There is a scene in the movie, *We Were Soldiers,* that shows an army veteran pushing another vet in a wheelchair. The two men are coming home from their tour of duty in Vietnam in 1968. As they walk through the airport with people passing them by, they receive no acknowledgement or even as much as a nod of thanks or gesture of encouragement. The camera zooms in on one soldier's face and you see a tear running down his cheek as if to say, "Isn't anybody thankful?"

Maybe 1968 and the unthanked soldiers from Vietnam were the beginning of our years one historian calls, *the unthankful society.* September 11th may have changed us and made us more thankful, yet for the Christian community, we are always to be thankful and encouraging one another because our God is the *God who gives encouragement.* Brothers and sisters, we all need encouragement and a thank you once in a while. A good strong "thank you" and words of encouragement go a long way toward building up one another in the faith, from the pastor who serves his flock to the Sunday School teacher who serves the class, to the person who cleans the church. Look for someone to encourage and thank today.

Look it up – **Isaiah 35:3; Philippians 2:1,2; Hebrews 3:13**

This truth for me – **Is there someone in your life that needs a word of encouragement today? Go and encourage.**

_____

_____

_____

Pray – **Thank the Lord for the ways He encourages you day by day.**

KEEP IN CIRCLES OF CHRISTIAN LIFE

Ezekiel 37:28 And the nations will know that I am the Lord...

The picture of the millennial age (the 1,000 years of Kingdom here on earth after Christ returns) is vivid in Ezekiel's prophecy. Also vivid is Ezekiel's use of the Hebrew terms, *qadash* and *miqdash*. These words translated are *sanctify* and *sanctuary*. They refer to an individual or a group of individuals who are observed as being clean or pure, and a thing or place being set apart as holy. The nation of Israel will be a holy people and be in a holy position, separate from the nations because God Himself will make them so, and through Israel He will declare His sovereign rule over His universe.

The Apostle Paul quotes from the Ezekiel passage in his second letter to the church in Corinth (2 Corinthians 6:16). In this present age, the Church—those who are in Christ by virtue of having been born-again—is the vessel through which God now declares His sovereign grace. Just as in the age to come when God will declare Himself through the sanctified vessel of Israel, He now declares Himself through His holy temple, the Church. It is no wonder 2 Corinthians 6 exhorts believers to be separate from the world's lawlessness and darkness; we are holy vessels, made holy by God Himself. Let the nations see God in us, who are sanctified by the cleansing blood of Christ.

*Look it up – **John 17:17-19; 2 Corinthians 6:17; Galatians 6:14***

*This truth for me – **Are you walking too close to the things of the world and are you spending too much time with unsaved people versus your brothers and sisters? What must change?***

_____

_____

_____

*Pray – **That God will give you a good circle of Christian friends to keep you accountable and enjoy Christian fellowship with.***

THE LEADERS GOD GIVES YOU

Romans 1:1 Paul, a bond-servant of Christ Jesus, called as an apostle, set apart...

Before the 19th century ended, theology was still regarded as the *Queen of the Sciences,* and ministers of the Gospel were considered to be a group of credible and scholarly men whose wisdom could be relied upon both in the sacred and secular worlds. However, in this 21st century, the consideration of religion and those who are called to serve the Church have sunk to an all-time low in terms of credibility and wisdom. With the recent tragic news of numerous Roman Catholic priests involved in child molestation cases, we clergy have again taken a broadside hit.

Yet today, God still recognizes us as His special servants, ordained to do His will, standing firm upon the Word of Life and sharing it with all. In the Apostle's letter to the church in Rome, he introduces his communication with a description of his credentials: one who serves the Church, a man called to his office, an apostle and a preacher set apart to share the Gospel. Our glory does not come from the world, but rather from the God of glory who says, *well done my good and faithful servant.* We are blessed to be recognized by Him! As a Christian, you need to honor your leaders and submit to them in the Lord.

*Look it up – **1 Corinthians 16:16; Hebrews 13:17; 1 Peter 2:13***

*This truth for me – **Do you have a problem with submitting to God-ordained leadership? If so, evaluate your heart against the word of God which calls us to submit to those who oversee.***

_____

_____

_____

*Pray – **For the leaders of your church and the will to honor them.***

OTHER-ORIENTED ATTENTION

1 Corinthians 13:5 ...it does not seek its own...

Love is as much a doctrine as reconciliation, justification and redemption; it is even what fuels such great doctrines of the faith. However, so often in the name of doctrine, we fail to love as Christ loved. But my focus is not on our failures in this area of love and theology but rather our failures in another area. One commentator on the 1 Corinthian passage says that when Paul wrote this, he may have had Barnabas in mind, the son of encouragement. Barnabas was always looking out for someone else's good. He is a good illustration of this *other-oriented love* Paul is speaking about.

Let me cut to the chase with an application of other-oriented love. Recently I observed, and others have told me, how difficult it seems to get people to return phone calls. It certainly is frustrating when you want to speak with someone about an important matter and not receive a return call. Imagine how missionaries feel when they try to set up meetings and contact pastors to come and share and do not hear back from those they contact. Does this happen? Yes, all the time. I know how busy we are and how many requests we receive for contact. However, whether we are pastors, ministry directors or workers in the church, we must try to keep in mind that the courtesy of responding to people, greeting and acknowledging them, are demonstrations of love.

Look it up – **Romans 12:10; Philippians 2:3; 1 Peter 2:17**

This truth for me – **Maybe you or I failed to return a call this week; it's time to show love and make that return call.**

_____

_____

_____

Pray – **For God to make you more sensitive and responsive to people when they contact you.**

THE CARCASS OF DEATH

Judges 14:9 ...he had scraped the honey out of the body of the lion.

I was 14 years old when my uncle finally allowed me to be with my cousins on the kill floor of our family's butcher shop (sorry for the graphic terminology). My first instruction was to learn the meticulous skill of skinning cattle. On that first day, I was standing by the open carcass of a steer which had just been lowered onto the skinning frame with its back on the frame and its hind legs sticking up. As I leaned over and began skinning around the hind legs, my cousins picked me up and hurled me into the open carcass. I was the runt of the family and they loved playing tricks on me. I will never forget the cold eerie feeling that made my skin crawl while rustling to get up and out of that dead steer.

Samson, when he had reached into the dead carcass of the lion, entered into a place of death where the child of God is not to enter. It was not just that he broke his Nazarite vow, but rather he was touching that which is an abomination to God—death and decay. The child of God who has been washed by the blood of the Lord and freed from sin and death is no longer to play around with the things of death. We, who are light, have been called out of darkness and are not to go back into the carcasses of sin and worldly lusts. Maybe there is a dead carcass you find yourself in. If so, run to the Lord and He, who went down into the carcass of death to destroy death, will lift you out.

Look it up – Leviticus 5:2; Matthew 23:27; Romans 14:14

This truth for me – If you find yourself involved with unclean things, what does the Lord want you to do?

_____

_____

_____

Pray – That if you have anything unclean in your life, God will help you to clean it out through prayer and repentance.

HOW DEEP IS YOUR LOVE

1 Samuel 18:1 ...Jonathan loved him as himself.

In reviewing the relationship that Jonathan, King Saul's son, had with David, I counted at least three times where the Bible stated that Jonathan loved David as himself. This type of love was a pure, selfless and unconditional love motivated by Jonathan's understanding of God's plan and purpose for David. Jonathan, who was the next in line to be the king of Israel, could have been jealous of David. But instead, Jonathan looked beyond his own promotion and promoted David, God's choice for king.

Do we allow jealousy to get in the way of God's plan? Jealousy can lead to anger, bitterness, and eventually murder. No matter what the source of jealousy, this dark emotion will end up hurting someone and harming our own walk with the Lord and His people. If jealousy is eating away at your joy and peace, then today give it over to the Lord and ask Him to replace your jealousy with a Jonathan-like love. When we love others as we love ourselves, we can defeat jealousy and find God's blessing and favor.

Look it up – **1 Samuel 20:1-17; I Corinthians 13:1-3; John 13:31-35**

This truth for me – **How far does your love go? Does it go to the point of being willing to love another more than you love yourself? What does this type of love mean to you?**

_____

_____

_____

Pray – **For the Lord to give you a heart of selfless love toward even those you may not like.**

FACE TO FACE WITH THE ALMIGHTY

Exodus 33:11 Thus the Lord used to speak to Moses face to face...

Have you ever thought about what God looks like, or desired a face-to-face time with God? The answer to such a question is biblically clear—*no mortal man can see the face of God and remain alive.* Man will only see God when this mortal life is over and eternal spiritual life begins. God's grace granted Moses a very limited exposure to His glory in order that Moses would not be consumed. Even this brief glance at the glory of God left Moses aglow when he came off the mountain. But more important is the fact that it was God's unmerited grace which allowed Moses the glance in the first place. Moses was a mere mortal and a sinner in the sight of God, yet God's grace came unconditionally to such a sinner.

My friends, it is still God's grace that bows to unworthy sinners in order that they may have a glimpse of Him through His Son and His Word. It is also unconditional grace which will allow the redeemed to see God face to face when they die and go to eternity. Our face-to-face is yet to come!

*Look it up – **Deuteronomy 34:10; Matthew 5:8; 1 Corinthians 13:12***

*This truth for me – **How can you gain a face-to-face with God through His Word? List ways the Word allows us to see God.***

_____

_____

_____

*Pray – **For your Bible reading to be more alive and experience God.***

NO, NOTHING BUT THE BLOOD

Revelation 5:9 ...Thou wast slain...

Liberal and Neo-Orthodox Christianity (the beliefs that deny the divine inspiration of the Scriptures and all that is supernatural in the Bible) would argue that the blood of Christ had no atoning value, and it is irrational to think that blood shed 2,000 years ago at Calvary can wash away a sinner's sin today. Yet, contrary to what liberalism might believe, the Bible states that without the washing of Christ's blood, all sinners, both 2,000 years ago and today, remain dead in trespasses and sin. To die without that cleansing flow being applied to your life means an eternity of darkness and torment.

The well-known hymn asks a biblical rhetorical question and then answers the question with a mighty response: *What can wash away my sin? Nothing! Nothing! Nothing! But the Blood of Jesus.* Christ revealed to the Apostle John, in the fifth chapter of the book of Revelation, a powerful worship service taking place in heaven. Gathered in worship were the four living creatures or most likely cherubim (angels), along with thousands of other angels, and twenty-four elders holding harps and bowls of incense. In the middle of this assembly was the Lamb of God, the exalted glorified Christ. All the praise of those gathered was bringing glory and honor to the Lamb. Why? Because He was slain and with His BLOOD, He purchased the elect from every tongue, tribe and nation. Is the blood insignificant? Not at all, rather it is the significant price paid for sinners like you and me.

Look it up – **Romans 5:9; Ephesians 1:7; 1 Peter 1:17-19**

This truth for me – **Do you accept the truth of Scripture that the blood of Christ cleanses us from sin? What is hard about this statement?**

_____

_____

_____

Pray – **Thank God for sending His Son to shed His blood and wash us white as snow.**

WE ARE PRONE TO WANDER

1 Kings 11:4 ...and his heart was not wholly devoted to the Lord...

In the past ten years, Attention Deficit Disorder (ADD) has been the diagnosis which doctors have pronounced on hyperactive children who have difficulty concentrating. For King Solomon it was not ADD that caused him to turn his concentration away from God, but rather it was sin. His sin specifically was his multi-affairs with many women from foreign nations who lured him away to their pagan gods and away from the true God of Israel. The comparison made here in the text is that Solomon was not devoted to God as was his father, King David, who was described in Scripture as being *a man after God's own heart.* What a contrast; Solomon was a man after his own heart's lust, and David was man after God's own heart. It is not that David was perfect and had no sin, quite the opposite. David sinned and did so to an extreme in the adulterous affair he had with Bathsheba and then a murderous plot to kill Uriah, Bathsheba's husband. The difference between David's handling of sin and Solomon's is REPENTANCE. In Psalm 51 David writes *...cleanse me from sin, for I know my transgressions...* There are times when we all turn our devotion to sin and we leave the God we love, whether for a brief time or for a habitual season. The key to turning our hearts back to God is true repentance. Do you have a case of Spiritual ADD? Is your devotion focused on something or someone other than God? Turn back to the God who loves you and is faithful to forgive a repentant heart.

Look it up – Psalm 119:10; Isaiah 35:8; James 5:19-20

This truth for me – Do you find yourself wandering from the Lord? When does this happen and what must be done to get back on the true path?

_____

_____

_____

Pray – For the Lord's strength to keep your heart and mind focused on Christ. And when you stray, pray for forgiveness.

GRACE AND MERCY KEEPS COMING

1 Peter 1:3 ...according to His great mercy...

I think of mercy differing from grace in that mercy is the form of love which God demonstrates toward a miserable and helpless sinner. Grace is that gift of God to show unmerited favor to the guilty sinner and perfect him in the perfection of Christ. Both grace and mercy rule out any human merit. None of us deserve or earn God's mercy and grace; rather, any input of human effort violates both the mercy and grace of God. A sinner is in a state of suffering and need, even though he may not know it. His case is one of helplessness and hopelessness. He flounders along in life trying to lift his futile condition through the means of *being* religious, holding to man-made philosophies, self-help exercises, and striving for achievement and success. Yet when the bottom line is calculated, he is still at a severe loss and remains helpless and miserable even though he might gain the whole world. The sinner needs God's grace to lift him from the sludge of sin and God's mercy to wrap him in true love. That true love of mercy is Jesus Christ. God, who is rich in mercy, cries out to the helpless sinner and says, come to Christ and see my love in Him who died for sinners. Christian, remember His great mercy and grace towards you. Sinner, cry out to Christ for mercy and grace in Jesus Christ

*Look it up – **Matthew 20:29-34; John 1:16, 17; Ephesians 2:4-9***

*This truth for me – **His mercy and grace are beyond comprehension. List how His mercy and grace blessed you today or this week.***

_____

_____

_____

*Pray – **Thank God for His merciful love and His unmerited grace that chose you.***

THE GOD WHO STANDS WITH US ALWAYS

2 Timothy 4:17 But the Lord stood with me...

Have you ever been left alone, feeling deserted by those who were nearest to you? The Apostle Paul relates such a time when he was imprisoned in Rome. He was about to make his defense to the Roman court when he looked around and saw that he was all alone.

Here are some lessons we can learn from Paul's lonely experience. First, don't get upset with people when they desert you. Paul said in verse 16, ...*may it not be counted against them.* In my own life I have discovered that in many cases when I find myself alone on an emotional island, it was God who placed me there so that I would learn how to depend solely on Him. Second, people, even the best, are not going to be as loyal as God. The parables of the earthly father and the earthly friend teach us that even the best of people will let us down (Luke 11:5-13). Thirdly, the only true one that you can depend upon in all circumstances is God. Here is one of those great, *but God* statements. Paul says that all deserted him, *but the Lord stood with me...* The Lord will always be there for His children, His presence especially felt when they need Him the most. In my favorite Psalm, David writes, *The Lord is my light and my salvation...For my father and my mother have forsaken me, BUT THE LORD will take me up* (Psalm 27:1,10). If you are His child, rejoice that He will forever stand by you. If you are not His child, He will be standing one day as your judge. Repent and call upon the name of Christ for salvation.

Look it up – **Psalm 16:9; John 8:29; 2 Timothy 4:17**

This truth for me – **Are you feeling lonely today or have you felt lonely in the past? How does knowing that Jesus is always with you help you in your loneliness?**

———————————————————————————————

———————————————————————————————

———————————————————————————————

Pray – **For a greater awareness of Christ's presence with you.**

TELL ME THE STORY OF SALVATION

Acts 14:27 ...they began to report all things that God had done...

Are you blessed by hearing the testimonies of the saints? I could sit hour after hour and listen to how God saves people. One Sunday afternoon in Chicago, the old-time evangelist, Billy Sunday, entered a saloon with several of his ball-playing friends. When Billy came out from the saloon, he ran into a group of people playing instruments and testifying of Christ's power to save. This scene and the message affected Billy. He turned to listen, repented, and believed unto salvation. He left his buddies and entered the Pacific Garden Mission. This mission might ring a bell for some of us because it is the mission that has produced, over the years, thousands of testimonies of God's saving grace in people's lives. On many Sunday evenings, I tune my radio to *Unshackled* and listen for another testimony of God's saving grace. It's usually not long before I fill up with tears of joy and thanksgiving for the way God works in saving people from sin and death. Have you heard a testimony lately and rejoiced in God's saving power? But more intimately, have you been a part of a testimony lately and used by God to lead someone to Jesus? Let's do the work of an evangelist and broadcast the testimonies of His grace to save.

Look it up – **Luke 1:69-77; 2 Corinthians 6:2; Romans 10:1**

This truth for me – **When is the last time you shared your testimony? Rehearse how God saved you.**

_____

_____

_____

Pray – **Thank God for His gift of salvation and pray for opportunities to give your testimony.**

GOD WORKS HIS WORK

Ephesians 2:10 For we are His workmanship...

Input, output... are the words in a children's musical. The concept is simple; what goes in affects what comes out. When a person is born-again, God puts a new regenerated life in that person. When a person is regenerated to new life in Christ, the old life is destroyed and all things become new. The Spirit's work of regeneration is nothing short of a most wonderful and miraculous work of God. To take spiritually dead and corrupt sinners and make them into saints who now love and adore God is amazing. To see and be a part of this amazing work of new life is a great privilege.

How do we take part? By witnessing and teaching sinners the Gospel. But by no means does the new believer reach perfection in this life. Rather he presses on toward the hope of eternal life when at that time he or she will be perfected. When people first take note of the new life in a believer, they are usually stunned and skeptical. Thank God that He sees our new life in Christ and is neither stunned nor skeptical. Why? Because He was the One who worked His work in us and gave us new life.

Look it up – **Romans 6:5; 2 Corinthians 5:17; Colossians 3:12-17**

This truth for me – **Do you see evidence in your life of the new things God has given you? New tastes and desires for His things? List them.**

_____

_____

_____

Pray – **Thank God for your new creation and pray for the Spirit's power to keep you growing in the grace and righteousness of Christ.**

CALLED TO CATCH

Luke 5:10 ...from now on you will be catching men.

The fishing partnership of Simon Peter, and brothers, James and John, had fished all night without success. But that morning, Jesus instructed Simon to go back out to sea and again put the nets down. Within moments the nets were filled beyond imagination; when they began to pull the fish in, the boats started to sink. This experience certainly would have been a great motivator to continue fishing and to watch their business prosper.

But God had a different plan. Jesus was going to take these seasoned and successful fishermen and retool them to catch men. It is one thing to catch fish and quite another to catch humans! First, the hooks are different. With men, you need the hook of the Gospel. Second, unlike fishing for fish, you don't catch men by human strength, but rather by the regenerating power of the Holy Spirit. Thirdly, men don't become passive like a fish who gives up after the fisherman battles the fish into exhaustion. Rather, a sinner's heart and nature is in constant rejection of the Gospel until God alone breaks that sinful nature.

These fishermen had a new enterprise in front of them, catching men, but, as they would learn, the catch would not come by their power but by the power of the God who saves His people. Those fishermen, like we, needed to depend upon the Holy Spirit as they cast the Gospel to sinners. Keep casting and God will bring in the catch.

Look it up – Jeremiah 16:16; Matthew 4:19-20; Luke 5:10

*This truth for me – **How much soul fishing have you done lately? What have you given up to catch souls?***

_____

_____

_____

*Pray – **For the Lord to bless you with catching a soul for the Kingdom this week.***

SERVING CHRIST, NOT OURSELVES

1 Corinthians 9:18a What then is my reward?

The preaching of the Gospel has become big business in America. Billions of dollars are spent in gospel TV and radio broadcasting, gospel cruises and vacation sites, gospel music and film, and other business endeavors with the name *gospel* attached. Those associated with these businesses prosper in the name of the gospel. Let me stop there and say that many of these businesses and people are credible people who love the Lord. My question is this—*Is the Gospel clouded by such enterprises?*

The Apostle Paul was very careful when he preached and shared the gospel. He handled this precious jewel of good news with integrity and a desire to keep the gospel free from entanglement to exploitation. Paul would be the first to say that those who preach the gospel *should get their living from the gospel.* But *gaining a living* and *living to gain* from the gospel are often confused in American Christianity. Paul refused to take pay for the gospel, rather he sought employment when needed in order to support his ministry and physical needs. Would that we would see more people like Paul who gave up his rights for the gospel and less of those who demand their due from the gospel.

Look it up – 1 Corinthians 4:11-13; 2 Thessalonians 3:10-12; 1 Timothy 5:17-18

This truth for me – **Do you give money to ministries that you know little about? List the credible ministries that you need to support and don't be fooled by those seeking selfish gain.**

_____

_____

_____

Pray – **For discernment to know what ministries you should support and those that do not deserve your support.**

AT PEACE WITH A GREAT GOD

Ephesians 1:11 ...having been predestined according to His purpose...

Whenever we see words in Scripture like *purpose, His will, preordained, plan* and *His counsel*, they should remind us that God is in total control of everything. His plan for His creation is and has been in motion throughout all of history. These words also alert us that in eternity past, the Godhead, Father, Son and Holy Spirit, *decreed* all that would come to pass. If there is even one loose particle in the universe that is out of control, then God isn't God. Nothing is outside of the decrees of God and therefore, we need not fear what we read in the papers about the chaos in the world, the horror of terrorist activities, or the tragedy of poverty and famine. Yes, God is even in control of all these negative aspects. When it comes to those who believe in Christ, in God's purpose and plan, we are His special people...special because He has predestined us to be like His Son, Jesus Christ, *...who are called according to His purpose...to become conformed to the image of His Son...* (Romans 8:28,29).

Child of God, be at peace. God is in control of all things even when they seem to be out of control. He is especially watching over you, because as a child of God you have been placed *in Christ*.

Look it up – **Psalm 103:19; Romans 9:15-23; Revelation 4:11**

This truth for me – **Is there something out of control in your life? What are you doing about it? Are you worrying or panicking, or are you trusting God?**

_____

_____

_____

Pray – **For God to give you a bigger vision of His greatness and sovereignty.**

THE TRIED AND TRUE WAY

Jeremiah 6:16 ...Stand at the crossroads and look...ask where the good way is, and walk in it... (NIV)

Each day we face life crossroads. We come to intersections—big and small—where we have the choice. We can say, "I will do what is right and good and do what will give God glory." Or, we can exercise our rationalizing capacities and decide that we are going to take the ungodly road which feels or looks best. For instance, it might be what we decide to do about the car that just cut us off, or the person who pushed his way in line at the check-out counter. Bigger decisions may be whether I should enter into a wrong relationship, have sex out of marriage, or take that cigarette, drug or booze into my body.

When the Jews were confronted with their big crossroad of following God or straying off to false gods and pagan relationships, they choose to turn away from God. The prophet, Jeremiah, says they declared, *We will not walk in it,* (verse 16). How arrogant and rebellious to say to God, "No, I will not take Your way." The judgment that fell upon Israel was justified for such treatment of God's grace and mercy.

Yet, how many of us do the same thing? It is impossible to choose God's way unless we have first been born-again and forgiven by God. But even this does not make it easy to choose the right way. When we come to life's crossroads, we must turn to God and ask Him for the power to walk in the right way.

*Look it up – **Psalm 81:13; Joshua 22:5; Micah 4:2***

*This truth for me – **Are you standing at a crossroad and trying to decide what to do? Make a list of reasons why you should take God's way.***

---

*Pray – **For wisdom and courage to make godly decisions.***

WHO ARE WE?

Romans 9:20 ...who are you, O man...

Jonah had it absolutely correct when he prayed from the belly of the fish, ...*Salvation is from the Lord* (Jonah 2:9). From beginning to end, the work of saving sinners is in the hands of God. Even the faith to believe and accept Christ is given by God alone. We may say, "You mean that my good works can't save me? My moral way of life? I must at the least believe and accept Christ on my own, mustn't I?" Certainly people will say, as Paul anticipated in chapter 9 of Romans, "God is not fair." On the contrary, God is fair and most gracious and merciful. All of mankind is destined for hell, but God saves a people to be His people and the glory of Christ.

Brother and sister, if God chose to save you, it certainly wasn't because you were good. As a matter of fact we all were children of wrath and by nature dead and corrupting, stinking in our sin (Ephesians 2:1-3). His grace alone saved us and we must say thanks by seeking to be holy people, spreading to everyone the good news of salvation in Christ. If you are reading this and are not saved, you know there is a hole yet in your heart that you cannot fill. Only Christ can give you life and give it abundantly. Cry out to God and ask Him for the faith to repent of your sins and believe upon the Lord Jesus Christ.

*Look it up – **Jeremiah 17:9; Romans 8:29-30; Ephesians 2:1-10***

*This truth for me – **Do you have thoughts of God being unfair and often ask "Why God." Think about how you tried to play god recently.***

---

*Pray – **Praise God for being so gracious and not giving us what we really deserve.***

THE WARMTH OF GOD

Isaiah 61:10 ...He has wrapped me with a robe of righteousness...

When I was in elementary school, the teacher would tell us to get our wraps and make sure we were wrapped up so the cold would not chill us. When cold weather is moving in, we better bundle up.

While thinking on this idea of being wrapped or bundled up, I couldn't help but praise God for the way He has wrapped up His children in the righteousness of Christ. No cold darkness anymore for those that are in Christ Jesus. No more fear of losing or having our robe of righteousness stolen away. Those whom God saves, He covers with all of the blessings of salvation in Christ. The Christian is adorned in the splendor of Christ like a bride adorned with jewels, awaiting her bridegroom.

What is our response to such a glorious position with God? *I will rejoice greatly in the Lord, my soul will exult in my God.* Yes, rejoicing and exultation within our hearts is the proper response. Today rejoice greatly, for He has come to you and adorned you in His splendor.

> *"He rules the world with truth and grace. And makes the nations prove*
> *The glories of His righteousness and wonders of His love..."*

*Look it up – **Isaiah 62:5; Hebrews 1:8,9; 2 Peter 1:1***

*This truth for me – **Are there times you feel like God is far away? Do you want to bring Him close? Believe that His righteousness is your comfort and warmth. How can you know His righteousness?***

---

*Pray – **For God to give you a real sense of His Love and the warmth of that love today as you spend some extra time in His word and in prayer today.***

IMITATE JESUS

John 7:5 For not even His brothers were believing in Him.

A now famous banker was once asked how he learned the banking business. The banker replied that when he started out as a messenger in the bank, one of the vice presidents came up to him and asked, "Son, do you want to learn banking?" The banker replied with an emphatic "Yes," and the vice-president responded, "Just stay by my side." It would be nice if we could say to a sinner, just stay by my side and through my example you will come to know Jesus. But even if we were able to live a sinless life and do all that our Lord desires of us, no one comes to Christ by even a perfect human example.

When Christ lived with His family and grew up with other siblings in the family, He was the perfect example to them of godliness, yet it is obvious that at the time of John's writing of this account in Chapter 7, Christ's earthly half-brothers were not believers. Jesus had given His own explanation of this in chapter 6 of the Gospel of John; *All that the Father gives me shall come to me...* Our Christian examples are useful in the Father's calling, and our witness of the Gospel is the essential means for the Father to call, but it must be the Father who calls and gives the dead sinner life to believe. My friends, we should model Christ, be good examples, proclaim the Gospel to the sinner, and then pray for God to work.

*Look it up – **Job 1:1; 1 Corinthians 11:1; 1 Peter 2:21***

*This truth for me – **Who was a good example of godliness for you? What can you imitate in your Christian walk?***

_____

_____

_____

*Pray – **That you might imitate Christ day by day.***

IS HELL REAL?

Matthew 25:46 ...these will go away into eternal punishment...

When is the last time you heard a series of messages on hell, God's wrath or eternal punishment? According to a series of articles in <u>Modern Reformation</u>, the topic of hell and its teaching is uncommon. There are those who sidestep hell, and focus on God's love instead of His wrath. They want to believe that everyone will be gathered up in God's love, exempt from damnation for their sin. Others provide an avenue through self-works where again the hope is that human works versus the righteousness of Christ will satisfy the wrath of God. Even some evangelical churches and theologians deny the eternal punishment of the unrepentant sinner.

One such recent thought on the subject is that the unrepentant sinner will be judged and then destroyed, or annihilated. The arguments behind the annihilation view have some biblical merit and are palatable because annihilation is quick and not an ongoing punishment. Yet, Jesus said that the punishment of the unsaved will be eternal. Eternal punishment will stand for eternity as a testimony of man's unrighteousness and God's perfect and glorious holiness. Praise God for the salvation that saves sinners from eternal punishment. For you who fear God's eternal punishment, repent of your sins, go to God, and ask for forgiveness and believe upon the Lord Jesus Christ for salvation.

*Look it up – **Matthew 25:41; 2 Thessalonians 1:9; Revelation 14:10***

*This truth for me – **How do you see the unsaved: as being OK or facing eternal punishment?***

_____

_____

_____

*Pray – **That God will give you eyes of grace to see the reality of where the unsaved are going and for the urgency to go and share the Gospel.***

A REAL PEST

Acts 24:5 *For we have found this man a real pest...*

The charge before Governor Felix was that Paul was a real pest. For me, twenty-two years ago, it was my mother-in-law. She came from an Italian/ Catholic background and had made her pilgrimage through various religious quests for peace in her life. Going through a divorce and left with the daunting task of raising four girls, she looked for help. God was wooing her to Himself and soon He sent a woman to explain the Gospel to her. God saved her and from the moment she was given a new life in Christ, she thanked Him by being His evangelistic pest. She became a godly pest at her job and to her clients, leading a number of them to the Lord. Her family was also pestered by her witness of the Gospel, and I became a primary target. Over and over she explained to me that I needed to be born-again. Whether on the phone, at my home, or out in the city, whenever I ran into her, she pestered me with the Gospel of Christ. Many times my reaction was like Felix's reaction to Paul, the pest, *go away...when I find time I'll get back to you* (see Acts 24:25). But God would not allow her to go away and soon God worked His work in my life. He forced me to face Christ; I needed to be born-again. He saved me and gave me new life and a call to ministry.

Thanks, Mom, for being a pest for Jesus! Who will we pester today about their need for Christ?

*Look it up – **Mark 16:15; Luke 24:47; John 20:21***

*This truth for me – **Write down the name of a person you can "pester" for the Lord.***

---

*Pray – **For the Holy Spirit to give you an energetic desire to share the Gospel.***

SATISFIED - INDEED

Luke 18:13 ...God be merciful to me...

The tax gatherer in this passage knew who it is that must show mercy in order to be forgiven; God and God alone! While the Jewish priests were praying their self-righteous prayers, God was convicting the tax collector with the understanding of what was needed for forgiveness. It is God's wrath that must be removed. The word mercy in this verse is sometimes translated propitious. It sounds like the word propitiation, which means to satisfy God's wrath. Christ's death and the shedding of His blood was the propitiation necessary for God to show His mercy on the elect sinner. Again, only God can convict a sinner's heart to cry out and see his or her need for mercy. Only God can satisfy God's wrath in order for mercy to be given to a helpless sinner crying out for salvation.

The nature of man seeking a self-righteous approach to salvation will say, "I am good enough, I have done enough good things and I have the faith necessary to go to heaven." The true and only way to God is through His Son, Jesus Christ, who is **the propitiation for our sins,** and satisfies the wrath of God being poured out upon all unrighteousness. Only Jesus can cover our sin and remove God's wrath from our lives.

*Look it up – **Psalm 103:13; Luke 6:36; Hebrews 2:17***

*This truth for me – **Write down all the ways God has been merciful to you, from the time He saved you up to today.***

_____

_____

_____

*Pray – **Praise Him for His mercy and thank Him for not giving you what you deserve.***

A DEEPER KNOWLEDGE OF HIM

Job 42:5 ...*now my eye sees Thee.*

How high is your view of God? In the clause preceding Job's statement, he confesses, *I have heard of you by the hearing of the ear...* Almost everyone with whom we come in contact will say that they heard about God, meaning that they know something about God and His character. Job now states that he has moved from that superficial state of hearing about God and thinking that he knows Him to the higher degree of seeing God. He saw God in a dark cloud, and here he is declaring that he now sees God deep in his soul. Job understands the mighty power of the presence of God. He had a perception of God but now He senses God's power, mercy, grace and sovereignty.

Knowing God on this higher level of intimate knowledge of God's power and grace should be each Christian's goal. The Apostle Paul stated this goal in this manner, *that I may know Him, and the power of His resurrection...* (Philippians 3:10). Paul wanted to know deeply that power that would one day raise him from the dead and present him in glory to the Father. In other words, he wanted a high view of God and a deep knowledge of Christ and salvation. What a quest, one which lasts for a lifetime—to know Him! May that high view of God and deep understanding of His might and mercy be our goal today.

Look it up – **1 Corinthians 13:12; 2 Corinthians 10:5;1 John 5:20**

This truth for me – **Do you really know God? What are some things that you really know about God and will bring you comfort and joy?**

_____

_____

_____

Pray – That your mind and heart will be filled each day with more knowledge about God.

HIS HOLD IS FIRM

Romans 8:38 For I am convinced...

Paul was convinced that when God saves people, they were saved forever. A Christian cannot lose his or her salvation! Is this a biblical doctrine? Yes! (Romans 5:10; 8:1, 27-30; Philippians 1:6; John 6:39; 10:28) Is this a theological doctrine? Yes! When looking at God's plan and purpose for saving a chosen person, His plan is to not only save but also to save for all eternity. This is grounded in God and not man. Just as sinful man could do nothing to save himself, the forgiven sinner can do nothing to "unsave" himself.

Wait a minute, do you mean that a Christian can sin and still go to heaven? Yes, a Christian can sin and even sin badly. This sinning may initiate God's discipline upon the Christian, bringing pain and struggle to his life. Or God may exercise His judgment by taking the physical life of the Christian, while sparing his eternal spirit. The salvation that begins with God's eternal purpose of saving sinners ends with God's eternal purpose in uniting the saved with His Son in glory. *For whom He foreknew, He also predestined to become conformed to the image of His son...and who He predestined, these He also called; and who He called, these he also justified; and who he justified, these he also glorified.*

*Look it up – **John 17:14; Ephesians 4:30; Hebrews 7:25***

*This truth for me – **Write down what you need to remember about the Lord when times come upon you that make you doubt your salvation.***

---

*Pray – **For the Holy Spirit to give you confidence in your salvation through Christ.***

A CHILD'S HEART

Psalm 51:5 ...I was brought forth in iniquity...

When my wife was pregnant with our third daughter, I accompanied her to the doctor and watched little Nina squirm around inside the womb. My thoughts were, "she is so cute." We were thrilled when we saw those ultrasound impressions of our daughter. Little did we think about the baby in the womb being a sinner. We tend to write off such reality with sentimentality, not wanting to face the sin in all of mankind, ...*through one man sin entered into the world, and death through sin; and so death spread to all men...* (Romans 5:12).

Yes, sin and death even passed to my little girl. This is why my wife and I shared the Gospel with our girls, telling them of God's judgment, the grace of God in Christ and their need of salvation through Jesus. We are all totally and completely depraved, void of any ability to please a Holy God and be saved. Only God can save the sinner and He does so through the work of Christ and the proclamation of the Gospel. I praise God that He saves through the witness of the Gospel.

Please don't let sentimentality or wishful thinking keep you from sitting down and explaining the Gospel to your children or other children. They are all sinners in need of salvation through Christ.

Look it up – ***Psalm 58:3; Matthew 18:3; John 3:6***

This truth for me – ***List the children with whom you have contact and think of how you can reach them with the Gospel.***

———————————————————————————————

———————————————————————————————

———————————————————————————————

Pray – ***For the salvation of children.***

TRUTH OR TOLERATION

John 4:22 You worship that which you do not know...

Tolerance is a powerful concept in society. In many churches the term has forged an entirely new way of dealing with religions that stray from historical biblical Christianity and condone sin. Today, tolerance goes so far as to accept sinful practices such as homosexuality, lesbianism and abortion. In some cases the rationale goes like this, "We should be tolerant because Jesus modeled a tolerant attitude toward those who differed with Him."

But did He? The answer is clear in—NO! He neither tolerated false teaching nor looked the other way concerning sin. In John 4 the woman at the well had sinful relationships with men, and she was a pagan worshipper. Jesus tolerated neither of her indulgences. Rather, He demonstrated a deeper love for purity and truth than a tolerance toward lies and sin by saying, *You worship that which you do not know...* In other words, "woman, your religion is totally false," and regarding her sin, "woman, you have been promiscuous with men" (verse 18). No tolerance here. Jesus confronted paganism and sin head-on, and He did it with true love, which seeks to set forth truth and holiness. One last thought: when setting forth truth and purity, we must remember to make sure our own lives are in tune with Christ.

Look it up – Isaiah 59:2; Ephesians 4:2; Revelation 2:2

*This truth for me – **What sin in your life or someone else's life are you tolerating? What needs to be done?** _____*

_____

_____

*Pray – **For God to give you discernment about sin and its evil.***

YUCKY MUST-DOS

Jonah 1:2 Arise, go to Nineveh the great city, and cry against it...

Have you ever been asked to do something that pushed you out of your comfort zone and even instilled fear in you? Did you want to run and hide? The flight syndrome is not uncommon to most of us. We often experience it when we are told to switch jobs and relocate, or when we are given a responsibility that we believe is too much for us. We may be infected when the Lord wants us to move into missions or help a church planter get a church started.

In the case of Jonah, he had to leave his comfort zone when God commanded him to *go to Nineveh, the great city,* filled with pagan people and wickedness, and preach against it. He must have imagined all kinds of negative things when he thought of having to tell such a people that they were evil and wicked. However, God deals with Jonah, and he goes and preaches, and the city repents. But then, Jonah becomes upset because God saved such evil people.

The point for this devotional is that there are things we know we must do that are uncomfortable and cause fear. In such situations, we must follow the path that Jonah took when he prayed, *I called out of my distress to the Lord, and He answered me.* If God has been telling you to do something that causes you concern, cry out to Him for the power to do what must be done.

Look it up – Matthew 6:34; Luke 11:28; Hebrews 11:24-28

This truth for me – List some things you did not want to do, but you had to do them. What will help you to obey, even when you don't feel like obeying? _

_____

_____

Pray – That God will give you His peace when an uncomfortable task comes your way.

SOLID GROUNDING

Titus 1:9 ...to exhort in sound doctrine and to refute...

The shepherd has two purposes for carrying his staff among the sheep: to direct the sheep and to ward off the wolves. In like manner, the pastor-shepherd has two duties: to gather and build up the church and to fight off false teachers and their heresies. Pastors do not carry spiritual staffs with them, but they are to carry the Word of God—the Bible—and be able to use its teachings for exhorting and defending the Christian faith. John Calvin wrote, *"...the first thing required in a pastor is, that he be well instructed in the knowledge of sound doctrine; the second is, that, with unwavering firmness of courage, he hold by the confession of it to the last..."* Holding to sound doctrine is not only knowing how to memorize and write down definitions. It is also demonstrating a working knowledge of sound doctrine when witnessing, teaching, preaching, and refuting. If we fail to hold forth the Word of God with sound teaching from a sound doctrinal perspective, we will fail in our most important calling—to glorify God and fully enjoy Him forever. All our planning and envisioning is futile unless it is girded and grounded in sound doctrine. This goes for the Christian church, the Christian home and our individual Christian lives.

Look it up – **Proverbs 4:2; 1 Timothy 4:6; 2 John 9**

This truth for me – **Are you still on the "milk" of the Word, or do you study the Word to gain understanding? What can you do to have a mind with sound doctrine?**

Pray – **For time to study and develop a mind that can share and teach with sound doctrine.**

WHAT, ME?

Acts 13:48 ...as many as had been appointed [ordained, elected] to eternal life believed.

What word in Christian doctrine has stirred the hottest cauldrons of debate? ELECTION! Why are so many Christians frustrated by this word that displays so meaningfully the grace, love, sovereignty, justice and mercy of our Father? Perhaps it is because they have been influenced more by tradition than the Bible, or have been taught by those who ignore election. But at the core of this antagonism is the nature and heart of man. From the beginning of humanity in the garden, man did not like to admit that he had nothing to do with something. To be totally dependent upon God was uncomfortable for Adam and Eve. They needed to be like God. This began the ball of *me-ism* rolling down the humanistic mountain and away from the peak of God's sovereignty. Of all the doctrines, we should be most humbled and joyous about election. King David danced before the Lord because the Lord had chosen him. Like David, we should rejoice because a holy God chose wretches as us!

"Do not be afraid to dwell upon this high doctrine of election. When your mind is most heavy and depressed, you will find it to be a bottle of richest cordial ...desire to have your mind enlarged that you may comprehend more and more the eternal, everlasting, discriminating love of God..." Charles Spurgeon

Look it up – **John 15:16; Ephesians 1:4; 2 Thessalonians 2:13**

This truth for me – **List what is positive about being God's elect and why God's election is something to rejoice about like David did.**

Pray – **Praise God for choosing you to be saved in Christ.**

WHO DO WE THINK WE ARE

Romans 8:28, Romans 10:14 …God causes all things…how shall they hear without a preacher?

Yesterday we looked at the positive grace that lies within the doctrine of election and predestination. We should rejoice in the understanding that God chose to save us. There is another positive side to election, yet on the surface it seems to be an *antinomy, or a contradiction of two principles, each of which is true.* How can a Sovereign God, who chooses those He will save, hold accountable the rest who are not saved? He *can* and *does* because He is God. All mankind is sinful and worthy of eternal death, but by His grace He saves some.

Regarding evangelism, there is also an antinomy. The Bible says that God does all the saving of a sinner, and He accomplished this through His chosen means—the preaching of the gospel. So, salvation is totally of God, and that salvation occurs through the preaching of the Gospel. Some may say, "Well, if that is what you believe, then I can just kick back and let God save." No! God not only saves the elect, He also provides the means, and that means is by every Christian sharing the Gospel with others. As we witness, God saves. Thus, another great joy of being among the elect is being God's chosen instrument. There is no greater motivation for evangelism than witnessing because we want to thank Him and show obedience for His choice.

Look it up – Exodus 33:19; Isaiah 61:5; Romans 9:15-24

This truth for me – With salvation, there is responsibility, the responsibility to be ambassadors for Christ. How will you be His ambassador today?

Pray – That God uses you in wonderful ways to call His elect into the fold.

PRAY FOR THE PLANTERS

2 Corinthians 11:27 I have been in labor and hardship, through many sleepless nights...

The Apostle Paul was an evangelistic church planter. He preached the Gospel to win souls to Christ and then formed these converts into local church bodies where he appointed elders to rule and govern. For all this Kingdom building, he suffered hardship and tension to the point of sleeplessness. One church planter said, "I didn't know how difficult church planting was until I lost sleep about it." A missionary who returned to the States and entered into church planting here stated, "People need to pray even harder for me now that I am here in America church planting."

Stop and think for a moment. Where would the Devil try his hardest to interfere with missions? My answer is church planting. The Devil does not want to see sinners saved or a new church started, especially in America. A baby church and its church planter are prime targets for the darts of the Devil. What is needed? Prayer! This is the cry from men who plant, "Were it not for the prayers of the saints, I would have given up church planting long ago." Church planters are a committed group of men who serve the Lord in building His Kingdom through church planting both oversees and here at home. Their challenge to all of us is to Pray! Pray! Pray! Pray for church-planting families: their needs, financial support, and most of all for souls to be saved through their ministries.

*Look it up - **Acts 13:1-3; Ephesians 6:19; 1 Thessalonians 5:25***

*This truth for me – **List a church planter that you know or know about. Find out more about him and begin today praying for this servant of the Lord.***

———————————————————————————————————

———————————————————————————————————

———————————————————————————————————

*Pray – **For a church planter and his church-planting family.***

THE PLEASURE OF GOD

Isaiah 42:1 Behold my Servant...My chosen one in whom My soul delights...

We take possession of those we love, i.e. *my* wife and *my* children. These close to us belong to us! The prophet Isaiah is referring to Christ, the Messiah, when he speaks of this servant in chapter 42. In the Trinity, the persons of the Godhead belong to each other; they are one in power, honor and glory. The Son of God, Jesus, belongs to the Father, and the Spirit to the Son and all to each other. In this possessive triune relationship, there is a very special relationship between the Father and the Son. This is not to minimize the Holy Spirit's relationship to the Son and the Father because He is mentioned in the text as the person of the Godhead who is with Christ and assists in the work of salvation. But the highlight here is the Father's delight in the Servant, Jesus Christ. He upholds or empowers Christ. This is seen in the times when Jesus limited His own omnipotence and glory and relied upon the Father. The Father also delights with deep affection for the Son. This must be the Father's delight in what the Son would accomplish at Calvary in dying for the sinners whom the Father seeks to save.

What does all this have to do with us? First, we should take note that if we are to please God, it must be through Jesus. It is Jesus who pleases the Father and in Him we are found pleasing. Second, it is the servant's attitude and life that delights the Father and empowers us to do His will. Thirdly, we who are saved are the possession of the Father; I am His and He is mine, no longer alone or without hope. Praise God!

*Look it up – **Matthew 3:17; Luke 3:22; 1 Peter 2:4***

*This truth for me - **How is your life pleasing to God? List some areas that please Him and some areas you need to work on.***

_____

_____

_____

*Pray – **That you will be a pleasing servant of God.***

THE JOY OF SUFFERING

Hebrews 12:2 ...for the joy set before Him endured the cross...

God taught me the meaning of giving thanks in 1980. I had been saved for about four months when I went to a prayer meeting at my home church. Giving thanks was a big part of my young Christian life, but what I would hear at that prayer meeting that night would change my entire understanding of thanksgiving. The pastor asked for people to share their thanks to God. A number stood and thanked the Lord for various things. Then the room became quiet, and the pastor asked if anyone else wanted to share. I heard the rustle of a dog in the back pews and knew that it was the blind girl I had met at the singles fellowship. She stood to her feet and said these penetrating words, "I don't know if I have ever done this before, but tonight I want to thank God for being blind." I was stunned for a moment at hearing someone thank God for the suffering in their life and to do it with such conviction and joy in their voice.

After prayer meeting I drove back home, crying most of the way while thanking God for the hard things that He brought into my life. He used those most painful times to save me, cause me to grow in His grace and love Him deeply. Christ thanked God by counting the cross joy and knowing what His death would mean to the Father: that God's people would be redeemed by the death of His Son. Are you thankful for pain, sorrow, or heartache? Will you trust God to use your pain to grow you in His grace?

*Look it up – **Philippians 2:8; Colossians 3:1; Hebrews 2:9***

*This truth for me - **What pain, sorrow or heartache will you thank God for?***

_____

_____

_____

*Pray – **That God will give you joy even in your sorrows and sufferings.***

GLORY IN THE TENT

John 1:14 ...we beheld His glory...

Have you ever slept in a tent? One impressive thing about tent sleeping is how dark it gets inside the tent. The Bible speaks about our lives, along with the world we live in, being as dark tents, pitch black because of sin and death. God became incarnate and dwelt among us in His own human tent. His humanity unlike ours, was perfect. He came to seek and save us from the darkness of sin and death. *...the Word (Jesus) became flesh and dwelt among us, and we beheld His glory, glory as of the only begotten from the Father, full of grace and truth* (John 1:14). *Dwelt* means to tabernacle or to pitch a tent. Jesus came to pitch His tent with us and to march into the darkness of our tents and shine His glory. Were it not for God's mercy and grace, we would still be in darkness and sin; our tents would be filled with despair and hopelessness. Christ comes into our dark tents and fills them with the glory of salvation. God became as a man, limiting His glory so that He could be like us in all things, yet without sin. He went to the cross and died in our place as the God-Man. In Christ we have forgiveness of sin and are brought to the Father. Is your tent still in the darkness of sin and death? Turn to the Light—Jesus Christ—repent of your sins and believe upon the Lord and be saved. Your tent will overflow with His glory and grace.

*Look it up – **Exodus 40:24; Galatians 4:4; Revelation 7:15***

*This truth for me - **Maybe you are a Christian and there are still some dark corners in your tent. List the darkness of sin you need to give to the Lord.***

_____

_____

_____

*Pray – **For those living in their dark tents of sin and for your dark corners.***

MY HOPE IS IN THE OMNI LORD

Philippians 2:10 ...in heaven, and on earth, and under the earth.

Well, that says it all, doesn't it? Christ is in control of everyone. This particular passage tells us that Christ will one day judge all people, no matter where they are. In other similar passages, we are told that Christ is over all things—circumstances and situations—both in the heavens and on the earth. In theological terms we call this Christ's sovereign control of all things and His providence in sustaining all things.

What can we draw from these truths? *First,* that Christ is in control of all things and there is nothing outside of the Lord's sovereign control. *Second,* because He is in control of all things, both good and bad, we can know that all things are working according to a perfect plan that was formulated by the Godhead before the creation of the world. *Third,* being a child of God, by having been born again through the work of Christ and the Holy Spirit, one can find peace in knowing Christ is in control of all things, even when the things in our personal lives seem out of control. *And finally,* knowing that all control has been rested in the hands of our Savior, we can worship Him with all our mind, heart and soul, confident in a living hope that He will bring all things to a good and perfect conclusion - *my hope is in the Lord!*

*Look it up – **Isaiah 45:23; Ephesians 2:10; Revelation 5:13***

*This truth for me - **What does the sovereignty of God mean to you? Name three positive things about God's sovereignty.***

_____

_____

_____

*Pray - **Thanking God that He is sovereign and knows all about you.***

GIVING YOUR ALL

2 Corinthians 8:9 For you know the grace of our Lord Jesus Christ, that though He was rich, yet for your sake He became poor...

The generosity of the Macedonia Christians that Paul is speaking to is an example of gracious giving. The supreme example that the apostle gives to substantiate his definition of gracious giving is the incarnation of the Lord Jesus Christ. Even though Christ was the glorious God of the universe, He humbled Himself to become flesh and save undeserving sinners.

Paul says, *"YOU know the grace of our Lord Jesus Christ..."* Yes, we as Christians do know that grace that gives generously, but do we model it in our lives? Are we gracious givers to the expansion of the Kingdom of God through financially supporting missions? Are we gracious givers of understanding and support to our pastors and leaders in our churches? God saved me later in my life and I didn't grow up in the church. When I came into the church, I thrilled at the helpful men whom God called to preach the Word. What amazed me, and still bothers me, is how so many Christians are critical of their pastors and leaders and lack the gift of grace toward the ones called to minister. Having been a pastor, I am fully aware that pastors are fallible men. Please be a gracious giver of your love and support. Finally, are we gracious givers of the Gospel? Christ became poor so we would become rich through His Gospel of salvation. Let us be amazingly gracious people as we reflect upon the Lord's incarnation and how He is so amazingly gracious.

*Look it up - **Philippians 2:5-7; Romans 15:13; 1 John 3:16-20***

*This truth for me – **What are some obstacles to giving generously? List some of the obstacles you face to giving generously.***

---

*Pray – **That you would be able to give generously in all areas of your life.***

THE LIGHT OF GRACE

John 1:14 ...glory as of the only begotten from the Father, full of grace...

Were it not for God's grace toward sinners, we would be left on our own to figure out how to escape sin and death. We have come up with some very logical and believable means for ridding ourselves of sin and death. We have concocted all kinds of religions that make us feel good and give us a false security. Brilliant individuals have formulated philosophies to sooth our searching minds and falsely give a temporal balm to our emptiness. Even some Gospel preachers say that all one needs to do is recite a Bible formula of the Gospel. God saves sinners, and God's salvation is rested in one way. The way is by grace alone through faith alone centered in Christ alone and by the means of the preaching of the Gospel alone. All of our foolish attempts to satisfy a Holy God and eradicate sin from our lives are empty efforts. *Glory as of the only begotten from the Father* appeared on that first Christmas day, and the light of Christ's grace was shown to a world in darkness. At the cross, that light of grace extinguished the darkness of sin and death, and it now shines in those who have been born-again in Christ. May the grace of our Lord and Savior, Jesus Christ, shine His light in all your lives, and may we live by grace, trusting in His power to overcome sin. *"Lord, in the strength of grace, with a glad heart and free, Myself, my residue of days, I consecrate to Thee."* (Charles Wesley, The Methodist Hymnal – selection #217)

Look it up – ***Galatians 1:6; 1 Timothy 1:14; 2 John 2:3***

This truth for me – ***Stop, meditate and dwell on Jesus and the grace He employed in saving you. Write a thank-you.***

_____

_____

_____

Pray – ***For God to give you a greater sense of Christ's glory and grace.***

WEIGHED DOWN AND LIFTED UP

Romans 6:2 ...How shall we who died to sin still live in it?

We were studying the doctrine of eternal security, or as some would say, *once saved always saved*. One of the students could not agree with the biblical evidence that when God truly saves a sinner, He secures that one in Christ. She explained to me that her husband had made a profession of faith and now was back to his old ways of sin. I could sense a real bitterness in her spirit toward her spouse, and it became evident that she had gone through some serious abuse. She wanted to believe her husband was saved but could not justify the way he acted.

When God saves a sinner, He does not perfect him here on earth. He does, in a spiritual positioning, place the forgiven one in Christ and give him all the benefits of a relationship with Christ, but perfection doesn't occur until God glorifies us in heaven. While here on earth, Christians constantly battle sin and come under attack by the Devil's temptation. But when Christians find themselves involved in sin, there must be repentance and God's forgiveness. While I didn't know the condition of the husband's heart, I did know that repentance was necessary, and I encouraged the woman to ask God to bring her husband to repentance. It may be that some of us are struggling with sin and are not a reflection of Christ. The cure is repentance and seeking God's forgiveness so that *we who died to sin will no longer live in sin* but *have life and have it abundantly*.

*Look it up – **Galatians 5:24; Colossians 3:3; 1 Peter 2:24***

*This truth for me – **What sins do you need to put away? List them and repent if necessary.***

---

*Pray – **For God to give you the confidence that you can overcome sin in His power and then do so.***

HANDLING THE WORD OF TRUTH

2 Timothy 2:15, 4:3 ...*handling accurately the word of truth...the time will come when they will not endure sound doctrine...*

John MacArthur, pastor of Grace Community Church in California and president of Master's Seminary, wrote in <u>Outreach</u> magazine: "*In the medical field the bar of medical qualifications is set extremely high in order to protect patients from malpractice. That doesn't happen in today's church... in the continuing explosion of independence that defines evangelicalism we have lots of ill-prepared or ill-qualified people with an awful lot of passion and zeal, but who maybe aren't as careful as they need to be in protecting the content of the message. What matters is that we get the Truth - the way God revealed the Truth - to the people. I'm not nearly as concerned with methods as I am with the protection of the essential message... if your people really come to know the Lord, as He's revealed in Scripture...you won't have to prop people up with 'half-time pep talks' about outreach. You won't have to depend upon methodology. We won't have to 'whip up' our people who are mature in the Lord to do evangelism. It will be just a natural overflow.*"

Pastors need to be diligent men of the Word, handling it accurately, and bringing God's truth to their people as revealed in Scripture. When godly men are properly handling the Word of God and feeding their flocks, God will bring forth His fruit in His timing through the people who are being equipped to do the work of ministry.

*Look it up – **Psalm 119:160; John 17:17; James 1:18***

*This truth for me – **Are you sitting under the true teaching and preaching of God's Word? Write down what makes for a good preacher.***

_____

_____

_____

*Pray – **For God to continue to call men who will be diligent students of the Word and able to teach.***

MISSIONS HERE AND NOW

2 Corinthians 5:10 For we must all appear before the judgment seat of Christ...

The theme of a mission's conference I once attended was *Living In The Light Of Forever.* The focus was living and serving NOW with eternal things in mind. I must admit that I lose sight at times of the eternal and get caught up in the here and now. Opportunities to speak with people about the gospel can pass by, and before we know it, we missed out on actually speaking to people about their future and what will happen to them when they stand before God in judgment. The unsaved will face a judgment of condemnation for rejecting Christ, while Christians will face judgment concerning how faithful they were to God and obedient to His will.

The best place to start living in the light of eternity is right here and right now. America needs Christians willing to begin living in the light of eternity in their own backyards. I recently lunched with a foreign missionary who is home and working with his mission board. I see more and more missionaries coming off the foreign field for all kinds of reasons, but could it be that God is bringing gifted missionaries back to kick start a mission's movement in the American church to reach the U.S.? I don't know, but praise be to God if this is the case.

Look it up – Matthew 9:37-38; Luke 24:47; Acts 1:8

This truth for me – Define **missions. Do you define it by geography or unbelief?**

_____

_____

_____

Pray – For God to open our eyes to see missions as meaning to go to all unbelievers near and far off.

THE ROCK OF OUR SALVATION

Matthew 16:18 ...and upon this rock I will build My church...

The building material used to lay a foundation and hold a house together is often concrete. Concrete gives strength to a building. Christ calls the substance that forms the building of the church, *rock*. This rock has had its share of interpretations. The Roman Catholic Church points to the Apostle Peter as the rock. Others argue that Christ is making a play on words here and is referring to Himself as the rock of the Church.

There are more views, but the interpretation I like is the one which states that the rock mentioned in Matthew 16 is the rock of *faith*. The faith expressed by Peter—Jesus is the Christ, the anointed Messiah—is a faith which can only come to a sinner by the hand of God. Christ is the sole builder of His church and the foundation of salvation upon which He places elect sinners to be living stones, but the concrete to the building process is *FAITH!* We are saved by faith, we are kept by faith, we have been justified by faith, and we are to live by faith and not by our own strength and power. Faith is the Christian's concrete. Your Christian life is being built up as a dwelling of God and faith is the concrete that Christ uses. *"My God shall raise me up, I trust Him with all."* (found in Sir Walter Raleigh's Bible, written the night before he was beheaded.)

*Look it up – **2 Samuel 22:31; Hebrews 11:1-3; 1 John 5:4***

*This truth for me – **Write down what your level of faith is today and where you are lacking in faith.***

_____

_____

_____

*Pray – **For the Holy Spirit to empower you with greater faith as you read, study and meditate on His word.***

SACRED AND SECURE

Colossians 3:12 And so, as those who have been chosen of God...put on...

God saved me! I was fully *in Christ* at the moment of my salvation. I was seated in the heavenlies, and was sanctified and baptized into Christ's death. My sins were forgiven and I was placed into His resurrection. Yet there were a lot of things that needed to be *put on*. When I walked into a local church, some told me they were not sure what to make of me, knowing my sordid background. Their eyes could not comprehend my position in Christ—but it was real and remains so. Through the Bible, the Holy Spirit showed me what to put on in my new life. The more I read the Scriptures, the more the Spirit said *take that off* and *put that on*. The Word and the Spirit's power and guidance took me, a wretch of a man, and began shaping him into what he really was, a child of God.

The progressive work of sanctification continues till the Father calls us home. Three things are very important. First, Christians must know that their *position in Christ* is complete and secure at the moment they are saved. Second, the work of sanctification is progressive. The Christian is called to put on Christ's new life through obedience to the teachings of the Scriptures. Thirdly, it is the Holy Spirit's assignment to come alongside the Christian, empower him, and assist him in his pilgrimage to glory; *keep seeking the things above, where Christ is.*

Look it up – **Leviticus 20:8; Ephesians 4:12,13; Hebrews 10:10**

This truth for me – **Write down three things that make you secure in Christ.**

_____

_____

_____

Pray – **For God to fill your mind with the greatness of your position in Christ.**

THE POWER OF PREACHING

James 1:18 ...He brought us forth by the word of truth...

How important is the preaching of the Word of God? Were it not for the Word of God preached, you and I would not have received the seeding necessary to begin the work of salvation in our hearts. Were it not for the preached Word, we would not have been made alive by the Holy Spirit and been given the faith to believe. Were it not for the preached Word, our new lives in Christ would look much the same as before God saved us. In your ministry as a pastor, Sunday School teacher, children's or youth leader, mother/father, or friend, is the Word of God taken seriously, studied diligently, and relied upon wholeheartedly? God brings forth His results in saving and conforming a people to the image of Christ, not by good oration or how we can dress up the Word in dramatic ways, but simply by how clearly and diligently we present the whole counsel of the Word of Truth.

I once heard R.C. Sproul say, "How in the world could I humanly manipulate or embellish what God has anointed and the Holy Spirit has empowered?" Is the preaching of the Word of God at the center of your church's pulpit each week? Parents, does the preaching/teaching of the Word of God have a daily place in the time you spend with your children? Christian worker, do you rush your assignment at church without having studied and prepared to teach the Word of Truth? Do you want to see God's results? Hold forth God's Word of Truth!

*Look it up – **Psalm 108:4; Matthew 22:16; Revelation 21:5***

*This truth for me – **What is your view of preaching? How can you get more from your pastor's preaching?***

---

*Pray – **For ears to hear and a mind to meditate on God's Word preached and for wisdom to carry the Word into your daily life.***

THINKING HIGH THOUGHTS

Ezekiel 37:6 ...I will put sinews on you, make flesh grow back on you, cover you with skin, and put breath in you that you may come alive...

WOW, now that is change—the regeneration of very dry bones. Many believe this prophetic vision pointed to God's eventual political and spiritual revival of Israel. While I agree with this, I have no doubt that this is also an Old Testament illustration of the spiritual regeneration that the Holy Spirit causes in the elect sinner when he is given the faith to believe the Gospel. As the Apostle Paul states, he is *a new creation...*

I have been reading my fourth biography of Jonathan Edwards, the brilliant 18th century pastor, evangelist, scholar and philosopher. This biography, written by Ian Murray, speaks about Edward's transformed focus. Murray writes about how salvation affected all of Edwards' life—from the most trivial to the most sublime. God caused the dry bones of the valley to come to life; he also wrought a dramatic change in one of America's most brilliant men of history. In the same manner, God caused a dramatic and complete change in your life at the time you were born again. Is that change evident? Do you see yourself as changed with new affections for God and resolves to live for Him? Do you see the world and all things in it through God's lens? If not, you very well may not be born again. If you are a believer and haven't grasped the magnitude of your salvation, you may need to clear away some clutter so that your view of God can catch His majesty.

*Look it up – **1 Chronicles 29:11; Job 37:22; Jude 25***

*This truth for me – **Write down what may be blocking your high view of God's majesty or write down what you believe about God's majesty.***

---

*Pray – **That you will have a high view of God's majesty.***

FOOLISHNESS TO THE PERISHING

1 Corinthians 1:22-23...Jews ask for signs, and Greeks search for wisdom; but we preach...

John Chrysostom, a 4th century preacher in the Cathedral of Antioch, was nicknamed *Chrysostomos* which means *golden mouthed*. John Stott names four chief characteristics of Chrysostom's preaching. First, he was "*biblical,*" preached systematically through the books of Scripture. Second, he was "*simple and straightforward.*" His presentation was literal and to the point with a focus on the life and times in which he lived. Thirdly, his "*moral applications were down to earth.*" Stott says, "*reading his sermons today, one can imagine without difficulty...the whole life of an oriental city at the end of the fourth century.*" Fourth, "*he was fearless in his condemnations.*" Because of his faithful and fearless preaching, he was eventually exiled from his pulpit.

Chrysostom was just one of many in centuries past who held aloft the Word of God. Today the preacher is challenged by a society who likes entertainment and brief sessions in front of a pulpit, a society that begs for activity and social fellowship without the patience to sit and listen to the teaching of the Word. We may not want to put all the influence of society on the congregation because many preachers have not taken up the challenge to be biblical, relevant and fearless in their preaching. While the American Church has much going for it—technology, resources and quality people— so often it seems to have little effect upon our secular society. Dr. Martyn Lloyd-Jones declared, "*I would say without any hesitation that the most urgent need in the Christian Church today is true preaching.*" I agree!

*Look it up – **Jonah 3:2; Isaiah 40:9; Mark 6:12***

*This truth for me – **Remember a good sermon you heard? What was good?***

_____

_____

_____

*Pray – **That God's word will change the lives of those around you!***

ARE YOU WITH ME?

John 7:52 ...You are not also from Galilee, are you?...

Every Christian experiences the struggle between flesh and Spirit. Each day we go through what the Apostle Paul says—*evil lies close at hand.* When we come to crossroads of decisions, as to whether we are to give in to the flesh (sin) or gain victory in the strength of the Spirit, it is like the question that was posed to Nicodemus from his fellow Pharisees, *Are you with us or with Jesus?* The Pharisees had enough of this so-called rabbi from Galilee. The time had come to rid themselves of Jesus. Nicodemus, a member of the Sanhedrin and a Pharisee, had first come to Jesus *by night* (John 3). In John 7 there is indication of Nicodemus gravitating more toward support of Jesus. Then finally in John 19, we see Nicodemus coming to claim the body of Jesus and prepare it for burial. John's usage of contrasts and imagery should not be overlooked. Nicodemus, the one who first came by night, very possibly now was in the light. By the time of Christ's death, I think he could answer, "I am with Jesus!"

Are you with Jesus or not when it comes to sin? If you are born again, you are with Jesus. The call for you now is to not let sin be master over you, but rather, in the strength of the Spirit, be victorious. The next time you come to that crossroad of flesh and Spirit, ask yourself the question, *"Am I with Jesus or not?"*

*Look it up – **Matthew 13:55-57; Mark 3;6; John 7:7***

*This truth for me – **How openly do you speak to others about Jesus? Write down some of your fears about standing up for Jesus.***

_____

_____

_____

*Pray - **For God to give you a greater understanding of what it means to "be with Jesus."***

LITTLE THINGS IN THE SIGHT OF THE LORD

Micah 5:2 But as for you, Bethlehem Ephrathah, too little...

Much of American society is caught up in the *bigger is better* syndrome. Robert Logan writes an interesting thought in his foreword to a book by Tom Nebel, <u>Big Dreams In Small Town Places</u>. Logan states, *"...we are called to develop a harvest orientation - and much of the harvest is found in smaller towns...Many people ask me, 'Where are there growing communities where I can plant?' But that's not the right question. The question we need to ask is, Where are there unreached people that I am equipped to reach..."* Interesting thinking, and it seems to fit with the Apostle Paul's argument to the Corinthians when he responds to the value given to *worldly thinking* in 1 Corinthians 1:26-31. Here Paul argues that God purposely elects unto salvation *not many wise... not many noble...but God has chosen...the (little) things that are not* so that all boasting can be in the Lord.

Many of us were nothing, yet God made us into a chosen race and a holy priesthood. All this was accomplished in little people like you and me so that God's good purpose of election would be realized and the proud wisdom of the world would be shamed. God selected Bethlehem for the birth of His Son, Nazareth for His home, and the Cross for His triumph. Little, unpretentious, and foolish places were God's choice for the Royal King Jesus. Nebel says in his book, "small town doesn't mean small church." I would like to add, small Christians don't mean small results. When we are trusting and serving Jesus, we can do all things through Him who gives us the strength to accomplish His will. ***Let him who boasts, boast in the Lord!***

*Look it up – **Jeremiah 9:23-24; Galatians 6:14; James 1:9-10***

*This truth for me – **When is the last time you boasted about yourself? What do you need to do when you find yourself boasting?*** _____

_____

_____

*Praise God – **For the little things that bring Him glory.***

THANK YOU LORD FOR SAVING ME

Titus 3:5, 8 He saved us, not on the basis of deeds which we have done...be careful to engage in good deeds...

How many people believe that their good deeds, religious heritage, or going to church will save them from God's wrath and judgment? Worldwide, most people believe that the good deeds they perform will save them and be pleasing to God. I have several questions for these people: (1) What type and how many good deeds are necessary to satisfy God? (2) Will good deeds cancel out the bad? (3) If good deeds save us from eternal damnation, then why did God send His Son to die for sinners?

The simple biblical answer is, God does not save on the basis of the good deeds that we do, but rather on the good and perfect deed His Son, the God-man Jesus Christ, accomplished. *But now apart from the Law (doing good deeds) the righteousness of God has been manifested...through faith in Jesus Christ for all those who believe...justified as a gift by His grace...a propitiation (satisfaction) in His blood through faith...Where then is boasting? It is excluded. By what kind of law? Of deeds? No, but by a law of faith. For we maintain that a man is justified (saved) by faith apart from works (deeds)...* (Romans 3:21-28). Where then do works fit into pleasing God? They are our response to Him for saving us. We thank Him for salvation by doing the good works that Christ did. There was only one good deed that satisfies God ... the sacrifice of His Son at Calvary. We trust by faith in Christ and what He did for us.

*Look it up – **Acts 26:20; Romans 4:2-5; Galatians 2:16***

*This truth for me – **Do you confuse good works with being the basis for your salvation? Define good works and what they mean to your salvation.***

---

*Pray – **For God to help you see that your good works are a way to thank Him for your salvation.***

WAITING, WAITING, WAITING...

Mark 4:27 ...the seed sprouts up and grows—how, he himself does not know.

There is the great temptation in the ministry of the Gospel to think that embellishment will enhance results. The church today has so many tools at its disposal for making the Gospel look attractive: attractive door hangers to draw attention to our church plants, eye catching mailers to inform people of our ministries. Special events have the best sound systems, special effects, and lighting. I was reading that the church super-sizing trend is on the rise. One such in the Southwest has a sanctuary, hotel, convention center, water-slide park, housing development and movie theater. Wow! *We've come a long way baby.*

Or have we? I am not one to throw off the tools that are at our disposal but I must regularly remind myself where my dependence must be centered. The Lord's parable about the seed and harvest is one biblical reminder that it is Christ who brings results and He does so through the faithful proclamation of the Word. It is not easy to solely trust in the spreading of the seed to produce results. Whether we are a minister preaching from the pulpit or a layperson sharing the Gospel on a park bench, there is the temptation to think that we must do something more than just simply sharing and explaining the Word. Yet, that is it—sharing and teaching the Word, and God then brings His growth. But how does He bring growth and what is the growth? God knows! Trust Him!

*Look it up – **1 Thessalonians 5:24; Philippians 1:6; Colossians 2:19***

*This truth for me - **Do you become anxious for God to act? What can you focus on while waiting for God to bring His results?***

---

*Pray – **For the wisdom and patience to see God work and bring His results to your life and walk with Him.***

JUMP UP AND GO

Matthew 4:20 And they immediately left...

My mother lived with our family while I pastored a Quakertown church. She became ill and I took her to the hospital. I thought she was suffering from a virus that had weakened her and would be back home in a few days. However, when the doctor came into the emergency room, he asked me if they should take any extreme measures to keep Mother alive. I was amazed at the question, but realized that at her age and with her heart condition, this was probably a normal procedure. Mother got settled into her room and I went home. Several hours later a nurse called and said that Mother was taken to intensive care and that her kidneys were shutting down. This call caused me to jump out of bed and rush to the hospital. Over the next four days her condition deteriorated, and with each phone call, I grew less desirous to go to the hospital knowing that it would be to watch Mother go into eternity. Then, that final call came and with trepidation I drove to the hospital. Soon my mother was in the hands of the Lord.

The call to serve the Lord should not be like the call to come to a deathbed and watch life leave someone's body. We should jump to the call to ministry and service for Christ. Serving Jesus Christ is done in thankfulness for what the Lord has done for us in saving us and giving us His righteousness.

Maybe I am writing to some of you who are not jumping anymore at the opportunity to serve the Lord. If this is the case, remember how the Lord immediately answered the call to go and die for you. This should make us jump up!

*Look it up – **Psalm 122:1; 1 Peter 4:10; Romans 12:11***

*This truth for me – **Is there a service I have been hesitant to go after? Write down why you are hesitant and how to overcome it.** _____*

_____

_____

*Pray – **For the energy and will to go about what the Lord wants you to do.***

DELIGHTFUL PRAYERS

Proverbs 15:8 ...the prayer of the upright is His delight

It is an amazing concept to think that the God of the universe, in His sovereign purpose and plan for His creation, says that He delights in the prayers of His children. What may seem at times as a simple and rote way of communicating with God, He sees our prayer as a delight. J. Oswald Sanders, former Director of China Inland Mission, woke early each morning to pray with His Lord. In his book, *Prayer Power Unlimited*, he wrote, *"God's will is what He sovereignly purposes and plans, and as such it cannot be improved. It is perfect...Prayer is the means by which our desires can be redirected and aligned with the will of God."* It is no wonder that when the *upright*, God's children, pray according to His will, they are a delight to Him. When we pray according to His will, we are acknowledging that He is Sovereign and that we want His perfect will to be accomplished in our lives and in His creation.

We may answer...*but I have difficulty in knowing His will and applying it to my prayers.* No need for worry. God has given us two ultimate helps for praying in His will—His Word and His Spirit. The Word is a light to our path for knowing the will of God. The Holy Spirit is, as the Puritan Thomas Goodwin declares, *"...the Intercessor within us, who searches the deep things of God, doth offer, prompt and suggest to us in our prayers those very things that are in God's heart..."* Stay in the Word and ask the Holy Spirit to guide you. May our prayers be the delight of the Lord!

Look it up – **Psalm 5:3; Romans 8:26; Hebrews 4:16**

This truth for me – **How is your prayer life? Do you think God is delighting in your prayers? What can you do so God will delight in your prayers?**

_____

_____

_____

Pray – **Today, right now, and envision God sitting with you and delighting in your communion with Him.**

I AM HIS AND HE IS MINE

Psalm 67:4 Let the nations be glad...

For whom did Christ die? Some believe that Christ died for everyone (*universal* or *unlimited atonement*). They would say that the extent of Christ's death is the same as the extent of salvation; everyone will be saved. Most, however, who hold to this belief would deny that all will be saved. Rather, even though Christ's death was sufficient to save the whole world, it was only efficient to save the elect. On the other side are those who say that Christ's death was only meant to save the elect (*limited atonement* or *particular redemption*). Augustine held this view, as did most of the Reformers and Puritans. There are ample Scriptures that are used to defend both views, (unlimited = John 1:29; 3:16; Titus 2:11; Hebrews 2:9 / limited = Matthew 1:21; 20:28; John 17:9; Ephesians 5:25).

The limited view is often said to be less than motivational for missions ... if Christ only died for the elect, how can we preach to all people, saying that Christ died for them? While the unlimited view is questioned—with some saying that if Christ died for all people then all will be saved—we know all will not be saved. We are to share the Gospel with everyone, not trying to figure out who is elect. Christ's death was effectual for those the Father chooses to save, and it would follow that the elect are the people for whom Christ came to die.

Knowing that Christ died for me should create in me a humble and sacrificial spirit. If Christ died for you, then live for Him!

Look it up – **Acts 20:28; Colossians 3:12; 1 John 4:10**

This truth for me – **Don't be confused about your salvation. List how you know you are saved?**

Praise – **God for His great work in saving you in Christ!**

THE SWORD THAT DIVIDES AND UNITES

Luke 23:12 Now Herod and Pilate became friends...

This sounds strange, but Christ can bring the worst of enemies together and unify them so that they will accomplish great things for the Kingdom. Perhaps you are familiar with the book and movie, *The Cross and the Switchblade*. It is the story of Pastor David Wilkerson, founder of Teen Challenge Ministries, and Nicky Cruz, a former New York City gang member. The first time they met on the streets of New York, Nicky told Brother Wilkerson, "You come near me...I'll kill you..." Nicky had sixteen stabbings to his record and was known as a vicious gang fighter. But the Gospel got hold of him and he became a servant of the Lord and a friend and associate to Pastor Wilkerson. This story of reconciliation happens over and over as the Holy Spirit changes lives.

The interesting effect of Christ upon His two judges, Herod and Pilate, is not one of reconciliation to each other through the love of Christ. Rather it is the story of two leaders who became unified over their disgust with Christ. The Jewish priests, the Gentile world of Pilate and Rome, and the hybrid world of Herod, were all against Christ. He was silent as all gathered in unity to hate Him, scourge and mock Him, and finally kill Him. The love of Christ manifested on the cross can reconcile enemies or it can reveal the enemies of God. Pray that those who are aligned against Christ because of their sin and depravity will hear the message of reconciliation.

Look it up – **Psalm 16:13, 14; Matthew 10:22; 1 John 3:13**

This truth for me – **Do you know someone who hates Jesus? How can you help people understand the love of Christ?**

_____

_____

_____

Pray – **That the Lord will make your testimony of Christ be true and faithful no matter what the outcome.**

SOVEREIGNLY ENERGIZED FOR THE GOSPEL

2 Timothy 4:5 ...do the work of an evangelist...

I would classify myself as holding to the Reformation doctrines of sovereign grace and Calvinistic theology. And I desire to evangelize and see people saved. Some might say that the latter does not line up with the former—how does one who holds to sovereign thinking, like election, have fervor to evangelize and see people saved? Because it is one's view of the sovereignty of God that makes evangelism either a human effort or God's means of saving His elect. For me there is no greater motivation to evangelize than the knowledge that a sovereign God has ordained evangelism as the means by which He saves and also as the ministry by which I can thank Him for saving me. Every Christian should be evangelizing as a thank offering to a most merciful God. Yes, I evangelize with a burden for the lost, wanting to see no one enter the eternal fires of hell. However, even greater than my heart for the lost is my desire to obey God and fulfill His commission to witness.

When is the last time you spoke one-on-one to a sinner about their eternal destiny? Was it yesterday, last week, a month or year ago, or has it been so long that you can't remember? The Apostle Paul, in his closing exhortations to Timothy, did not leave out the need for Timothy to be evangelizing. We need to be evangelists. Ask God to lead you to a sinner this week to whom you can witness and, Lord willing, lead to Christ.

Look it up – **Matthew 11:25-30; Romans 11:33-36; Acts 13:48**

*This truth for me –***What holds you back from witnessing and what gets you motivated to witness.**

Pray – **For a greater sense of God's sovereignty and a greater burden for the lost.**

GIVING WAY TO FOOLISHNESS

Proverbs 25:19 Like a bad tooth...is confidence in a faithless man...

I have been blessed with a good set of teeth. I believe that I have had only one or two cavities and one wisdom tooth extraction. I remember being on a hospital visitation and seeing a man in his bed cringing in pain. I thought to myself that this man must have undergone some extreme surgery. When I questioned a nurse regarding his condition, she told me that he had just returned from having his wisdom teeth removed. At that moment I thanked the Lord for having a good set of teeth.

The writer of Proverbs uses the two characteristics of a bad tooth to describe an unfaithful person—painful and useless. Trusting in a faithless person is like trusting in a bad tooth—they give you pain and are good for nothing. It is especially painful when a *righteous person* or a believer gives way to unfaithfulness. To see a Christian move from a committed faith in the Lord to a place of apostasy and loss of integrity is most painful. Watching a once-faithful brother or sister give way to sin and no longer serve the Lord is like experiencing the pain of a rotting tooth. Two things to consider: first, who do you trust? Our trust must ultimately be in the Lord. He will never give pain to the one who trusts in Him. And second, maybe you or an acquaintance has become like a bad tooth. If so, just as extraction is the solution to a bad tooth, so repentance is the cure for a life gone astray.

*Look it up – **Luke 12:20; Ephesians 5:17; 1 Peter 2:15***

*This truth for me - **Is there a foolish person in your life who needs prayer or assistance? How can you provide help?***

_____

_____

_____

*Pray – **For the Lord to help those you know who have turned to foolish ways.***

PRAYER OPENS GOSPEL DOORS

John 1:41 He found first his own brother...

It is a normal response for a Christian to want to find someone and tell them about Christ. When Andrew and Phillip met Jesus, it was normal for them to go and tell others. In contrast, it is abnormal not to want to tell others of Christ. If we, who have been saved by grace and experienced the love of God poured out in our souls, lack the desire to evangelize, there is something abnormal about our Christianity. *"The impulse to evangelize should spring up spontaneously in us as we see our neighbor's need for Christ...and have felt any measure of gratitude for the grace that has saved us..."(J.I. Packer - Evangelism And The Sovereignty Of God).* This evangelistic spontaneity, if not present in us, is to be fostered by prayer. If we find the obstacles of false shame, shyness or busyness getting in the way of evangelizing, then the way to break down these barriers is to pray to the Lord of the Harvest. Ask Him for opportunities to witness and the courage and strength which the Holy Spirit will give to those who ask. I find that if I go through a period when I have not witnessed to someone or led a person to the Lord, prayer is the means by which God opens the doors of opportunity. I am praying now that when I go to make more contacts this week, the doors to witness will be wide open. Expecting God to answer this prayer, I am looking forward to rejoicing for having had the privilege of sharing Christ. Pray today for a witnessing opportunity.

Look it up – **2 Thessalonians 3:1; Ephesians 6:19; Colossians 4:2-4**

This truth for me – **List the ways that you can improve your prayer life.**

_____

_____

_____

Pray – **For the Holy Spirit to give you fervency in your prayers to go out and about with the Gospel.**

GRADUAL BUT SURE

2 Peter 3:18 But grow in the grace and knowledge of our Lord...

Certain types of tests are now being administered in schools to determine how students are developing and grasping what is being taught. The government has set some standards for achievement, and if school districts don't meet those standards, federal support is in jeopardy. As a Christian, how would you like to be tested in order to determine whether or not you are growing in your knowledge of God and becoming more like Christ? I don't know of any such tests, and if some exist, I would question the results. Just as salvation is the internal working of God in the heart, so is our progressive sanctification. But this does not mean that Christian growth cannot be seen or experienced. We should be able to look back over the past years since becoming a Christian and see more Christlikeness in our lives, more knowledge of God and the teachings of Christ, more peace and security in our relationship with the Lord, more love and hope, and more usefulness in service to Him.

The Apostle Peter's exhortation in verse 18 is a good conclusion to this letter that seeks to stir up the Christian mind by way of remembering the teachings that produce virtue, confidence, humility, love and hope. Christian growth is always centered in the Word of God and the believer's mind and heart. Even though Christian growth is gradual, it is sure when centered in the Bible and lived out in action. Grow, grow, grow *in the grace and the knowledge of our Lord.*

*Look it up – **Isaiah 40:30; Romans 4:19-20; 1 Corinthians 14:20***

*This truth for me – **List areas of your Christian walk where you want to see growth. Meditate on ways to grow in those areas.***

_____

_____

_____

*Pray – **That the Holy Spirit will help you grow to be more like Christ.***

BLOW SPIRIT BLOW

John 3:8 The wind blows where it wishes...

One evening when I sat down to dinner with my family, it felt a little stuffy in our kitchen, so I opened the window. I started to see the curtain move and then a beautiful red flowering plant my wife had sitting on the sill began to sway. The fresh cool breeze that poured through the window caused me to pause and think of how wonderful the blowing of the Holy Spirit is in our Christian lives. From the moment the Spirit poured out His regenerating work in our dead hearts, we were made aware of the miraculous and sovereign work of God. God's work in saving sinners and sanctifying us is so quiet and powerful, it cannot be detected by noise or audacity. Rather it is experienced and seen like the gentle wind that moves a curtain or causes a flower to be animated.

When Elijah was depressed by what he perceived as ungodly and apathetic times in the lives of his people, God reminded him of His sovereign control over all things. God was not in the strong wind that collapsed the mountains before Elijah. He was found in *a sound of a gentle blowing*. May the wind you see and feel remind you that God is in control and His Spirit is at work in and around you. Be filled with the gentle breeze of His Spirit today.

Look it – **Psalm 104:3; Ezekiel 2:2; John 4:23, 24**

This truth for me – **Look for the movement of the Spirit in your mind and your walk. Write down how the Spirit is leading you.**

_____

_____

_____

Pray – **That you will witness the Spirit's leading in your life and in the lives of those around you by your, and their growth in grace.**

GOING HOME

John 17:5 And now, glorify Thou Me together with Thyself, Father...

There is nothing like going home after a long trip and settling down into your own bed and the comforts of familiar things. When the Lord left His glory to come to Earth, we are told in Philippians 2 that He *emptied* Himself. Christ left His glory to become the bond slavery of humanity. Try to think of infinite and unbounded divine existence confining itself to the limitations of a human body and living in the surroundings of first century Israel. There are no analogies to compare with this humility on the part of our Lord. God becoming like us, leaving His glory for the humiliation of the cross, is a subject for meditation. It is no wonder that on the night He was betrayed, He prayed in great anticipation of returning to existence with His Father in glory.

When Ascension Day comes around, remember it! The celebration of this event allows us to participate in the joy the Lord had in going back to the Father. It reminds us that the work of salvation is completed and our Mediator is interceding for us with the Father. Also, Ascension is our living hope that we will see Him face to face in Heaven.

> *"Jesus the Savior reigns, the God of truth and love; when He had purged our stains He took His seat above: Lift up your heart, lift up your voice! Rejoice, again, I say, rejoice."*

Look it up – **Luke 24:51; Acts 1:9; Ephesians 4:8-10**

This truth for me – **List how important it is for you to know that Christ stands in glory to intercede for you.**

_____

_____

_____

Pray – **That you will have peace in all things knowing your Savior stands in glory making intercession for you.**

A TIME FOR TURNING

Acts 26:16,18 ...*I have appeared to you, to appoint you...to open their eyes so that they may turn...*

When driving, have you ever turned from going in one direction and started to head the opposite way? I have a tendency of doing this when my thoughts drift and I find myself several miles past where I had planned to exit off the road. I then have to turn around and go in the other direction. In the Bible this motion is defined as repenting or turning. In the original language of the New Testament, the word used for conversion is also used for turning or repenting. The Apostle Paul stated to King Agrippa that he was appointed by God to turn people or to convert people to Christ.

The term **conversion** is not an acceptable word in today's tolerant society. To say that we are out to convert people to Christ is offensive to many. What right do you have to convert someone from what they believe? Don't you have any respect for a person's personal beliefs? As difficult as it may be for some to understand, God Himself charges His children to seek to convert people to Christianity. Why? Because Christ has the only answers to life: *He is the way, the truth, and the life.* The Apostle Paul was appointed to convert people to Christ and so, too, is every Christian. No, we cannot do this in our own power. We are given the commission to proclaim the message of conversion: the Gospel of Christ's saving grace for sinners. When we proclaim the Gospel, God saves His people. Do you have a fervor for evangelism and to seek converts? Christ did...the apostles did...and so should we!

*Look it up – **Jonah 3:10; 2 Corinthians 7:10; Revelation 2:5***

*This truth for me –**What was it like when you "turned" to Christ. Remember how glorious.***

_____

_____

_____

*Pray – **For the many unbelievers that you know who need to turn to the Lord.***

BE HOLY ALL YOU SAINTS

2 Timothy 2:19 ...*The Lord knows those who are His...*

If people are lost while traveling and then find themselves on the right road to get to their destination, will they seek to be lost again or try to follow the road that leads to their destination? The answer is obvious: they seek to stay on the right way and do all they can to make sure they are moving toward their destination.

When sinners are saved, it is because God elected them unto salvation and sealed them unto eternal life. The saved are heading to glory and nothing will intercept that pilgrimage. But some would say, "Doesn't election then make the saved lazy and negligent toward God and the command to be holy?" No! The elect know they are on the right road to God and will seek to stay on that road, diligently striving to serve Him who saved them. They will not seek to be lost again but rather, they will go after holiness. The Puritan, John Owen, from whom I borrowed the illustration of the road, wrote, *"Those ordained to salvation were also ordained to be holy."* The Apostle Paul concludes his statement in verse 19 by saying, *The Lord knows those who are His, let everyone who names the name of the Lord abstain from wickedness (be holy).* Holiness is the proof of election, and election is the motivation for holiness. *MAY THE ELECT BE HOLY!*

*Look it up – **Leviticus 20:7; Ephesians 5:26, 27; 1 Peter 1:15***

*This truth for me – **Describe what glory will be like when you arrive.***

_____

_____

_____

*Pray – **And thank God for the promise and secure hope of glory.***

PEACE OF LIFE, NOW

John 14:27 Peace I leave with you; My peace I give to you...

In the Old Testament, God called the promised land of Canaan the place of rest where He will eventually bring peace for the Jews. With today's news of the conflicts in Israel and Palestine, it is hard to imagine that one day the Lord will bring rest and peace to those lands.

When Jesus promises peace to His disciples, John states that He is saying that the peace He gives will provide a rest for the soul. This peace is contrasted to the confusion and affliction we often face. Peace doesn't mean that our lives are void of tribulation and affliction. The context of John 14 seems to promise the follower of Christ that affliction and tribulation are at home with the Christian. But there will never be peace or the prospect of peace in a life that is without Christ. For those of us in Christ, peace is promised by none other than Christ Himself. Yes, peace is not only a possibility but it should be realized, and the fruit of Christ's peace, joy and faith are to be a significant part of our Christian lives.

Are you troubled today and frustrated or confused about something? Are these negative feelings causing you to be depressed? Through prayer and meditation in the Word, seek the peace that is yours in Jesus.

*Look it up – **Judges 6:24; Romans 15:33; Hebrews 13:20,21***

*This truth for me – **What things are causing you anxiety? List some and then think about how God's peace can help.***

_____

_____

_____

*Pray – **For God to show you His peace through His word and your position in His Son, Jesus.***

FILLING UP WITH THE WIND OF THE SPIRIT

Acts 2:2 And suddenly there came from heaven a noise like a violent, rushing wind...

One of the most refreshing feelings I experience is that of a strong wind sweeping upon me. The wind is a refreshing and restoring agent to a weary body. After exercising outdoors my body becomes tired and my mouth is dry. But when a cool wind starts to blow across my sweated forehead, it is very refreshing. How invigorating it feels.

The wind reminds us of the Spirit's work in regenerating sinners and giving them new life. In the same way many of us, as Christians, need the wind of God's Spirit to renew our fervor for spiritual things: Bible reading, prayer, church attendance, and especially personal witnessing and evangelism. When the Spirit of God swept through the hearts of the apostles on the day of Pentecost, they were filled to the point of rushing out into the streets, glorifying God and sharing Jesus. Could it be that we are not seeing conversion growth in the American church because we are not filled with the Spirit? Filling is the one work of the Spirit that we have something to say about. We can't seek the baptism, or sealing, or indwelling, or the gifting of the Spirit; God does all this for us. But we are to seek to be filled. My friend, let us seek to be filled today with the Spirit of God and see God save sinners. Filling takes a yielded and holy life, ready for the unction of the Spirit. Are we yielded and holy? Be filled - TODAY!

*Look it up – **John 3:34; 1 Corinthians 2:9-10; Ephesians 5:18***

*This truth for me – **How yielded are you to the Lord? List areas of your life you need to release and have God handle.***

_____

_____

_____

*Pray – **For the filling of the Spirit and the necessary yielding you must do.***

NO SURPRISES WITH GOD

Exodus 4:11 Who has made man's mouth? Or who makes him dumb or deaf, or seeing or blind? Is it not I, the Lord?

One Sunday evening on my way home, I listened to a so-called "Bible teacher." I had complained about this man's teaching to the radio station manager. Here is what the man stated one particular time about God: "*God acts contingent upon our behavior...we at times may surprise God.*" He went on to compare Genesis 1—where he stated that everything God made was good and perfect— to Genesis 6, stating that when God saw that man had become totally wicked, He was so *surprised* by this wickedness that His reaction was to destroy all mankind and try again.

By this time I had enough of such teaching and turned off the radio. The Bible is clear that God is *not* surprised by anything that man does. God has ordained all that takes place in His world and works all things out to His glorious plan and purpose. Even when we see things evil and confusing, God is not fooled. He is in control and will settle all evil by His justice, and provide grace and mercy for His will to be accomplished. God reminded Moses that He was the God of ALL. Don't make excuses for God; He is in control. He is in control of your life; trust Him and wait upon Him.

Look it up – Psalm 93:1; Romans 11:36; Ephesians 1:9-11

This truth for me – Do you believe God is in control of all things? Where do you struggle with this truth?

_____

_____

_____

Praise – God for His sovereign control of all things and His peace that comes in knowing He is above all.

MOVING TOWARD WHO WE ARE

Hebrews 10:14 For by one offering He has perfected for all time those who are sanctified [being made holy].

Here is one of those *incomprehensible* statements in Scripture—two truths that just don't seem to go together in our finite minds. How can something that is perfect still be in the process of being made perfect or *holy?* An artist friend of mine once told me, "Rembrandt's paintings are perfect. There is nothing more to add or alter in the master's art." This is the way that most of us think about perfection. What possibly could be added to something that is perfect?

The Christian is called *perfected* by the writer of Hebrews. Christ offered Himself on the cross and purchased our perfection. This we call *justification.* But He also purchased our ongoing process of being made holy, and this we call *sanctification.* One writer says, *"the work of forgiveness and the work of making one holy can never be separated."* Believer, in Christ, you and I are perfect in the sight of God, because Christ purchased us and presents everyone of us before the Father as forgiven saints. We are also being made holy into the likeness of Jesus. Here is the application of this incomprehensible truth. Rejoice and live in thanksgiving for the gift of forgiveness in Christ, and with every breath and thought, live to the glory of God.

*Look it up – **Romans 6:14; Colossians 3:10-12; 2 Thessalonians 2:13***

*This truth for me – **We all know we have not yet been glorified, that is, perfected in heaven. But in Christ we have His perfection given to us. Meditate now on your position in Christ and your calling to grow and mature in grace.***

_____

_____

_____

*Pray – **For strength to put off the old person you were and be who you are in Christ.***

LEAVING WORSHIP WITH THE WORD

Nehemiah 8:9 ...For all the people were weeping...

While driving to a church on Sunday morning, I turned on the radio and heard Dr. James Boice say, "...will you leave worship this morning different than when you came in?" This remark made me think!

The people who had gathered to hear Ezra stood to their feet when he opened the Scriptures, and for six hours they heard the reading and explanation of the Word. The outcome of that was dramatic! The people were pierced to the heart and repented and wept over their sin. The reading of God's Word, accompanied by explanation and exhortation, caused the people to leave that worship experience different than when they arrived.

In worship, I am blessed by good music and innovative presentations. But what affects me the most and leaves its lasting impression is the hearing and preaching of the Word. The divine instruments of preaching and exhortation were what changed a wretch like me into a new creation and what keeps fashioning me into the image of Christ. It is not enough to leave worship feeling good. Our minds must be changed and conformed more to the things of God. There will be times when the Word of God preached will not allow us to leave worship feeling good and other times when the Word will thrill us and bring great joy. It is the hearing of the Word, preached and taught, that changes us for eternity. Be changed this week through God's powerful Word.

*Look it up – **Mark 16:15; 1 Corinthians 1:17-21; 2 Timothy 4:1,2***

*This truth for me – **Are you attentive to the preaching of the Word of God? In what ways is hearing the preaching of the Word changing you?***

---

*Pray – **For the Holy Spirit to make you even more attentive to the preaching of His Word.***

GETTING COMFORTABLE WITH SIN

John 16:8 ...convict the world concerning sin...

It is obvious that the work of the Holy Spirit is to convict us of our sin. But, you may ask, don't we know we are sinners? Why does the Holy Spirit have to convict us of our sin? It is not that we don't know we are sinners, but rather that we are helpless in our sin, and we are comfortable being sinners! By nature we are sinners and can do nothing about it without the Holy Spirit's work of conviction. He causes us to be born-again with new life from God so that we recognize our sin and repent, then recognize the Gospel and believe. Only God, the Spirit, can do this work of salvation.

Some time ago I heard an advertisement for a new TV show about homosexuals. The show's commentator said, "We are here and we are queer. Get used to it." He didn't have to tell people to get used to sin—we have gotten used to SIN! The Christian is not to *get used to sin*, but rather to flee from it, and in some situations, confront it. As children of God, we must not get used to sin! If we do, and put our blinders on, we partner with sin. May the Holy Spirit do His job of convicting, and may we never *get used to sin.*

Much forgiven, much delivered, much instructed, much enriched, much blessed, shall we dare to put forth our hand unto evil? God forbid!
C. Spurgeon

Look it up – ***Genesis 4:7; Psalm 51:3; Romans 5:12***

This truth for me – **How comfortable are you with sin? Can you list some sin you have accepted and how you will deal with it?**

_____

_____

_____

Pray – ***That the Lord will always give you discernment about sin in you and around you.***

YOU CAN THROW IT AWAY

Ephesians 4:24 ...put on the new self...

Old habits are hard to break! You heard this adage and you know that it is true, even impossible in some cases, for those who do not have Christ in their life. But for the Christian, we are commanded to put on the new life we have received in Christ and put off the old. With certain old things that tag along after salvation, this may be difficult, but not impossible. God would never tell us to do something that could not be accomplished. The key to putting off the old and putting on the new is to depend upon God's power and not our own. No, I don't mean sit back and let a thunderbolt from God hit you so that you will throw off that old habit, action or attitude. But rather give forth your own effort in putting on your new life in Christ, then see how God will add His power to change you. Here are some thoughts to ponder from our passage in Ephesians: Put on the new self which is already yours (Ephesians 4:24; Ephesians 2:4-6). Put on the new self which is a continuous action till we get to glory (Ephesians 2:10; 4:17; 5:2). Put on the new self which is in Christ (Ephesians 2:20-21).

No old way is too difficult for God to take away.
No old thought is too entrenched for God to erase.
No old sin is too binding for God to forgive and cleanse.
No old lust is too strong for God to destroy.
God in you, the hope of Glory!

Look it up – **Romans 6:6; Ephesians 4:20-24; Colossians 3:9-10**

This truth for me – **What is still hanging on to you from your past that is not glorifying to the Lord? Name it and state how you will throw it away.**

Praise – **God for your new self in Christ and pray for His help to throw off the old ways.**

MY GUIDE AND MY HELPER

1 Kings 11:6 ...and did not follow the Lord fully...

Reading through 1 Kings, I was again astounded by the story of Solomon's calling to be king, the blessings he received from the Lord (particularly wisdom), and the riches that he amassed. I was perplexed as to how Solomon, in all his wisdom, could mess up! The glamour of foreign women and the false gods they brought into Solomon s life and the nation of Israel were his undoing. How could someone with such God-given wisdom fall prey to intermarriage with pagan women and the adoption of false religions? It happened because the human heart is prone to wander and move its attention from God and His truth.

How many of us think that we know the Bible well enough, or think we pray often enough, or believe we serve the Lord diligently enough? Looking at Solomon's life can tell us that the Lord demands our *full* attention to His directives for our lives. But how in the world do creatures, weak as we are, have the power to *fully* follow the Lord? It happens when we turn to Him, ask for His assistance, and trust by faith that the Holy Spirit will be our helper. No one can *fully* obey and follow the Lord unless the Spirit is his helper and the Bible is his guide.

Look it up – **Job 28:28; Proverbs 9:9; Luke 18:18-22**

This truth for me – **How well do you follow the Lord? When do you put your wisdom before the Lord's wisdom?**

_____

_____

_____

Pray – **For God's wisdom to prevail in your life.**

BE OF SOUND DOCTRINE

I Timothy 4:6 ...of the faith and of the sound doctrine...

"*The deplorable condition in which I found religious affairs during a recent visitation of the congregations, has impelled me to publish this Catechism... Alas! What misery I beheld...the people seem to have no knowledge whatever of Christian doctrine...*"

This is Martin Luther's opening to his introduction for his Small Catechism. I find it interesting that instead of placing the blame for such doctrinal ignorance upon the people, he places it upon the elders (bishops). "*Ye bishops! what answer will you give to Christ for having so shamefully neglected the people and paid no attention to the duties of your office...you do not take the least interest in teaching the people...*" Luther's condemnation for such neglect of doctrine falls upon those called to preach and teach.

Today, we are inundated by so-called teachers and preachers who are not sound in doctrine. But it is of no concern to many Christians because they cannot distinguish between sound and bad doctrine as long as they are getting an emotional charge from what they hear. The church in America is in need of hearing sound doctrine. Luther understood that this is what leads to godly living, "*...so that they (the Christians) may know how to distinguish right from wrong in their conduct...*" Is there a connection between the worldliness of the American church and its lack of understanding sound doctrine? Maybe so!

Look it up – Proverbs 4:2; Titus 2:1; 2 John 9

This truth for me – How would you describe your knowledge of sound doctrine? List some ways to improve your mind with sound doctrine.

Pray – For God to lead you to good sound teaching of the truth.

COVERED WITH EVERLASTING LOVE

Genesis 3:21 And the Lord God made garments of skin...

The end result of God's cursing of Adam and Eve is this *skin* illustration of God's grace. Just as God provided the garments of skin to cover the first couple, He would also send His Son to be killed and whose blood would cover our sin. The Old Testament gives us this mysterious and veiled picture of the atonement. These skins came from an animal that evidently was killed by God. As Adam and Eve walked out of the garden, covered with these skins, they also walked with the promise that God would provide the necessary sacrifice for mankind to take away their sins. Adam and Eve were no longer blessed with perfection. They were now sinners and under the curse of God, yet they were given a promise of life by God's grace. Adam believed that promise.

As Christians—figuratively speaking—we too walk in skins. We are covered by the shed blood of Jesus Christ and walk in the skin of new life in Christ. There are many who remain under the curse of sin and death. Those of us, covered in Christ, must seek to bring the Gospel to those walking in spiritual darkness. Share today the grace of our Lord and Savior, Jesus Christ!

Look it up – John 1:29; Hebrews 9:11-14; 1 Peter 1:18, 19

This truth for me – Because we are in Christ, our sins are covered by His blood. Meditate on what this means to your present Christian walk.

_____

_____

_____

Praise – God for His forgiveness in Christ and for the cost Christ paid on the cross to set you free from sin.

THE FUEL OF OBEDIENT THANKSGIVING

1 Corinthians 9:16 ...for I am under compulsion; for woe is me if I do not preach... Acts 26:2 ...I consider myself fortunate [happy]...

Why does the Christian Church witness and evangelize? Many say it is because it has a passion for lost souls. Others say that evangelism is the fulfillment of the Great Commission. While both reasons are good, they may not be the ultimate basis for evangelism. I have seen people lose fervor and passion for souls when they experience little results. Some have grown cold to missions because of a lack of accomplishment or because a mission board changes direction. What then provides a more solid and lasting base for evangelism?

Some reformed theologians have said that the motivation for evangelism and missions is *obedience*. God's means for saving His elect is evangelism and God commissioned His church to be witnesses. Another view is that we evangelize because we want to *thank God and praise Him* for what He has accomplished in salvation and the best way to be thankful is to be witnesses of His grace. I believe both obedience and thanksgiving provide a lasting commitment to evangelism and missions. Obedience keeps us witnessing, *woe to me if I do not witness.* Thanksgiving keeps us praising God and wanting Him to be known. We should be happy to share the wonderful grace of our Lord. Be **obedient** to the charge to witness and **thankful** that you can share Christ, the glorious Savior, with others.

*Look it up – **Psalm 1:1-3; Psalm 50; Psalm 103:2***

*This truth for me – **How have you been obedient lately to witness? Write down what being thankful means to you.***

---

*Pray – **For a heart that is always thankful for the great grace God has extended to you, and be obedient to His desires.***

MY LIFE IS ALL YOURS

John 3:16 ...He gave His only begotten...

I would sum Christianity up in one word: *sacrifice*—God's sacrifice for His children and the Christian's charge to sacrifice for others. I have been reading the history of the *U.S. Life Saving Service*, the forerunner to the Coast Guard. Those who served were some of the most courageous and rugged individuals in this country's history. Day after day and storm after storm, the keepers and surf men of the life saving stations would search our coastlines for ships and crews in distress and then provide the assistance necessary in order to rescue lives. Joshua James, the most famous keeper in American history (Massachusetts Humane Society and Point Allerton Life Saving Station), saved hundreds of lives. In the terrible hurricane of 1888, Keeper James was on duty constantly for days, attending to six wrecks and saving 29 lives. The accounts of these rescues are amazing, and the courage and stamina of this man was incomprehensible. In 1902, he died on duty at the age of 74. A brief eulogy was presented by his superintendent, "...*He was a man of the highest character ... he lived up to the Life Savers Motto, We must go out but we don't have to come back...*" On the morning Joshua James died, he saw an approaching storm and his last words were, "*The tide is ebbing.*"

Spiritually speaking, our society's tide is ebbing and it needs to see sacrificial churches and individuals that will be a safe haven in the storm. Ask yourself, *how is my church living out a testimony of sacrifice? Am I living a sacrificial life?*

*Look it up – **Psalm 54:6; Romans 12:1; Ephesians 5:2***

*This truth for me – **List the ways you have given yourself up for the Lord and others.***

_____

_____

_____

*Pray – **For the Lord to have you see the ultimate glory of living sacrificial.***

THE GAME IS AFOOT

Ephesians 5:17 ...understand what the will of the Lord is.

Most of us at some time or another ask, *How do I determine what the Lord's will is for my life?* Every Christian faces this question at some juncture of their walk with Christ. There have been writings and exercises that are helpful. One such work is, <u>Finding The Lord's Will</u>, by Dr. Bruce K. Waltke. He writes, *"God guides us first through His Word, then through our heartfelt desires, then the wise counsel of others, and then our circumstances. At that point we must rely on our own sound judgment...God gave each of us a brain and He expects us to put it to good use."*

I agree with Dr. Waltke's formula and would add the need to be patient in prayer. I don't know of one occasion in my life where, after doing what Dr. Waltke suggests, I didn't have to pray and wait upon the Lord. Finding the Lord's will at times is not as hard as we believe. Many of the crossroads we face and the decisions we need to make are clearly mapped out in God's Word and can be discovered by study and meditation. Others are more vague, needing deeper study and proper counsel. Take note that the common thread here is the Bible. *God's Word is the answer to understanding what the will of the Lord is in all things.* Finding the Lord's will may be a painstaking and mysterious endeavor, but its result is *peace!*

Look it up – ***Deuteronomy 4:29; Proverbs 2:4, 5; Acts 17:27-28***

This truth for me – ***Have you found God's will for your life? How do you search for God's will in everyday decisions?***

Pray – ***That when a decision needs to be made, you will first seek God's will.***

THE QUESTION OF LOVE

John 21:15 ...*do you love Me more than these...*

My youngest daughter and I would meet each morning before school to have a time of devotions. At some point we went through the book of John. One morning as we read the interrogation that Christ had with Peter concerning Peter's level of love for the Lord, my daughter asked, "why did Jesus ask Peter so many times if he loved Him?" I answered, "He wanted Peter to understand what it really meant to love Him." Peter's love was not yet at the level of being fully committed to Christ.

I wonder how many of us would give the same answer as Peter did if the Lord were to stand in front of us and ask us if we loved Him. Would we say, "Yes Lord, come on, you know that I love you, didn't I ask you into my heart and am I not born-again? Haven't I been serving in the church and trying to do what is right?" We might even think to ourselves, *What more does He want from me?* The *more* that Christ wants is everything; yes, everything—our total devotion, our total attention! Don't misinterpret this and think that the Lord wants us to spend every waking hour involved with a church program or an activity. He wants our minds and hearts to be filled with His Word, His faith, His love, His hope, and His Spirit. How would you answer the Lord's question today, *Do you really love me?*

Look it up – **John 15:9-13; John 16:27; Philippians 1:9**

This truth for me – **Measure your level of love for Christ and others. Write down some of your thoughts.**

_____

_____

_____

Pray – **That your love for the Lord and others will grow.**

GOOD, EVIL AND GOD

Luke 22:22 ...as it has been determined...

Does it make you uncomfortable to think that God determines ALL things, even the things that we might consider bad or evil? Even those who hold to strong views of God's sovereignty tend to shy away from the word *determinism*. Gordon Clark in his book, <u>Religion, Reason, and Revelation</u>, writes, *"for some reason it seems to them (certain Calvinists) an unpleasant connotation. However, the Bible speaks not only of predestination, usually with reference to eternal life, but it also speaks of the foreordination or predetermination of evil acts..."* When I discuss with people the subject of good, evil and God, I often have to ask, "Either God is sovereign over all things or only some things. Which is it?"

I believe the God of the universe, who sent His Son to be crushed on the cross of Calvary and endure such horrible brutality for me, is in control of ALL things no matter how uncomfortable some aspects of His sovereignty might seem. Since God determined the betrayal and death of His Son, then we must believe that He has determined ALL things. This should not make us feel uncomfortable but just the opposite. The God of love, justice, patience, kindness, gentleness, peace, and truth is in control of everything! That means that even the worst evil is being fashioned according to His good and perfect plan. If you don't believe this, just ask Joseph, who knew this truth so well, *...you meant evil against me, but God meant it for good...* (Genesis 50:20).

Look it up – Psalm 145:9; Lamentations 3:38; Romans 8:28-32

This truth for me – Trying to understand why God allows evil is disturbing. Write down some ways God uses evil for His glory and plan.

Pray – That God will give you a better understanding of His mercy and grace.

MIRROR, MIRROR IN THE WORD

Hebrews 4:1 *Therefore, let us fear...*

Self-examination is a productive exercise. Whether pertaining to our family, job, marriage, friendships or ministry, it is good to evaluate how we are doing. Our salvation is another major area that needs self-examination. The Scriptures are replete in telling Christians they are secure in Christ and sealed in the Holy Spirit. In Romans 8, the Apostle Paul wrote that the Christian has eternal salvation and will never face the condemnation of God. This same apostle—along with the writer of Hebrews—warns and exhorts the Christian to *...take care...lest there be in any one of you an evil, unbelieving heart...* Hebrews 3:12. How do we put such statements together? If we are saved and secure in such a salvation, why examine ourselves?

First, because self-examination reminds us that we are saved. Second, because it helps us to reflect on the wonderful work of grace that God has wrought in us. Third, it allows us to see what sin, or attack of the devil, may be causing us to doubt our salvation. Fourth, self-examination takes away doubts. And lastly, for those who think they are saved because of their works, it may awaken in them a real need for the Gospel.

How do I examine myself? First, through the Word; it is a spiritual mirror! Next through my works—what I do and how I live indicates if I have a real faith! Finally, through my appetite—for what do I thirst and hunger? The things of God or the things of this world?

Look it up – **Song of Solomon 7:26; 2 Corinthians 3:18; James 1:23,24**

This truth for me – **When is the last time you did a self-evaluation? List areas in your life that need to be evaluated.**

———————————————————————————————

———————————————————————————————

———————————————————————————————

Pray – **That the Holy Spirit will assist you with a spiritual evaluation.**

FROM THE DEEP PIT TO LOFTY GLORY

Romans 7:24a Wretched man that I am!

A correct view of one's own sin will lead to gaining a correct view of God's powerful grace. The Apostle Paul writes that he is a wretch, dead in sin and *the chief sinner*. He also possesses the highest esteem for God's saving grace—see his doxology at the end of Romans 11.

The Puritan, William Perkins, in his commentary on Galatians, writes about those who believe their own will or good works, coupled with God's grace, can save them. *"...The (one who rejects salvation by grace alone) ascribes his conversion not wholly to grace, but partly to grace, and partly to nature, or the strength of man's will helped by grace."* Ian Murray says that the reason anyone would think he is saved by his own will helped along by God's grace, *"...lacks a true knowledge of sin."* I agree! If you don't understand sin, then you will not understand God's saving grace.

Justification by faith alone is an unwelcome, humbling belief. Human nature rejects it and seeks its own ways of solving the problem of sin. Only when we see the ugliness of sin, its nature to reject the Savior, and the impossibility of doing anything humanly to be saved, will we understand God's grace. Thank the Lord for the ability He gives to know that we who were once dead in sin are saved by His mercy and grace alone. If you are not saved, cry out to God and ask Him to give you the faith to see your sin, repent, and believe on Jesus Christ.

Look it up – **Romans 3:10; 1 Timothy 1:15; Colossians 1:12**

This truth for me – **Remember your sinful condition before you were saved. List the ways God lifted you up.**

_____

_____

_____

Praise – **God for redeeming you from sin and giving you the title "saint."**

NAME ABOVE ALL NAMES

Ezekiel 20:9 ...I acted for the sake of My name...

King Solomon wrote that a good name is better than gold. Some names like *Rockefeller* or *Gates* summon great amounts of wealth. Other names like *Mother Theresa* or *Gandhi* stir people's adoration. Still other names like *Hitler* or *Mao* elicit anger and fear.

There is one name that carries with it an infinite and ultimate understanding— the name of our true God, Jehovah. God will not allow His name to be considered in any terms other than *holy, just, gracious, righteous, longsuffering;* these names indicate His perfections. The prophet Ezekiel records God's response to the nation of Israel when it discredited the name of God. He said, *I acted for the sake of my name...* God will not allow man to bring His name into ill repute—it must remain high and lifted up.

It is our privilege and challenge to lift up the name of God. Some may say they are doing that in church by their praise and worship. Maybe so, but are we unashamedly lifting up God's name in the workplace, in school, in every aspect of life?

What is the solution to a low consideration of the Lord's name? We could take on the assignment the Lord gave to Ezekiel, *Therefore, son of man, speak to the house of Israel, and say to them, Thus says the Lord God....* Perhaps as we speak the Word to another, the name of God will be lifted high again.

Look it up – **Psalm 20:7; Exodus 20:7; Revelation 14:1**

This truth for me – **What names of God mean the most to you and list why?**

Pray – **That you will be bold in naming the name of God among your unsaved associates.**

AWAKEN US TO DELIGHT IN YOU

Joel 2:14 Who knows whether He will not turn and relent, And leave a blessing behind Him...

Many Christians are earnestly praying for revival to come to America. My favorite definition of the word *revival* is *the return of life.* The implication is that something has died or is near death, but a miracle caused the once-dead thing to have life. Another good term that has been used regarding spiritual revival or revival in the church is *awakening.* Some have studied the history of revivals and the writings of those like Jonathan Edwards, who was intimately associated with revivals and awakenings. He states that you cannot stage revivals with a series of meetings or by exercising some spiritual formula. John Armstrong speaks of revival in these terms, *"A sovereign intervention of the Holy Spirit of God...powerfully sweeping across the visible church in blessing the normal ministry of the Word of God, and prayer, in the lives of both believers and new converts..."* Note Armstrong's focus: the *Holy Spirit* supernaturally blessing the normal ministry of the *Word, and prayer.* I believe that the normal ministry of the Word is the primacy of preaching and the normal ministry of prayer is its place of priority in the church. But sad to say, this may not be the case in most churches. If revival is to come, there may first need to be a return to the primacy of preaching and prayer before we can ever expect to receive a supernatural blessing. Are you ready for revival? Do you have a hunger for the preaching of God's Word and a thirst for times of prayer?

*Look it up – **Psalm 85:6; Habakkuk 3:2; Hebrews 8:10-12***

*This truth for me – **Revival begins with you. How are your reviving your worship through prayer and the Word? List ways you will seek revival.***

_____

_____

_____

*Pray – **For God to stir through His Spirit a revival in the church, your heart and your home.***

MATCHING WORDS WITH ACTIONS

Matthew 3:8 Therefore bring forth fruit in keeping with your repentance.

For those who take on a new position or career, changes must be made. I prayed for a brother who lost his position in computer programming and is now working in maintenance. Significant changes have occurred in his life.

When God saves a sinner, significant changes occur. The change is so significant that the Apostle Paul describes it in terms of the person becoming *a new creation.* If people truly repent and turn from their sin, their lives demonstrate such a turning. There are people who say that they are born-again; they have asked God to forgive them, yet their lives show little, if any, change. If God saves a person, He changes them and gives them a new life with new desires. We have every reason to be concerned for people who say they are Christians but have no desire to fellowship with other Christians, go to church, read the Bible, witness, pray, or hunger to know their God more and more. We should not be fooled or take it for granted that people are Christians if their lives don't portray a thirst for God. This could be a deadly assumption. A Christian will be a new person with new tastes, new desires, new loves and new priorities. The old things will continually pass away.

Look it up – Ezekiel 11:19; 2 Corinthians 5:17; Ephesians 4:24

This truth for me – List what you thirst after about God and your relationship with Him.

Pray – For God to increase your desires for Him and His people day by day.

HE IS ALWAYS THERE FOR US

Psalm 13:1a How long, O Lord? Wilt Thou forget me forever?

I've heard of defendants on trial for violent crimes say, *"I let my anger get the best of me."* All of us know how easy it is to allow this to happen. When we feel sad, we speak words of despair, and when we are upset, we speak words of malice. In the case of King David writing Psalm 13, he laments over his enemies and their oppression toward him. The beginning of the Psalm is a good example of how we can easily jump to false conclusions. Was God far from David? Was God hiding from the king and not wanting to help him in his troubles? The answer to both questions is *NO!* The Bible is clear to tell us that God always dwells with His people. The Scriptures remind us that God is near; He is omnipresent, in all places at all times. He never hides from us and is ever present in our times of joy and struggle. Yet, many times our feelings try to tell us just the opposite. "Where is God when I really need Him? God is not interested in my meager plight!" This kind of thinking is false and not in line with the way God has revealed Himself to us in the Bible. Rely upon His Word and not your feelings. It didn't take David long to recognize the truth: *But I have trusted in Thy lovingkindness; my heart shall rejoice in thy salvation. I will sing to the Lord, Because He has dealt bountifully with me* (Psalm 13:5,6).

Do you find yourself flooded with feelings that are dictating a false thinking about God and plunging you into despair? Don't despair, the Bible holds the truth about our God and is filled with truth. Trust in the Word of God and not the word of self.

Look it up – **1 Kings 19:11; Joel 2:17; John 8:19**

This truth for me – **Have you ever cried out like the Psalmist, "How long, Oh Lord?" How did the Lord help you see Him again?**

Praise – **God that Christ never leaves us or forsakes us.**

GOD HAS MADE US TO FALL UPON THE LAMB

John 1:29 ...Behold the Lamb of God who takes away the sin of the world!

There is an old story of a carpenter in Germany who was working on a church steeple. He suddenly lost his footing and fell to the ground. On the grass below was a flock of sheep grazing. The man landed on one of the sheep and his life was spared ... but the lamb perished! In deepest gratitude for the lamb's sacrifice, the man carved in one of the stones above the doorway to the church a beautiful lamb and put the words of John 1:29 beneath the figure.

I will always remember vividly the night that God caused me to *fall upon the Lamb* and cast my sins and burdens on the precious Savior, Jesus Christ. I give thanks to God for all things in life, but my greatest gratitude is for sending the Son to be the Lamb that takes away even the darkest of sin - our rejection of the Christ. In these words, *Behold the Lamb of God...* spoken by John the Baptist, there is both declaration and amazement. *Behold,* it is the Savior, He is here and He will carry away our sin and open the way to the Father. May your Christian heart jump with such declaration and amazement for the Savior who has come to you and saved you from your fall to damnation. For those who may read this and are not saved, only Jesus can catch you from an eternal fall to Hell. Believe upon the Lord Jesus Christ, repent of your sin, and be saved.

Look it up – ***Genesis 22:7,8; John 1:35,36; Revelation 5:12***

This truth for me – ***Jesus broke your fall into damnation, and in doing so, He died so you may have life. Meditate on this and then write a thought.***

_____

_____

_____

Pray – ***For a heart as tender and sacrificial as the Savior models for us.***

ABLE TO SAVE AND SATISFY

Genesis 3:15 ...He shall bruise you on the head, and you shall bruise him on the heel.

It is proper to capitalize the pronoun *"He"* in this passage. It is a direct reference to Jesus Christ. Here, God curses the serpent and we learn that the serpent (the Devil) will be ultimately defeated by the *seed of a woman*—meaning someone who will be born as a man. Then in this verse, we read that this one who is born of a woman will be powerful enough to crush the Devil on his *head* and forever do away with Satan, sin and death. If you were to reference this with the similar New Testament statement in Romans 16:20, you would discover that it is God the Son who will crush the Devil.

From this earliest mention of the Savior in Genesis 3, we are to realize that Jesus Christ is the *God-Man* sent to save us from our sin by defeating Satan, the world and sin. He will do this by His death on the cross. He will be bruised on His *heel (the cross)*, but by this bruising He will totally defeat the Devil.

This brings us to the incarnation of Jesus Christ, the God-Man. On the cross the *Divine Savior* suffered and died to forgive us our sins and the *Perfect Human* gave His life in our place to satisfy a Holy God. We rejoice that the God-Man came to earth to go to the cross and there to suffer and die to forgive us and be our perfect sacrifice. He stood in our place to do what we cannot accomplish. He alone is both God and Man. Incomprehensible? Yes, but true.

Look it up **Luke 9:20; 1 Timothy 2:5; 1 John 4:2**

This truth for me – **Christ is both God and Man. How do you understand this truth? What does it mean to you?**

———————————————————————————————

———————————————————————————————

———————————————————————————————

Pray – **For understanding of this great truth that Jesus Christ is the God-Man.**

IN LOWLINESS THERE LIES GREATNESS

Zechariah 9:9 ...He is just and endowed with salvation...

In this prophecy from Zechariah, one sees the contrast between the great Grecian king, Alexander the Great, and the Messiah King.

I have a tendency to lean toward the underdog in a battle. My first experience watching a boxing match came when I was twelve years old. My buddies and I went to the local gym to watch the Friday night fights. When the boxers were announced, into the ring walked a very muscular young man with obvious power. Behind him walked his opponent, who was skinny and weak compared to the strong man. My friends began to debate how the muscular man would pulverize the skinnier man. In my heart I felt the same thing, but my underdog prejudice forced me to hope the skinny man would win the fight. The starting bell rang, and the two men came to the center of the ring. The strong man was clumsy and his bulky muscles inhibited his ability to punch with speed or accuracy. Within forty seconds of the first round, the quickness and agility of the skinny fighter confused Mr. Muscles. The underdog landed a lightning fast left hook to the jaw of the hulk and knocked him out. The fight was over.

In comparison to the power and might of Alexander, Zechariah tells us that the Messiah, **Jesus Christ, the God-Man**, will conquer and bring salvation through the humble means of His sacrifice. The greatest fight over sin and death was achieved by Jesus Christ's humiliation on the cross. God brings great things to pass by way of humble circumstances.

*Look it up – **Proverbs 15:33; Daniel 4:37; Micah 6:8***

*This truth for me –**List ways God has taught you humility. What are its benefits?***

_____

_____

_____

*Pray – **And repent of those areas of your life where you put self first.***

A KINGSHIP BEYOND COMPARISON

Matthew 2:2a *Where is He who has been born King of the Jews?*

Our eternal hope is settled in God's faithful promise that He will save His elect, the *heirs of the promise*. The writer of the book of Hebrews says that because we have the promise of salvation secured in God, it is *an anchor to our souls*. What wonderful symbolism for how secure we are in the salvation that God has provided. This security is rested not in anything that we have accomplished or possess, but rather our anchor is attached to Jesus Christ, the King of the Jews.

The book of Hebrews also speaks of a King named Melchizedek, meaning *King of Righteousness*. Hebrews tells us to observe Melchizedek's greatness. This Melchizedek, spoken of in the Old Testament, was a sign of the true King who would come to earth and fulfill the promise of God to save His people. Jesus Christ, King of the Jews, came to earth in the line of Melchizedek to bring peace and righteousness to hearts of the heirs of the promise.

Do you have God's hope anchored to your soul? Do you have peace with God and possess His righteousness, knowing that when you face Him you will face Him in Christ and be acceptable because your faith is rested in Jesus? Trust in the Lord, the King of Peace and Righteousness.

*Look it up – **Zechariah 9:9; John 1:49; Hebrews 8:1***

*This truth for me – **Knowing that you follow the King of Kings makes you royal and acceptable to the Father. Write down a few praises for such a position.***

_____

_____

_____

*Praise – **The Lord for granting us participation in His royal entourage.***

STILL TIME BUT DON'T WAIT

Matthew 25:31 ...the Son of Man comes in His glory...

The Kingdom of God is near. Most Christians do not keep the Lord's return in the forefront of their thoughts. We also tend to ignore His judgment. One of the supreme purposes in the Lord returning is that He will take His rightful place on the throne of glory and there mete out His judgment on all the nations and all of mankind. Whether we might believe this judgment in Matthew 25 is exercised at the beginning of Christ's 1,000 year Kingdom reign or at its end, it is confirmed that there will be a final judgment for all. The *goats* in this passage are those doomed to eternal damnation, and the *sheep* are all who belong to Christ by virtue of believing the message of the Gospel. Christ will be bringing judgment. Just as we are exhorted to be ready for His return, we are also to be ready for His judgment.

If today you are not a believer in Christ for salvation, you are doomed, but it is not too late to repent and believe upon the Lord Jesus. If you are a sheep but need to deal with sin in your life, then do it now before He returns. Today is the day of salvation and the day of repentance!

*Look it up – **Luke 12:45, 46; 1 Thessalonians 3:13; 2 Peter 3:3-9***

*This truth for me – **Are you ready? What do you need to do to be ready for the Lord's return?***

_____

_____

_____

*Pray – **That you will be ready for Christ's return when all things will finally be brought into line with His righteousness.***

POWERFUL RESOLUTIONS

Philippians 3:10 that I may know...the power...and the fellowship...

Have you ever made New Year's resolutions? Many of us make resolutions to take steps or make changes in our lives. I often think about what new things and changes need to take place in my life. I also think about what new things and changes need to take place in the church. Evaluation and the setting of goals are positive, and as Christians, we need to *press on* toward becoming more like Christ every day.

Two words are significant in the Apostle Paul's writing in this section of Philippians: *power and fellowship.* Paul set forth his own life resolutions here. He first wanted to know the dynamic resurrection power of God. The word he uses here for *power* is our English word *dynamite.* Paul resolved to know the dynamite power of God in overcoming sin and fighting the good battle in order to press on. The word in the original language for *fellowship* is *koinonia.* This word has the sweet understanding of a close relationship to something or someone. Paul resolved to desire a sweet fellowship with the sufferings of Christ, a resolve to grow in faith and holiness. No matter what we may resolve to change in our lives, consider Paul's resolutions - *to know the power of His resurrection and the fellowship of His sufferings!*

Look it up – ***Judges 5:15; Psalm 17:4,5; Psalm 63:4***

This truth for me – ***List several things you want to resolve to know about the Lord or do for Him.***

———————————————————————————

———————————————————————————

———————————————————————————

Pray – ***That the Holy Spirit will give you the power to accomplish what you resolve to do.***

JUST A PRAYER AWAY

Psalm 22:2 ...thou dost not answer...

There are moments in life when we feel abandoned. Christians can come to the place where they don't sense the attention of their God and cry out in distress seeking to hear from Him and yet He remains silent. The Psalmist has this feeling of abandonment, *"...I cry by day, but Thou dost not answer."* In the pastorate you counsel with Christians that have come to this place of feeling that God has left them, and the only real counsel to give is to remind the depressed person that God never leaves or forsakes His children. Yes, God is silent at times, but He is never far away. I believe that God's silence is not a sign of withdrawal, but rather a means He uses to grow our faith and trust in Him. *To trust in God, even when it feels like He is not there, is God's testing of our faith to wait for Him to act.* The psalmist comes back to reality and states in verses four and five, *"...They trusted, and Thou didst deliver them... In Thee they trusted, and were not disappointed."*

Our Lord, in His human spirit, had feelings of abandonment. This Psalm begins with the words, *My God, My God, why hast Thou forsaken me.* These are the words spoken by Christ from the cross. It was soon after these words that Jesus said, *Father, into Thy hands I commit my Spirit.* Christian, if you are feeling today that God is far off, be reminded by His promises that He is near you. Commit your mind and pain into His capable hands and He will deliver you.

Look it up – **Psalm 73:28; Isaiah 58:1; Hebrews 4:16**

This truth for me – **Think of those times you felt all alone. God was near – how is He near to you now?**

_____

_____

_____

Pray – **Thanking God for His nearness to you in all things and at all times.**

HE SAVES AS WE SHARE

Matthew 9:35 And Jesus was going about all the cities...

As we continue to read on in this passage, we discover that Jesus was not merely visiting all the cities but was ministering in the cities. Are you a busy person? Many of us would answer this question with a "yes." Our busy lives get in the way of some very important priorities: time with our families, our spouses, our friends, and the proper time to care for our own spiritual and physical needs.

But the priority I want to address is *taking the time to share the Gospel with those around us who are going to an eternal hell.* You could argue that there may have never been anyone as busy or as fixed on a purpose as Jesus Christ, yet He never lost sight of His foremost directive – *to seek and save those who are lost* (Luke 19:10). Are you too busy to share the Gospel? When is the last time you spoke with someone about eternal life and the need for Jesus? A Christian cannot save anyone, but we are the means by which God saves. God has planned to save His elect from *every tongue, tribe and nation,* and He has ordained His children to be the instruments of saving grace. He saves as we share. Are you sharing Christ with the lost? Do so today and rejoice in this great privilege.

*Look it up – **Luke 14:23; John 10:10; 2 Corinthians 5:20***

*This truth for me – **He saves as we share. What does this mean for you?***

_____

_____

_____

*Pray – **For God to give you time, energy and a plan to reach souls for Christ.***

SECRETS RESERVED FOR GOD

Romans 11:33 ...How...unfathomable His ways!

When I begin my classes on *God, Christ, Holy Spirit and Salvation* at the schools where I teach, I show the students this verse in Deuteronomy 24:24: *The secret things belong to God...* I want the class to understand that as finite human beings we are dependent upon God's revelation to know the truths He wants us to know about Himself and His creation. Precise knowledge of God comes from the Bible. But the Bible is limited in that it tells us all that God wants us to know but leaves *out secret things* known only to God.

This truth may be both comforting and disturbing. It should comfort us to know that God is selective in what He reveals, and when He withholds certain things, He does so for our wellbeing. There are times when we may become disturbed not knowing why God allows seemingly negative things to happen, or why God chooses to act in ways that on the surface may look contrary to His love and grace. At these times we must remember—like the prophet Isaiah did—that God's ways are not our ways. *God's ways are always perfect, just, and loving even when they seem the opposite.* The child of God must remember that *from Him and through Him and to Him are all things. To Him be the glory, AMEN!*

Look it up – **Psalm 139:6; Job 11:7; Jeremiah 23:24**

This truth for me – **What most confuses you about God? List how you will trust God when He is incomprehensible to you.**

_____

_____

_____

Pray – **That God will give you faith to trust Him even when things seem confusing.**

YOU CANNOT FOOL GOD

John 6:64 But there are some of you who do not believe...

Were you ever fooled by someone? You thought one thing about them and they turned out to be the complete opposite. I would imagine that we all have had such an experience with a co-worker, friend or relative.

It seems that there were a number of people in the crowd of so-called *disciples* (*John 6:60*) who were trying to fool Christ. They heard His teaching but hearing did not bring faith, but rather grumbling and arguments. They may have had an academic or experiential knowledge about Christ and His doctrines, yet did not believe by faith in the Lord and He knew it, *For Jesus knew from the beginning who they were who did not believe in Him...* Not only is this good evidence that the God-Man, Jesus Christ, possessed the divine quality of omniscience (all-knowing), but also is a proof that Christ truly knows the human heart.

You can't fool God! Yet there are people in churches who try to fool God by religious and ritualistic efforts. A person cannot believe in Christ unless he is given that faith to believe, *...no one can come to Me unless it has been granted him from the Father (John 6:65).* You may truly believe because God has worked His work in you, but you may be trying to fool God by covering up sin. *You can't fool God!* You may not be a Christian. Your attempt at fooling God through religion or ritual will cost you dearly—your eternal life. **You can't fool God!** Turn to God, and seek His forgiveness. He is faithful; He will forgive.

*Look it up – **Psalms 2:4; Proverbs 3:34; Galatians 6:7***

*This truth for me – **Was there a time you thought you fooled God or held something back you thought He would not know or you didn't want Him to know?** _____*

_____

_____

Pray – That the Lord will keep you honest and open with your sin before Him.

FREE, FREE AT LAST

1 Corinthians 6:20 ...you have been bought with a price...

Slavery is not a pleasant topic. In my estimation, the darkest time in our country's history was when the institution of slavery was a part of our culture. But as dark and heinous as slavery was, even darker is the slavery that all humans face with their own sinfulness. The Bible is not only clear in calling all of us sinners, but also correct in describing our sin as making us dead. John Gerstner, the theologian, said that *the sinner is like a rotting, walking corpse and a stench in the nostrils of God*—a rough statement but biblically true. Not only are sinners dead, they are also enslaved. The total depravity into which we are born renders us totally helpless. We have no free will; our will is shackled by sin. With such a depraved nature, our only choice is to turn from God and seek our own way.

The solution to such a helpless condition is the mercy and grace of God through His Son Jesus Christ. Christ died for sinners, paying the price that we could not pay for our sin debt to God. This is called redemption. The blood of Christ is His payment for our sin, and when God saves us, He cancels our sin debt because Christ paid it all. Charles Spurgeon says that we owe everything to God's love in saving us but we owe nothing to His justice because that has been satisfied. Christ settled the wrath of God against us and we are free ... free indeed! If you are born-again, you are free in Christ. Claim it and don't live like a slave to sin. If you are not born-again, you are a slave to sin. Repent and believe that Christ paid for your sins and cry out to God for His forgiveness.

Look it up – **Romans 8:15; Galatians 5:1; Hebrews 2:14,15**

This truth for me – **List the ways Christ has set you free and how you feel now compared to how you felt when you were unsaved.**

_____

_____

_____

Praise – **God for the freedom you now have in Christ from sin and death.**

KNOWLEDGE NEEDS ACTION

Ephesians 1:17 That the God of our Lord Jesus Christ, the Father of glory, may give you a spirit of wisdom...

Do you possess knowledge or wisdom? A former professor defined wisdom as *knowledge in action*. I would agree with such a definition. We all know of people that have attained a great deal of knowledge but know little about how to apply such knowledge in a productive manner. To ask God to give you wisdom is a great privilege that is given to the child of God. We are told in the book of James that when we ask for wisdom, God promises to give it to us. WOW, I can ask God for wisdom and He will give it to me! Yes, but remember what you are asking for. When we ask for God's wisdom, we are not merely asking for knowledge that fills our heads. Rather we are asking God to give us the ability to live in His will and His desires. Here is an example. When I ask God for the wisdom to handle a problem, He gives me the wisdom needed to take the action that will glorify Him. Do you have a concern today, a problem needing attention, or a question begging an answer? Every Christian needs God's wisdom. Ask Him for His wisdom today and then put it into action.

Look it up – ***Psalm 37:30; 1 Corinthian 2:6-9; James 1:5-8***

This truth for me – ***Where are you lacking wisdom? Write down what is perplexing you and then ask God for the wisdom to act.***

_____

_____

_____

Pray – ***For the Lord's wisdom to handle the challenges you are facing.***

THE WEIGHT HAS BEEN LIFTED

1 John 2:2 And He Himself is the propitiation for our sins...

What is the heart of the Gospel? In other words, what does the Gospel, the core of salvation, rest upon? J.I. Packer writes in his book, <u>Knowing God</u>, that the heart of the Gospel is *propitiation,* the doctrine of Christ's shed blood which takes away sin and satisfies the wrath of a Holy God. Were it not that God (Christ) died for God (the Father) and shed His perfect cleansing blood, we would still be dead in sin and God's wrath would still be poured out upon us.

Even though the word *propitiation* appears only three times in the Bible, the Scriptures are saturated with the understanding of propitiation as the basis of salvation and the Gospel. Wherever you see the shed blood of Christ, you see propitiation. Christ died to take away wrath and give freedom from sin and damnation. Whenever we preach the Gospel, the blood propitiation must be the central part to consider and convey. Without the shed blood of Christ, we have no Gospel and we have no salvation. Praise be to God for sending the Son to die and bleed for sinners and to be the complete and worthy sacrifice to the Father.

> *...Lord I believe Thy precious blood, which at the mercy seat of God*
> *forever doth for sinners plead, for me, e'en for my soul was shed...*
> (Zinzendorf, 1739)

Look it up – **Romans 3:21-15; Hebrews 2:17; 1 John 4:10**

This truth for me – **What does it mean to have God's wrath taken from you? How will you repay Christ for such an act of mercy?**

_____

_____

_____

Pray – **For those around you who are still under God's wrath for their sin and rejection of Christ.**

STAND FIRM IN THE KNOWLEDGE OF GOD

Daniel 3:16 ...O Nebuchadnezzar, we do not need to give you an answer concerning this.

Have you ever been threatened? Most of us probably have not experienced a threat, especially a threat that concerned our lives. But if we had, I wonder how we would respond to such an unsettling thing. Daniel's three young compatriots, Shadrach, Meshach, and Abednego, were under a decree by the king to bow down and worship a golden image every time they heard the sound of music trumpeted in the streets of Babylon. In defiance of the decree and loyalty to God, they disregarded the order and refused to worship the idol. For this, the king threatened that they be thrown into the fiery pit and executed. In light of this threat, their response is quite calm, controlled and indifferent. They stood firm in the knowledge of their God and His ability to either deliver them or, if that were not His will, to take them home to be with Him.

Their response is not only amazing but it demonstrates something else. These men knew their God. Today, we who know God are content and calm no matter what we face. Knowing God is evident in the way we handle the tests of life. How well do you know Him?

*Look it up – **Hosea 6:3; 2 Corinthians 4:6; 1 John 2:3-6***

*This truth for me – **How well do you know God? List areas in your life that are weak because of lack of a knowledge of God.***

_____

_____

_____

*Pray – **For more of a desire to know the Lord through His word and prayer.***

MAYBE TOMORROW?

Luke 12:45 ...my master will be a long time in coming...

When the cat's away, the mice will play. We all are familiar with this little ditty that describes how, when authority is absent, chaos exists.

By contrast, Christ describes a faithful and sensible steward as one who takes care of business even when authority is absent. In the parable of Luke 12, the steward, who is in charge of all his master's servants and possessions while the master is gone, takes advantage of the master's absence and beats the servants and embarks on promiscuous partying.

Two things need to be captured from the parable. First, we need to be ready for the Lord's return by acting faithfully and sensibly while He tarries. Second, we need to realize that Christ has given His church great spiritual wealth, and to whom much is given, much is required. Our human tendency is to put off until tomorrow what should be done today. Each of us has at least a little bit of procrastination in us! One thing we cannot put off until tomorrow is being faithful and sensible as we wait for the Lord's return.

Look it up – Joshua 24:15; Luke 14:16-21; 2 Corinthians 6:2

This truth for me – Meditate on what the Lord has given you and then evaluate how faithful and sensible you are with His great possessions and promises.

_____

_____

_____

Pray – That you will do what is necessary to serve and please the Lord each day and not put off what needs to be done.

PREPARE TO RESPOND

1 Peter 3:15 ...give an account for the hope that is in you...

Have you ever seen the movie *The Passion?* Some time ago, at a lunch with fellow pastors, there was conversation about this movie. It was noted that the film made an impact for the Gospel. One pastor shared that he heard a woman say that at her beauty parlor, the conversation revolved around the death of Christ. This brother then asked, *"When is the last time a group of women at a beauty parlor discussed the death of Christ?"* If this kind of thing occurs because of any responsible movie about Christ, it can only assist the church in its effort to bring the Gospel to people. I hope we are praying for God to touch lives through such films.

There is another question that I hear people asking when they hear or watch something about Christ. The question is, *What is this all about?* Well, maybe they don't ask this question so directly but it is certainly on the minds of some. I pray that Christians will have good biblical answers when questions about Christ arise. God helps us in our evangelism by providing things that stir people's minds to think about life and death, eternity, Christ and God, and other spiritual topics. We don't need to go into big productions to stir people to think about these things. We only need to be ready and prepared to give an answer when God gives us the opportunity to speak with people about Christ. Look today for open doors to talk about Jesus.

Look it up – Philippians 1:7,8; Colossians 4:5,6; Jude 3

This truth for me – Are you ready and prepared to give a biblical answer to those who ask you spiritual questions? List how you can be prepared.

_____

_____

_____

Pray – That you will have a ready and prepared heart to answer people's questions about God and life.

PURITY, HOLINESS AND HONOR

Ezra 7:9 ...the good hand of his God was upon him.

I, along with many of you, praise God for the freedoms we experience here in the United States of America. Our freedoms have been secured by the many who have fought and given their lives in the wars that have challenged our freedoms, and by many godly individuals who have lived their lives in step with God's mercy and justice.

God's hand was upon Ezra, and this unction of divine presence caused King Artaxerxes to show tremendous favor toward Ezra and the nation of Israel. But let me point out the clause which follows our lead passage, *...for Ezra had set his heart to STUDY the law of the Lord, and to PRACTICE it, and to TEACH His statutes and ordinances in Israel.* Ezra dedicated himself to God's Word in study and practice, and God showered His blessing upon Ezra and the nation of Israel. God also moved the king to show favor toward the Jews.

As followers of Christ, we need to be concerned and alert when it comes to the ungodly swings in government and laws. Yet there is an even greater responsibility than alertness and involvement, and that is holiness. May the RED remind us of the blood of the Savior who died to give real freedom to sinners. May the WHITE call us to live pure and holy lives that God will honor and bless. And may the BLUE be a reminder that our home is ultimately not here but above the heavens with our Lord! Have a great 4th!

*Look it up – **Isaiah 35:10; Mark 10:45; Romans 5:6-8***

*This truth for me – **We thank the Lord for the dedication of the soldiers who fought for our country's freedom, and especially for Christ who fought to make us eternally free. Write down what this means for you personally.***

---

*Praise – **God for our country's freedom and the freedom we have in Christ.***

THE GREATEST SUFFERING

Luke 22:44 And being in agony He was praying fervently...

The physical anguish our Lord suffered at the hands of the Romans and the Sanhedrin was revolting. However, the Lord's spiritual anguish should have as significant an impact on us as the physical torture He endured. In the account of our Lord praying in the garden immediately before He was to be betrayed and arrested, Luke uses strong words to describe this time of prayer, *being in agony...* The physical brutality Christ endured during His course of the beatings and floggings could be endured by a human. But no human has ever endured the spiritual or emotional torture that our Lord experienced in His conquering of sin and death. Christ agonized over the thought of having to take sin upon Himself and face the separation there would be for that brief moment in all of eternity between Him and the Father. Our Lord's words on the cross take this agony to its pinnacle, *My God, My God, why hast Thou forsaken me?* Martin Luther wrote, "God forsaking God, who can understand this?" We cannot comprehend the spiritual anguish that Christ experienced on the cross, but we can be thankful that He did it for us sinners. He, the precious and perfect King of Kings, agonized and suffered to carry my sins away.

> *What Thou, my Lord, hast suffered was all for sinner's gain:*
> *Mine, Mine was the transgression, But Thine the deadly pain.*
> *Lo, here I fall, my Savior! Tis I deserve Thy place;*
> *Look on me with Thy favor, Vouchsafe to me Thy grace.*
> (from the hymn *"O Sacred Head, Now Wounded"*)

*Look it up – **Psalm 6:6,7; Romans 5:7,8; 1 Peter 2:21-23***

*This truth for me – **Meditate on the depth of Christ's spiritual suffering. Write how His sufferings affect you.***

_____

_____

_____

*Pray – **For your life to be poured out to others in need.***

THE MIRACLE OF LIFE

Mark 2:12 ...We have never seen anything like this.

Have you ever been amazed by what Christ can accomplish? Christians have their own personal testimony of what wonderful and surprising things the Lord has done in their lives. The healing of the paralytic was an amazing miracle that Christ performed in the midst of the crowd gathered in Capernaum. Miracles are amazing and they prompt the response, *"I never saw anything like that."* But we must be careful when we say that something is a miracle or when we look for the miraculous in place of exercised faith.

Does God still perform miracles? I am sure that He does, and one of His ongoing miracles is His saving wretched sinners and making them into saints. I have never witnessed a dead person raised from the grave, but I have seen the spiritual dead made new in Christ by being born-again. Every time I see God save His elect, I can say with the crowd, *I have never seen anything like this.* **There is nothing, in my estimation, that compares to witnessing God give saving faith to spiritually dead sinners so that they can believe the Gospel and receive Christ as their Savior.** When is the last time you witnessed God's miraculous saving power? May we not lose sight of our duty to give witness to the Gospel. *Go and preach the Gospel....*

*Look it up – **John 4:46-54; Ephesians 2:1-3; Hebrews 7:25***

*This truth for me – **What miraculously happens when Christ saves a person?***

_____

_____

_____

*Pray – **For the miracle of new life to come to the unsaved you know.***

THE APPLE OF HIS EYE

1 John 4:9 By this the love of God was manifested in us...

When someone—a cherished daughter, a beloved parent—has a very special place in our life, we might say, *"She is the apple of my eye."* In the case of Jesus Christ, we are the apple of His perfect eye, the ones He desires to call unto salvation by virtue of His sacrificial death on the cross. Before the earth was established, the elect of God were the object of His great affection (Ephesians 1:3,4) and the joy set before our Lord as He hung from the cross of Calvary (Hebrews 12:2). While some may take issue with the doctrine of *particular redemption* or *limited atonement*, the essence of this doctrine is the great love God has for a particular sinful people who are predestined unto a salvation grounded solely in the love, mercy and grace of God. Jesus' love for His sheep is overwhelming. He is the *Shepherd* of the sheep and they find direction in Him (John 9:1-4), and the *Door* for the sheep and He opens the way to salvation (John 9:7). He is the *Good Shepherd* who lays down His life as the perfect sacrifice for the sheep (John 9:10-15). Are you saved by grace? If so, then you are the apple of God's eye, graven on His hands, all this because God chose you and called you, in Christ, not by any merit of your own.

> *In this is love, not that we loved God, but that He loved us and sent His Son to be the propitiation for our sins. (1 John 4:10)*

Look it up – **John 10:14,15; Romans 8:32,33; 2 Thessalonians 2:13**

This truth for me – **How does it make you feel to be God's special child? Write out your expressions.**

Praise – **God for His special love for you.**

RENEWED LOVE

Hosea 3:1 ...Go again, love a woman who is loved by her husband, yet an adulteress...

Humanly speaking it is very difficult to love someone who has been unfaithful to you. Adultery is the ruin of marriage. It is such a wedge that even the Lord allowed divorce in the case of adultery. Unfaithfulness to God is also a huge wedge between God and His children. Israel's unfaithfulness was evident in its constant seeking after idols and its intermarriage with paganism. God disciplined Israel to such an extent that they were forced into exile, but never totally abandoned from God's restorative grace. God promises to lead Israel to be alone with Him in the desert where He will speak kindly and tenderly to His people and offer new hope, prosperity, and a new covenant relationship (Hosea 2). The illustration of this renewed relationship is God's command for Hosea to go after Gomer, his unfaithful, adulteress wife, and love her. This love was to symbolize the Lord's love for His unfaithful people. If you have strayed from God and have not come to God for forgiveness, then it would be wise to understand the warnings of God's discipline and the grace of God's love and take the proper steps to be renewed. The way to spiritual renewal and salvation is to repent and turn to God, who is forever faithful.

Look it up – **2 Chronicles 29:6; Hebrews 10:29-31; 1 John 1:9**

This truth for me – **List the ways God has been faithful to you when you were unfaithful.**

_____

_____

_____

Pray – **For the Lord's strength to remain faithful in your walk with Him.**

BLESSED BEYOND MEASURE

Ephesians 1:3 ...who has blessed us with every spiritual blessing...

Occasionally upon making a significant purchase, I have looked back and thought that I should have gone for that little extra feature. Fortunately, as Christians, we don't have to look back to the day of our salvation and wish that we would have acquired that something extra. In Christ we were given everything necessary for our spiritual well-being at the time we were saved. We are in need of nothing! Notice that the Apostle Paul says we have received *every* spiritual blessing. He doesn't say that we were blessed with some but have to work out the rest, or that we only received what we were worth—for in and of ourselves, we are not worthy of any spiritual blessing. We have received *every* spiritual blessing! Please take note that these blessings are *spiritual*, not material; they come from God the Holy Spirit. They are blessings that should elicit our praise and thanks. What are the blessings? They are listed in the text:

election - being chosen by God to be holy and saved forever
adoption - He made us His sons and daughters and heirs with His Son Jesus
redemption - He delivered us from sin and death
forgiveness - God cleansed us totally
sealing – we have the Holy Spirit who authenticates us as belonging to God.

Isn't this a great foundation to praise God? Praise Him for *every* blessing that is yours by virtue of Christ's death.

Look it up – **Psalm 84:4; Ezekiel 34:26; Romans 5:1**

This truth for me – **List some recent blessings that the Lord has given you.**

_____

_____

_____

Praise – **God for all His blessings and how sufficient they are.**

IN CHRIST WE ARE LOVED

Isaiah 42:1 Behold, my Servant, whom I uphold; My chosen one in whom My soul delights...

At a conference I once attended, the speaker reminded us that when we think too much of ourselves as Christians, God will see to it that we are put back in our place—an interesting thought and quite true. God loves us, calls us His children, gives us the rights of His Kingdom, blesses us beyond all human imagination, and assures us that we will always be His personal cherished possession. These are great truths to claim and rejoice in, but let us never forget that we are the delight of God because we are in Jesus Christ. If God had not saved us and applied the atoning work of Christ's death to our lives and placed us fully into Jesus' death and resurrection—not to mention imputing all of the Lord's righteousness to our account—we would still be dead in our sins. God delights in His Servant, the Servant who suffered and died to satisfy God's wrath and forgive us our sins. No man could die His death; it was the *death of deaths*. God upholds and delights in Jesus, and if we are in Him by virtue of God causing us to be born-again, then we too are the Lord's delight. *Delight in the Lord because He delights in Christ in You!*

*Look it up – **1 Kings 10:9; Psalm 37:4; Isaiah 42:1***

*This truth for me – **God delights in us through Christ. List ways you can delight in God today.***

_____

_____

_____

*Pray – **For greater knowledge of God so that you can delight more and more in Him.***

THE RAPTURE OF PRAYER

Hebrews 5:7 *...with loud crying and tears...*

There is no greater model for prayer than Jesus Christ. He gives us examples of the posture of prayer. He prayed while standing, kneeling, and falling on His face. He prayed in secret, in the morning, in the evening, before and after small and great achievements, and under the pressures, sorrows, and joys of life. He prayed with thanksgiving, glorifying His Father, in intercession, and with great attention to the Father's will. He lived praying and died praying. Need we turn anywhere else but to the Lord when we look for an example of prayer and how to go about this blessed communion with the Father? Prayer is that great avenue of communication to the Father that His children have with Him. We should love to pray and love to commune with our Father in the intimacy of prayer. May our prayers be without ceasing, spontaneous throughout the day and filled with joy in knowing that not only are we speaking to the God of the universe but also that He is listening. In J. Oswald Sanders' book, *Prayer Power Unlimited,* he quotes S.D. Gordon:

> *"The Lord Jesus is still praying...Thirty years of living; thirty years of serving; one tremendous act of dying; nineteen hundred years of prayer. What an emphasis on prayer!"*

*Look it up – **Matthew 6:6-7; Luke 6:12; Hebrews 4:16***

*This truth for me – **How is your prayer life? List ways you can build up your prayer life.***

_____

_____

_____

*Pray – **And pray and pray and pray!***

MERCY AND ME

Psalm 41:1 How blessed is he who considers the helpless...

On my drive home one day, I saw a young woman walking through the main street of our little town. I often see her making the trip to and from the grocery store where she works. She bags my groceries and it is obvious that she is handicapped and a little slow. The quality of her life that stands out to me is her quiet and simple manner. She goes to work, does her job and walks home after she is finished. There is probably more to her life, but this is what I see, and in these observations I am reminded of several things. First, how thankful I am for the blessings God has given me and the abilities with which He has blessed me. Second, how precious the helpless and less able are in the sight of God and should be to us, also. Finally, the challenge of making mercy an active and regular part of my life. Isn't it true that for most Christians we do mercy as part of a program rather than a part of our lives? There is nothing wrong with programs that show mercy, but for the Christian, mercy is to be a natural flow of the Spirit's movement in us. As a Christian we all must be more aggressive as instruments of mercy and we must be more considerate of the *helpless*. Our Savior is our greatest example of how to *do mercy* as an integral part of His life and ministry.

*Look it up – **Micah 6:8; Matthew 9:27-30; 2 Corinthians 8:9***

*This truth for me – **How can you show mercy? List some ways you can show mercy in your normal walk of life.***

_____

_____

_____

*Pray – **For keen eyes and a soft heart to do mercy whenever and to whomever.***

EMBRACE ALL THAT IS GOOD

Romans 12:9 ...Abhor what is evil; cling to what is good.

In an age that decries all forms of discrimination, we may lose sight of the truth that true love *does* discriminate. Love discriminates on the basis of good and evil; evil is to be abhorred. The term *abhor* means to find things abominable, rotten or horrible. But what is evil in the sight of God, and what should be considered evil by the Christian? In a general statement, all sin is evil in the sight of God and all sin should be considered evil. The Bible clearly spells out what God finds abominable. It would serve us well to regularly review those things that He abhors, so that we neither take them lightly nor tolerate them. For instance, we are in a numbing down era where we are inundated with an avalanche of attempts that tell us there is nothing wrong with homosexuality and abortion. But God clearly says these are sinful and evil acts and we should abhor them. Real love loathes evil and clings to the good even while seeking ways to demonstrate Christ's love to those who are enslaved in sin. Homosexuality and abortion are only some of the many sins that have become acceptable.

However, don't lose sight of the other directive, *cling to what is good*. God is good! We can know good by understanding what He declares to be good. Cling to His Word and evil will be clearly spelled out, along with how God wants us to apply His goodness.

Look it up – ***Proverbs 3:3; Proverbs 19:8; Philemon 6***

This truth for me – **List any sin that you have accepted and not seen as evil and write down what you need to do about your acceptance of sin.**

Pray – **That the Lord will give you a mind and heart that will acknowledge sin and deal with it in a godly way.**

A PATH PUT DOWN BY GOD

Colossians 2:23 ...self-made religion...

We are constantly trying to bridge the gap between ourselves and God! However, as Romans 3:23 states, all these efforts fall short of reaching their goal of peace with God. Why? Mainly because they are *self-made* ways rather that *THE* way God designed through His Son, Jesus Christ. This way is one of death, and no one wants to walk that *green mile*—that walk a death row prisoner takes to his execution. When a sinner is called of God to be cleansed by the blood of Christ's death, he walks that green mile of grace, and is set free!

God's way to salvation and peace is not on a rose petal covered path, but rather on a road of pain and suffering. Jesus suffered and died for sinners. There is no other way to God than through Christ. It is not an attractive notion to be cleansed by the *blood* of Christ, but it is God's way and the only way we are finally taken off the green mile and placed on the heavenly path. No self-made religion, tradition, or self-sacrifice will please God. God is pleased with His religion, one that is centered in His Son and was worked out on the cross of Calvary. Are you trying to make a path to God through your own ideas and efforts? How futile! God has made that way through His Son, the Lord Jesus Christ.

*Look it up – **Isaiah 1:14; Acts 19:19; 1 Timothy 4:3***

*This truth for me – **When do you have trouble staying on God's way? List the ways you stray and what needs to be done.***

_____

_____

_____

*Pray – **For the Holy Spirit to give you the strength to walk on in the way of the Lord.***

PIERCED TO THE HEART

John 16:8 And He, when He comes, will convict the world concerning sin...

I find it difficult, if not impossible, to convince a person of sin. We may be an instrument to lead a sinner to righteousness, but it is the Holy Spirit who works on the sinner's heart to bring conviction and repentance. This is one of the powerful responsibilities that the Holy Spirit was given—a key reason He was sent by Christ, *to convict sinners regarding sin.*

We should be thankful that the Holy Spirit accomplishes this because, first, we often take a step back from confrontation. I don't know many Christians who relish the idea of having to go to someone and tell them that they need to repent of the sin they are committing. Second, because He can do a job that we cannot do. His conviction brings true repentance. You and I can get fooled by people, but no one can fool the Holy Spirit. Third, the Holy Spirit knows how to bring a person to repentance and then to healing after the stinging pierce of remorse and guilt is sensed. But we must not relax and think that if conviction is the job of the Holy Spirit, we have no part. The spiritual Christian is God's instrument to lead sinners to the Lord. It is our responsibility to go to sinners, preach repentance and then wait upon the Holy Spirit to bring conviction.

> *"...Oh wind of God, come bend us, break us, till humbly we*
> *confess our need; Then in Thy tenderness remake us..."*

*Look it up – **John 16:8-11; Romans 8:14; 1 Thessalonians 1:5***

*This truth for me – **Remember when the Holy Spirit convicted you of a sin? Think about this conviction and how it was used to help you.***

_____

_____

_____

*Praise – **The Lord for sending the Holy Spirit to convict sinners to salvation and Christians to repentance when sin enters into their lives.***

ME OH MY, OH GOD

Psalm 115:1 Not to us, O Lord, not to us...

Matthew Henry comments on verse one with this exhortation, "*All the good we do, is done by the power of his grace; and all the good we have, is the gift of his mere mercy, and he must have all the praise.*" Henry's statement flies in our faces of self-kingdom building. Is God's agenda more important than mine? Are His plans more of a priority than my plans? Do I see myself as part of a greater purpose than my little world? These are questions very relevant to the Christian living in today's self-glorifying, self-kingdom building and self-accumulating culture of *meism*. What commitments will keep a Christian from the influence of a self-centered culture? First, there is the need for a return to *sacrificial living*. Most American Christians must return to a life clearly seen as a love sacrifice for the glory of Christ. Second, we need to be *satisfied* and fight off the temptation to accumulate. We should ask ourselves, *do we really need all this?* Third, we must ask, *what do I treasure?* At the center of the Kingdom is King Jesus! Therefore, we must also have the King at the center of our lives. What kind of King do we serve? One who gave Himself up on a cross to set us free. When we live for Jesus, we find true freedom.

Look it up – **2 Corinthians 3:17; Ephesians 1:22; Philippians 3:20,21**

This truth for me - **Are you free, truly free in Christ? List what things of this world are enslaving you.**

_____

_____

_____

Pray – **That the Lord will have you see more and more of Him and less and less of you.**

HIS PLAN OUR MEANS

Nehemiah 2:20 ...The God of heaven will give us success; therefore we His servants will arise and build...

Many Christians interpret these words as an indication that God will take care of things, so why do anything. Others will begin working and in time forget that their work is truly God's work. *God not only ordains the ends of all that He purposes and plans, but He also ordains the means to reach His ends.* In this theological premise, two truths stand out. First, God is in sovereign control of all things, even the way He wants His plans carried out. Second, He gives us the privilege of serving Him and being the means for carrying out His plans. This truth should not produce complacency or overwork. Rather, His sovereignty and our God-given ability to follow should produce a motivation to please God and peace in knowing that serving Him is not done in our own strength. In evangelism, God saves through our witness of the Gospel. In worship, God shows us how to worship Him and become His instruments of worship in all of life. In holiness, God makes us holy in Christ, yet we must be holy in this world as He is holy. In our relationship with God, we must remember that God is faithful to accomplish His plans, and we must not work in our own strength, but ask Him for His power to carry out our part of the means in reaching His goals. Years ago, our minister of visitation used to say after we spent time in prayer, *"...arise and be doing."* We would pray to know God's will and then go about doing His will in His power!

*Look it up – **Matthew 11:25-30; Romans 10:14-15; 2 Corinthians 5:18***

*This truth for me – **What are you doing for the God who saved you? Describe how you are His instrument of grace.***

_____

_____

_____

*Pray – **That you will be sensitive to the Lord's leading and doing His will.***

MY HOPE IS IN THE LORD

Colossians 1:5 Because of the hope laid up for you in heaven...

Hope is often thought of as an invisible entity which borders on the idea of believing in things that may or may not occur. *I hope I will get married* or *I hope I will graduate.* But Webster says that hope is *an expectation of getting what is desired.* This is not the type of hope we have as Christians. Yes, our hope of eternal life is an expectant hope but it is *not* a hope that we may or may not realize. Our hope in Christ is *firmly secured* in the promise of the Gospel and established in heaven for each Christian. Our hope is a *living* hope and evidenced in the resurrection of Christ *(1 Peter 1:3).* We do not hope in something that is dead, but in One who is alive and standing at the right hand of the Father. Our hope does *not disappoint* because it is firmly rooted in the love of God *(Romans 5:5).* Our hope is an *anchor of the soul,* one which gives us access into the presence of God *(Hebrews 6:19).* And take note of the text in Colossians, *because of our hope laid up in heaven,* we also have a strong faith in Christ and the ability to love our fellow Christians.

How is your hope level today? If you are born-gain, you have been born unto an eternal hope that is firmly rooted in God the Son, Jesus Christ. If you are not born-again, you are *hopeless.* Without Christ there is no hope! May you be filled with His firm hope today.

> *"His oath, His covenant, His blood, support me in the whelming flood;*
> *When all around my soul gives way, He then is all my hope and stay."*

*Look it up – **Psalm 31:24; Romans 5:2; Colossians 1:3-6***

*This truth for me – **Is your hope in the Lord firmly rooted? List ways you can show your hope in Christ.***

_____

_____

_____

*Pray – **That as you read the Bible, it will give your hope a solid foundation.***

IT'S ALL ABOUT GOD'S POWER

Philippians 1:18 ...Christ is proclaimed...

Paul was not worried about the wrong motives of some who were preaching the Gospel. He says, ...*whether in pretense or in truth, Christ is proclaimed.* This statement reveals the power of the proclamation of the Gospel versus the need for man to be the powerhouse. The effectual power of proclaiming the Gospel rests in a sovereign God and not in fallible man. Yes, a preacher must have certain gifts to be a good preacher and certain competencies, but *we must not mistake gifts and competencies, or even charisma, for the innate power that preaching has.*

In the Old Testament God told Ezekiel to go and preach to dry bones. The symbolism is quite easy to understand. The bones represent spiritually dead Israelites and their need for revival. God's means to revive dead Israel was through the proclamation of the Word, and the Spirit using that Word to bring life to dead bones. Every time you hear the proclamation of the Bible, you are hearing the power of God that leads sinners unto salvation and molds Christians into the image of Christ. What a privilege to preach the Word and what a comfort to know that it is God who brings the power to His preached message. *It does not depend on me, but God!*

Look it up – **Romans 1:15,16; 1 Corinthians 2:1-5; 2 Timothy 3:14-17**

This truth for me – **Do you understand how powerful the Word of God is? List how powerful the Word is and how you can better share it.**

Pray – **For the Holy Spirit to help you build your knowledge of the Word through study and reading and then, that you will share it with others.**

A MOSAIC OF ONE

1 Corinthians 12:20 ...there are many members, but one body.

Do you ever get the feeling that there is a *them-and-us* attitude in the Church of Jesus Christ? But rather than putting ourselves into categories, the Bible clearly states that we are *ONE in Christ*. The Apostle Paul, writing to a very divided church in Corinth, reminds them that they are one, though they are all different sorts of people. What better metaphor to use than the human body. No one can argue that our physical bodies are an amazing creation of God and that God fashioned our bodies in precise unity. Our body works in a very miraculous manner, and all this work is done in unity even though our body parts vary in extremely differing ways; diverse yet one. Therefore Paul states, *..if one member suffers, all the members suffer with it; if one member is honored, all the members rejoice with it.* Which is more difficult: to suffer with another member of the Church or to rejoice with another member? Some may find it difficult to rejoice because of jealousy, bitterness or anger. Or some may not be willing to suffer with another member because of arrogance, selfishness or an *I-told-you-so* attitude.

When a Christian is struggling and suffering, how long does it take for Christians to respond? As individual Christians, we are called to come alongside brothers and sisters that suffer. ***WE ARE ONE!***

Look it up – **John 17:21; Galatians 3:28; Ephesians 4:1-6**

This truth for me – **List the ways you can help build unity in the Church.**

_____

_____

_____

Pray – **That you will always try to be a part of building unity among Christians.**

REJECTED BUT DIVINELY LOVED

Luke 10:16 ...and the one who rejects you rejects me...

Have you ever been rejected? When people say they don't want us or what we offer, we may feel sad and depressed. No one was more rejected than Jesus Christ when He walked the earth. As Christ established the Church, every group He encountered rejected Him: the leading rulers like Herod, His own family, His hometown neighbors, the Romans, the Sanhedrin, and even His own disciples. Yet, He was focused on His mission and did not lose heart. His eyes were fixed on the love of His Father and the desire to defeat sin and death and bring His Church home.

When people reject us or our Christian testimony, we must remember that in this world we will face rejection like our Savior did. But the real rejection from the world does not relate to us, but rather to Jesus. The world still rejects Him because of its depraved nature and helplessness to change. It is only the power of God that brings change. If you feel rejected, turn to Jesus Christ; He is the One who accepts you in His love. If you feel rejected for proclaiming the Gospel, remember it is not *you* they are rejecting, but the Lord Himself.

*Look it up – **Jeremiah 8:9; Luke 17:15; 1 Peter 2:4***

*This truth for me – **How does it feel to be rejected? Where must you focus when people reject your witness for Christ?***

_____

_____

_____

*Pray – **That you will not be ashamed of the Gospel and not fear rejection.***

THE KING'S ROBE

Isaiah 61:10 ...He has wrapped me with a robe of righteousness...

There are many credits and debits associated with the Christian life: things that God has taken away from us when He saved us and things that He has added to our new lives in Christ. John Armstrong writes, *"Christ did much more than to just die for our sins. If Jesus had only died for our sins, then we might avoid the fire, but would we have the holiness required to be welcomed into heaven?" (Reformation Revival Journal - Spring 2003)*

Not only must the wrath of God be removed from our sinful lives, we also must be made presentable to God. Christ's atoning death satisfies God's holy wrath, but having our sins forgiven was half the issue; the other half was to be made holy. Just as it was Christ who took our sins, it was also Christ who gave us His righteousness because we have not even the slightest ability to make ourselves holy. We call this the *imputed righteousness* of Christ. He *robes* us, completely covering us with His righteousness, so we can stand before God robed in the righteousness of Jesus Christ—the only One who is completely acceptable to God. WOW, what a Savior!

*Look it up – **Genesis 15:6; 1 Corinthians 1:30; Philippians 3:8,9***

*This truth for me – **Define righteousness and how the change that Christ made in you affected you.***

_____

_____

_____

*Praise – **God for covering you with His righteousness.***

THE HEART OF RITUAL

Romans 2:29 ...*circumcision is that which is of the heart...*

What value is there in rituals and religious activity? Going through the elements of religious rituals may make a person feel good. I remember going to Mass on many occasions before being born-again and coming away feeling that I had done a good thing and that God was pleased with my participation in the rituals. Rituals make people think that God demands such acts to satisfy His anger.

Another false rationale regarding the practice of religious acts is that they make a person better than one who does not perform the rituals. If we had time to comment on the entire section of Romans 2, we would see clearly that unless God changes a person's heart, all the religious acts and rituals in the world are meaningless. Every person falls short of what God demands. He demands *perfection*, the perfect keeping of the law, not rituals or religious acts that sinners perform. Only one man kept the Law of God perfectly, the God-Man, Jesus Christ. This is why *we must trust by faith* in Christ and not in our works.

Has God changed your heart? If so, then do your religious acts as symbols of praise and thanksgiving. If you are not saved, then cry out to God and repent of your sins and ask Christ to forgive you.

Look it up – **Isaiah 1:11-17; Romans 2:28-29; Colossians 2:13-16**

This truth for me – **What religious rituals do you think are necessary to practice?**

_____

_____

_____

Pray – **For greater understanding of the supreme sacrifice of Christ.**

IN PURSUIT OF THE BEST

1 Timothy 6:11 ...pursue righteousness, godliness, faith, love, perseverance and gentleness.

During times of conflict, we hear a lot about the military and what our soldiers are doing. Reports tell us how our troops are pursuing the enemy. As Christians we are involved in the battle of spiritual warfare and are encouraged to pursue certain objectives. We are to be pursing those objectives not for the purpose of destruction, but rather so we are prepared and equipped for the *good fight*.

What are we to pursue? We are told to pursue *righteousness,* put simply, doing what is right according to Christ, even when we don't feel like doing right. Next we are to pursue *godliness* or being godlike. In short, we are to mimic Christ in all of life. Third, pursue *faith,* trusting God to help you to be faithful and biblical in your commitments and your walk. Pursue *love.* The Apostle Paul outlines what love is all about in 1 Corinthians 13. If I were to sum up Paul's description of love, it would be to show sacrificial humility toward one another. Finally, pursue *gentleness.* Even soldiers can be gentle, and in the Lord's army this is a requirement. These may be difficult pursuits for us, but when the battle gets tough, look to the General—the Lord Jesus Christ—and ask for His strength to give you victory.

*Look it up – **1 Timothy 4:8; Romans 14:19; 2 Peter 1:5,7***

*This truth for me – **Out of the list of virtues given above, what do you need to pursue now?***

_____

_____

_____

*Pray – **For the diligence to pursue the godly virtues that will make you more like Christ.***

HOLY AND SET APART

Nehemiah 12:30 ...the Levites purified themselves; they also purified the people, the gates, and the wall.

A dedication service is held for the purpose of setting apart, either as a special place, event, achievement, or for someone to be consecrated for a special task. When the rebuilding of the wall around Jerusalem was completed, the Levites (priests) gathered the people together and held a joyous celebration of thanksgiving for God's provision and protection in rebuilding the wall around the city. A most important part of this dedication service was purification. The priests, the people, the gates, and the wall were most likely sprinkled with blood or water, and in doing so, they were symbolically set apart for God. To participate in setting people and things apart unto God, the individuals as well as the things themselves need to be holy. In order for the Jews and the wall of protection to have God's blessing, they needed to be pure.

When we dedicate a child in our churches, there is the call for the parents and the home to be set apart unto God. When we dedicate a church, there is the call for those who minister in the church to be holy and the things that go on inside the walls to be holy. God may have called you to a project or task and the first thing to understand is the need to be holy if the project is to have the Lord's blessings. God is more desirous of holiness than mere productivity.

*Look it up – **Genesis 4:4-7; Psalm 51:17; Romans 6:13***

*This truth for me – **Are you ready to serve the Lord? What, if any, areas of your life need to be made holy so your service is blessed?***

_____

_____

_____

*Pray – **For a holy life and service unto the Lord.***

THE BLESSINGS OF RECEIVING AND GIVING

Psalm 49:17 ...when he dies he will carry nothing away...

After John Rockefeller died, a reporter asked his secretary, *"How much did Mr. Rockefeller leave in his estate?"* The secretary answered, *"All of it."* How true, and the psalmist sets this truth forth in the words, *when he dies he will carry nothing away.* This is a good reminder of several simple but pointed truths. First, only things stored away for heaven will last. Our faithfulness and obedience to God and a life lived sacrificially for the Kingdom is a sampling of things that will last eternally. Second, be careful how much emphasis you place upon the world's riches and accumulating things that fade away. Third, take death seriously. The Lord can call at any moment— be ready. Fourth, guard your heart and mind from lusting after someone's accomplishments and riches. And finally, honor the Lord in all you do and all you accomplish. Put Him first in your agenda along with His Kingdom enterprises.

I know every mission agency director feels the same way I do when it comes to asking for financial support. It is not a comfortable request to make. You and I have heard many times that the American Church has enough money to finance all the mission endeavors in which we are engaged, and more. I believe this analysis is true, and if all of us might see more clearly that when we die we will leave everything here, we may consider the needs of the Kingdom in a more prioritized manner.

Look it up – ***Psalm 49:5-9; Jeremiah 9:23; Mark 12:41-44***

This truth for me – ***List ways you can better use your resources for the Kingdom of God.***

_____

_____

_____

Pray – ***For the wisdom to use your resources as a blessing for His Kingdom.***

IS IT REAL?

1 John 4:1 ...*test the spirits to see whether they are from God...*

"God acts contingent upon our behavior...we may surprise God...God doesn't know what will happen..." These are some of the teachings I heard a radio preacher state during his broadcast. Are these statements true and consistent with the orthodoxy of our faith and doctrine? NO, not at all. Many preach and teach the same sort of false doctrines, yet there seems to be little outcry from believers concerning such false teaching. Why?

One of the most significant and sad reasons is that many Christians can't tell the difference between true and false teaching. They lack discernment. The other reason is that a dangerous complacency is hovering over Christianity, a complacency that says *if it looks good and makes me feel good, then it must be true.* John demands that the Christian *test the spirits, because many false prophets have gone out into the world.*

More testing, and less surface acceptance, needs to be done. Dig into what you hear to see if it is of God and true. If you lack the tools or understanding, then acquire the necessary learning and study the Scriptures. Or you can go to a trusted brother or sister who has a proven understanding of truth and false teaching. God holds us accountable with His truth. He desires His children to be able to discern truth from lies.

Look it up – ***Matthew 5:19; 1 Timothy 1:3-7; Hebrews 13:9***

This truth for me – ***Have you ever got caught up in false teaching? List ways you can test the spirits.***

Pray – ***For godly discernment, and motivation to regularly study the Scriptures.***

CALLED TO A VISION OF SERVICE

Nehemiah 2:12 ...what my God was putting into my mind to do...

When God calls a man to ministry, He also puts into the man's mind a vision for what He wants him to accomplish. I sensed this in every calling to ministry, whether as a pastor or as mission board director. It was exciting to see the vision for ministry that God wanted to accomplish through me. It is not always easy to translate that vision to others and have them catch the vision, but if God puts it into your mind, He will also establish it in the minds of those that you are leading.

For Nehemiah, rebuilding the wall around Jerusalem and having an obstinate people catch his vision was a formidable task. Yet, as you read the story of Ezra and Nehemiah, you find no evidence of them swaying from the vision of rebuilding the wall and reviving the people to walk with God. The people catch the vision and respond over and over with submissive obedience.

It is a wonderful blessing when people you are leading catch the vision God placed on your mind and heart. I trust that this vision is from God, and in His time you will see how much a blessing it is to serve Him by following His vision. Maybe you have not sensed God's calling you to use your gifts for service. Pray and seek His leading.

Look it up – **2 Samuel 7:8,9; Isaiah 6:1-13; Hebrews 5:1-4**

This truth for me – **What has God called you to do for Him? List your thoughts.**

_____

_____

_____

Pray – **For God to make clear to you what He has for you to do in service to Him.**

NOW GO AND DO IT!

Joshua 1:9 Have I not commanded you? Be strong and courageous...

On the surface God's command to Joshua may seem callous. Joshua is about to enter Canaan, a land filled with detestable things and fierce people. Joshua must have been troubled about the task of wiping out all the people in these city states. God's counsel is a command. What kind of counsel commands someone to just go and do it? I have had people come into my office looking for help when facing a formidable obstacle in their lives. What would their reaction have been if I had simply said, *"I command you to be strong and courageous and now go do what you have to do?"*

This may sound like some cold advice, but we need to see the prelude to this counsel that God gives. First, God reminded Joshua that the land he was to conquer was already theirs because God had *given it to them.* Second, God promised Joshua that He would *be with Joshua and not fail or forsake him.* Third, God gave Joshua the key for success—*obedience to God's Word.* And the conclusion to these promises is, *I command you to be strong and courageous, now go do it.* The command from God is not as callous as we may have thought. When God commands us to do what He wants, He also gives us all we need. What is God telling you to do? Read His promises and study His Word for direction. Now go and do it.

*Look it up – **Deuteronomy 31:6; Daniel 10:19; John 14:31***

*This truth for me – **Have you been hesitating to do something you know you must do? List how you can let God strengthen you.***

_____

_____

_____

*Pray – **For the Holy Spirit to empower you to do what you need to do.***

GOD'S ABOUNDING GRACE

Matthew 9:17 Nor do men put new wine into old wineskins...

In Bible times the skins of animals were used to store wine and other liquids. When a skin became hardened over a period of time, it was marked so that new wine would not be placed into the old hardened skin. If it were, the obvious would occur. The new wine—still in the fermenting process— would expand and make the old skin burst.

Our Lord's picture is clear when applying the illustration to grace and the law. Christ was introducing the understanding that the Kingdom of God is built solely upon the grace of God and not on keeping of the law. Salvation was and always is grounded in the justification of a sinner by faith alone through grace alone. Trying to make works or ritual the foundation of salvation is useless and ineffective. If we try to find justification before a holy God through our own efforts, we will eventually burst into eternal damnation. The grace of God fills a new heart regenerated by God.

If you are trying to find salvation through your old efforts of works and religiosity, you will be disappointed. If you are a Christian and attempting to please God through your works, you will also find yourself pouring your efforts out on the ground. Trust in the Lord completely by faith and then live by the same faith that saved you. The grace of God is *new every morning* and is given to us over and over. Praise His Holy Name!

Look it up – **Luke 5:36-39; Romans 5:20; James 4:6**

This truth for me – **What may you be carrying over from the past that needs to be tossed? List those things that do not fit any longer in your Christian life.**

_____

_____

_____

Pray – **That you will be able to throw off the old and put more of the new things of God in your life.**

THE GLORIOUS WAY TO GOD

Ezekiel 14:20 ...they could not deliver either their son or their daughter...

The prophet Ezekiel wants Israel to know that salvation before a holy God is an individual matter. No one can ride the coattails of another into a right relationship with God, even if that person is as close as a father or mother. Salvation is a matter between a holy God and each individual He created. The sinner can only find forgiveness if he or she goes to God and seeks God's cleansing of the sin through Christ.

We all are sinners worthy of eternal death and this means that every man, woman and child stands accountable before God. It would be comfortable to have someone stand in our place and say, "*they are with me, God, please let them in.*" But the fact is that this is not the case. The only one that God will accept as our guarantee is Jesus Christ. If a sinner is to find peace with God and come into His righteousness and be saved, Jesus Christ must stand in his place and plead his case. With Jesus as our advocate, the Father must accept us. In Christ we are saved.

Is there anything we can do to help another person come to God? Yes, Yes, Yes! Christians are the means by which God will save. It is our testimony and our witness that God will use to save sinners. We are a most important part of the salvation plan. We cannot take sinners into heaven, but we can tell them about the God of Heaven and His Son, Jesus Christ, who died to save them. We can't carry a sinner into Heaven, but we can carry the Gospel to a sinner.

Look it up – **John 14;1-6; Acts 2:21; 1 Timothy 2:5**

This truth for me – **How can you witness to someone who thinks they are OK with God because they come from a Christian family?**

_____

_____

_____

Pray – **For God to help you realize that you are His means to save.**

GREAT GLORY IN SMALL THINGS

1 Kings 19:12 ...after the fire a sound of a gentle blowing.

The Strong Little Church was the title of a communication I received some time ago. The article stated, *"Small churches outperform larger churches in seven out of eight categories...We measured eight quality characteristics: empowering leadership, gift-oriented ministry, passionate spirituality, functional structures, inspiring worship services, holistic small groups, need-oriented evangelism, and loving relationships. Larger churches do better than smaller churches only in creating more inspiring worship services."* (Interview with Christian A. Schwarz, Leadership Journal, Fall 1999)

When Elijah was most likely looking for another powerful experience like he had on Mt. Carmel to get him out of his rut, God gave him a gentle blowing wind. There is nothing wrong with being a small denomination or a small church, unless the smallness is caused by a lack of vision, disunity, or sin. I hope that none of these apply to your church, but having stated this hope, we still need to continue to evaluate where we stand in each of these categories. Schwarz, at the end of the interview, says, *"...church growth and health should concentrate on healthy, small churches that can multiply and give birth to other small churches."* It may not be the big things that most impress and glorify God, but the gentle things that *blow* in and out of our lives to His glory.

*Look it up – **Proverbs 30:24-28; Matthew 25:23; James 3:4***

*This truth for me – **Do you get caught up with the bigger is better mentality of our age? List what small things are blessings to you.***

_____

_____

_____

*Pray – **For eyes to see God's greatness in small things.***

A JOB LEFT UNDONE

Judges 1:27-33 ...did not take possession...did not drive out...

When you see an unfinished task, how do you react? Could you care less or are you like I am? Seeing a task unfinished makes me nervous and upset. When the Israelites were given entrance into Canaan, they were commissioned by God to be His instrument of justice on the pagan Canaanites and destroy them entirely. But the Jews failed in this charge, neither driving out the Canaanites nor taking complete possession of the land. The consequences were that Israel abandoned God, adopted pagan foreign gods, and incurred God's chastisement and judgment. All this because a job was left unfinished.

God is a finisher. He doesn't leave loose ends and tasks unfinished. God's plan and purpose for His creation is clearly defined as having a completion, *I am the Alpha and Omega... the beginning and the end (Revelation 22:13)*. When God set forth His redemptive plan of salvation, He outlined its beginning in His eternal decrees and its completion at the cross, *...it is completed (John 19:30)*. Because God completes His tasks, He expects His people to complete the tasks He gives them to accomplish.

What task has God given you to accomplish? Some are clearly given: live holy like God is holy, be not of this world, love and care for one another. Other tasks are more personal. Maybe it is giving up that sin you are clinging to or serving Him with more fervor and attention. Whatever the task, the question lingers, will we finish what God has called us to do?

Look it up – Proverbs 16:9; Isaiah 14:27; Ephesians 1:10

This truth for me – Do you have a task left undone? How will it get done?

———————————————————————————

———————————————————————————

———————————————————————————

Pray – For God to give you the strength to complete your tasks.

A REVERENT FEAR

Jeremiah 2:19 ...the dread of Me is not in you...

NO FEAR!!! This has been a motto for our culture and we have seen it lived out in all segments of society. I have an urban school teacher friend who says that his students have no fear of the consequences of their actions. Punishment was once a deterrent to crime but as one young criminal said when interviewed in a detention center, "*...I got the dude, who cares if I have to do time...*"

If a good sense of fear is fading away in our society, how does it affect our view of God? It can affect us in the same manner it affected the Jews during the days of the Prophet Jeremiah. The result of a people without a fear of God is wickedness and apostasy. This was Israel's outcome because of their lack of a reverent fear for God and His ways. When a people fail to fear God and are wicked and apostate, God disciplines and judges them. God is the same today as He was in the days of Jeremiah. He has not deviated from bringing judgment upon those who fail to acknowledge and obey Him. We don't like to mention judgment in our Christian circles or from our pulpits for fear of offending someone. But a healthy and reverent fear of God has much better results than a condescending fear of man. May God grant us a good clear understanding of righteous fear and may we live holy before a holy God.

*Look it up – **Genesis 42:18; Isaiah 57:11; Matthew 10:28***

*This truth for me – **What is your reverent fear level for God? What does this fear level look like in your life?***

_____

_____

_____

*Pray – **For a reverent fear of the Lord and His power and judgment.***

CHOSEN BY GOD'S MERCY AND GRACE

Deuteronomy 29:4 ...the Lord has not given you a heart to know...

Scripture after scripture affirms God's sovereignty and His election of His people. I find it hard to study a passage and not sense the greatness of God and His almighty purpose and plan to save His people and keep them holy for the future wedding feast with His Son.

As I was sharing with a sincere and wonderful Christian, I mentioned the word *election*. I could tell that the mere mention of that word took her mind off the focus of the text we were discussing. Why are Christians so jolted by the doctrine of God's sovereign choice of His people? Some Christians cannot think of God being merciful and loving if He chooses some and not others. Other Christians believe that if you hold to the teaching of election, then you will not be on fire for missions or witnessing. Still others find it hard to believe that man has no say in the work of salvation other than believing, which a sinner can only do if God has elected to ...*give him a heart to know!*

It didn't take long for me to know God's sovereign choice. Only God could save a sinner like me and give me the faith to believe. He elected me and I knew it was pure grace, not anything of me. Thank the Lord for His election of you. As a faithful response to such a great mercy, serve and love Him with all your heart, mind, and spirit.

*Look it up – **Ephesians 1:4-13; Colossians 3:12; 1 Peter 2:9***

*This truth for me – **Does the doctrine of election disturb you? List the positives of God's choosing you.***

---

*Pray – **That God will give you a clear understanding of His grace, mercy and sovereignty in election.***

A LIFE THAT PLEASES GOD

Revelation 11:7 And when they have finished their testimony...

In your neighborhood or at your work, have you spoken recently about Jesus' saving power, or introduced someone to Christ and the Gospel? It seems apparent that we are not being an army of witnesses. Some churches are growing, but one must wonder what is the cause of this growth. Is it evangelism and conversion, or revolving-door Christians seeking a comfortable spiritual experience?

When I arrive in heaven, I hope I have the opportunity to meet the two witnesses of Revelation 10. When the end times appear, these two will have a tremendous ministry for about four years and then face the wrath of the Beast as it comes up from the abyss with terrible vengeance on the witnesses and finally kills them. They will not only face the terror of the Beast, but even as their bodies lie in the streets after being killed, the people will ridicule and mock them. But in the end, as always, God will have the final say as He brings them back to life and takes them home to heaven. Such is the course of life for those who please God. Those who powerfully tell of Jesus face antagonism and mockery, but in the end they are pleasing to God and will be rewarded in glory. *Be a witness today and be pleasing to God.*

Look it up – **Proverbs 16:7; 2 Corinthians 5:9; 1 Thessalonians 2:4**

This truth for me – **What is it about the witnesses of Revelation 10 that is so pleasing to God, and how can you be this pleasing to Him?**

_____

_____

_____

Pray – **For your life to be pleasing to God and that He will expose what is displeasing.**

THERE IS SOMETHING ABOUT A NAME

Isaiah 9:6 For a child...a son...Wonderful Counselor, Mighty God, Eternal Father, Prince of Peace.

What is in a name? In the case of Jesus Christ, EVERYTHING! The Lord's names not only tell us of His greatness and perfections, but also remind us of how precious and mighty He is. I cannot help but be amazed at the number of times various names are given for the Lord Jesus Christ. In this Messianic prophecy from Isaiah, we can count five names, or six if you think that wonderful and counselor refer to two names. Each name describes a particular aspect of our Lord's mission and character:

Child - so He could be like us and be our perfect substitute
Son - who was the obedient law keeper so that our guilt would be taken away
Wonderful Counselor - who supernaturally holds all truth and wisdom in His possession
Mighty God - who is able to forgive and grant eternal life to the repentant sinner
Eternal Father - who is the father of eternity and provides for all His children's needs
Prince of Peace - who brings peace in all its magnificence, to our heart and mind.

Rehearse the names of Jesus, and may your life be blessed with His presence.

Look it up – **Genesis 17:1; Psalm 50:1; Matthew 6:9**

This truth for me – **What names of God are meaningful to you and why?**

_____

_____

_____

Pray – **For a fresh new look and joy in God's names.**

A LIFELONG GROWTH IN CHRIST

2 Corinthians 4:16 ...*our inner man is being renewed day by day.*

On vacation our family relaxes by the ocean. I will often float along on my back enjoying the coolness of the water and its salty splash on my face. I become so relaxed that on many occasions I have turned over to discover that I had drifted a distance away from my starting point.

John Owens, the magnificent Puritan thinker writes, *"The work of holiness is secret and mysterious. As the outward man is slowly dying, we are not often aware of it, so it is with the growth of grace in the inward man."* It may not always be apparent that we are making any headway in our Christian lives because we fail so often and sin so frequently. When we face storms and trials, we think that we should have been stronger in the faith. We hear the stories of other Christians who have suffered for Christ and accomplished great things for the Lord and say to ourselves that we are nothing compared to such martyrs. Yet the truth of the matter is that every child of God is being moved along by the work of grace through the Holy Spirit. In Christ we are being *renewed day by day.*

Yes, we may face struggles and storms in our spiritual walk but as Owen writes, *"...backslidings are occasional and abnormal to the true nature of the new creature...a disturbance to the ordinary work of grace."* Our growth is the work of the Holy Spirit. Our duty is to yield to that work and be holy; sanctification is a lifelong work.

*Look it up – **Hebrews 6:1; Philippians 3:12; 2 Peter 3:18***

*This truth for me – **Are you growing in Christ? What might be hindering your growth?***

_____

_____

_____

*Pray – **For the Holy Spirit to help you grow in grace.***

GOD CALLS THE LOWLY

Micah 5:2 ...Too little to be among the clans of Judah...

Every so often we hear the stories of how great things come from little places. There are some small towns in western Pennsylvania that produced some of the best professional football players in the history of the National Football League. Joe Namath, Joe Montana and Tony Dorsett are a few of them.

When it comes to food, there are little towns and villages that are famous for their food products. The small towns around Lebanon, Pennsylvania produce a lunch meat called Lebanon Bologna, and it is world-famous for its smoky and meaty taste. In a small row home in my home town, there was a tiny bakery that only baked one fabulous product, an old-style rye bread.

We have a God who likes to take the places, things and people of no distinction and produce His greatness in them. In the beginning of the first letter to Corinth, we learn that God takes the *things (people) that are not* and uses them to confound the world by working His grace in their lives. In selecting a place for His Son, the Lord of the universe, to be born, He chose the insignificant hamlet of Bethlehem. But God even went to the extent of having the Savior born in a barn to the humble, lowly Joseph and Mary. There are times that you may feel insignificant and useless, yet in Christ you can find your significance and importance. To be a child of the King and a servant in His Kingdom are our most important roles.

*Look it up – **Ezekiel 17:24; Mark 4:31; 1 Corinthians 1:26-31***

*This truth for me – **List how God has used you to serve Him and His Kingdom.***

---

*Praise – **God for calling you and using you to build His Kingdom.***

THE GREATEST THING IN HISTORY

Luke 2:15 ...Let us go...and see this thing that has happened...

It is interesting that the shepherds responded to the angel's announcement by wanting to go to Bethlehem and see a *thing*. In the original language of the New Testament, this *thing* could be understood as a *word or utterance*. On the surface, Luke's usage of *thing or word* might sound out of place. However, if you consider what the shepherds heard from the angels about the baby born in Bethlehem, then their going to see a *thing or word* is not so awkward.

In John 1:1 we read, *In the beginning was the Word, and the Word was with God, and the Word was God.* If you read on, there is no doubt that *Word* is referring to Jesus Christ. The shepherds were heading off to see God, the incarnate truth from heaven who was born in lowly Bethlehem. Jesus is the *Word of Truth!* He is the *Word of Life!* He is the *Word of Creation!* What a tremendous *thing* was in store for the shepherds. The shepherds would behold Truth, Life and Power all wrapped up in a baby who was lying in a manger. The shepherds returned to their hillside, *glorifying and praising God.*

Is this your response to knowing Christ's truth, life and power in you? Don't take lightly the great work of God in your life. Glorify and praise Him. If you are not saved, fall on your knees and cry out to God for salvation; repent and believe on the Lord and be saved.

Look it up – ***2 Corinthians 4:2; 1 Thessalonians 2:13; Ephesians 6:17***

This truth for me – ***How has God's Word led you this week? List the ways.***

_____

_____

_____

Pray – ***For the Word of God to guide your every thought and action.***

THE FOUNDATION FOR PATIENCE

James 5:7 Be patient...

There are Christians who are reluctant to pray for patience, knowing what is attached to such a prayer request. James connects patience with suffering and endurance. He is not the only scripture writer to do this. The Bible is replete with exhortations to understand that as we endure the trials of life, God is building our patience. I would prefer that patience would be produced by some sort of pleasing activity, but real patience is the outcome of waiting upon the Lord to give His direction and relief in hard times. How does one endure to the point of being patient? First, *by example.* The example of others is a stimulant. James gives Job's trials as an example. The outcome of Job's trials was for him to see God's mercy and compassion. Second, we endure *by prayer.* Again, James exhorts that when we suffer, we are to pray... and pray hard! Third, a person should endure *by self-evaluation.* It is good and productive in times of trial to look inward. Some of us face trials because of sin. An evaluation of our lives, and confession if needed, will prepare hearts for the reception of God's mercy and compassion. Lastly, it is *by faith in God* that we endure. Don't only look *to* God but *at* Him. He is the almighty Sovereign of the universe who has all our trials in the palm of His hand. *Oh God, Thou art awesome...* (Psalm 68:35).

Look it up – **Romans 5:3; 2 Thessalonians 1:4; Hebrews 4:14-16**

This truth for me – **We are all impatient at times. What things make you impatient and how have you learned to be patient?**

Pray – **That God will give you the perseverance to go through your trials.**

THE BEST REASONS TO HARVEST

Matthew 9:37 ...The harvest is plentiful, but the workers are few.

What a bittersweet statement! The sweetness is in the fact that God has His elect scattered all over the world. They are awaiting the sending of the Gospel and the Holy Spirit's regenerating work in their lives. The bitter part is that workers (sent ones) are needed to go and bring the Gospel to every tongue, tribe and nation, beginning here in the cities and towns of America. Some would say that if there are so many God has chosen to be saved in the world, why not let God save them? Why plead for workers? We plead for workers, even knowing that God will save His elect, because workers of the Gospel are the means by which God will save His chosen people. It is legitimate to plead for harvesters to go into the fields and to pray for God to raise up harvesters.

What is it that motivates a person to go out into the harvest fields? Is it the lost condition of sinful mankind? Is it the plea that if we don't go, how will they be saved? Being moved by humanity's lost condition is a good reason to go into the fields. But there are even greater reasons. Workers should be motivated by *obedience* to the command to go, *thanksgiving* for the great grace shown to them as sinners, the *compassion* demonstrated by Christ, and the knowledge that *going and preaching is God's plan and means to save.* Pray for God to raise up workers for the Gospel who are motivated by obedience, thanksgiving, Christ's compassion, and a knowledge of God's plan and purpose.

*Look it up – **Psalm 107:1-3; 2 Corinthians 9:13; Philippians 2:8***

*This truth for me – **Think about what will encourage you to go and harvest souls.***

_____

_____

_____

*Pray – **For your heart and mind to obey, with thanksgiving, the command to go.***

NO ROOM TO BLOW YOUR OWN HORN

Romans 3:27 *Where then is boasting...*

If man were to have any part in appropriating his own salvation, he certainly would boast about such ability. But just the opposite is true; *the just shall live by faith,* not works. Even faith is not by man's conjuring it up on his own. Faith must be totally of God or else man would say, "But it was *my* faith that saved me," rather than giving God the glory for giving the gift of faith to cry out and believe. We must recognize that the bottom line about salvation, faith and belief, is that it is *all about God!* Any degree of man's involvement would trigger the sinful self-righteous nature that lives within every sinner. This sovereign thought of God drives me to be thankful and obedient, unlike the thinking that makes me believe I had a part in my salvation. Total dependence upon God leads me to praise Him with *all* my being, serve Him with *all* my energy, and love Him with *all* my heart.

Christian, a holy and sovereign God bent low to reach you, pull you out of the mire of sin and death, and place your feet on the rock, Jesus Christ. Cast off any thoughts of self-righteousness and fall low before Him!

Look it up – **Proverbs 25:14; Jeremiah 9:23-24; Ephesians 2:9**

This truth for me – **When have you boasted about something or been arrogant? What is worth boasting about? Think about it.**

Pray – **For a humble spirit that always recognizes the cost of your salvation.**

OUR GLORIOUS FUTURE

Psalm 84:10 ...a day in Thy courts is better than a thousand outside...

The three ultimate questions in life are: *Where have I come from? What is my duty?* and *Where am I going?* No other faith but Christianity gives a definitive answer to all three: we have our origins in a creator God, our duty now is to glorify God, and our hope for the future is eternal life in Christ Jesus. Most people are only interested in the here and now. Henry David Thoreau was not interested in his past or his future destiny. He once stated, *"One world at a time."* One reason why people don't care to look ahead to their future is because they have no assurance of what their eternal future will hold for them. Many *hope* they will end up in a place that is good. Others take a very dismal view of their destiny. A friend once said, *"I'm bound for hell because God would never want me."*

Christians are given many very beautiful pictures of their future with God in His heaven. One such view is here in Psalm 84. It reveals to us that the heaven of which we are certain is infinitely better than even a lifetime of the best this earth has to offer. It's hard to imagine that our best times and experiences in this life cannot even compare to one small moment in heaven. Why is being in heaven so much better? Simple, *because God is there!* When we are called home, we will be with our Savior Jesus Christ. Nothing can compare with that moment when we are face to face with Christ. Live today with the glory of God in your sights!

Look it up – **Psalm 24:7-8; Matthew 5:3; John 11:40**

This truth for me – **Describe what you believe being in glory will be like.**

_____

_____

_____

Pray – **That God will give you a thirst and desire to see His glory.**

GOD SEEKS A HEART THAT FEARS HIM

1 Kings 5:13 ...King Solomon levied forced laborers from all Israel...

The fear of God is the beginning of wisdom..." The man who wrote these words in the Proverbs is the same man who enslaved his people to build the temple and his own palace. It is the same man who took twice the amount of time to build his house as he did to build the Temple of God, and he also built his house larger than the temple. It is the same man who married an array of pagan women and brought their idolatry to the nation of Israel.

OK, why this history lesson on King Solomon? Simply to say that wisdom and the fear of God go together. A person can have superior wisdom, as Solomon possessed, but not have a reverence for God and His ways. One can even be theologically astute and know much about the Bible, but not have a heart that fears (reverences) God. Biblical and theological knowledge are then mere academics. The end result for Solomon was God's judgment on his loose and selfish life. God took his kingship and divided the prosperous nation of Israel into two weak nations with ungodly leaders for the most part. Maybe the greatest condemnation of Solomon was that the temple he built, along with his lavish palace, was stripped and destroyed. *God is a seeker of hearts bowed to Him and His ways. Fear the Lord and be wise!*

Look it up – **Proverbs 16:6; John 9:31; Hebrews 11:7**

This truth for me – **In what ways do you fear God? List the ways God is to be feared (reverenced).**

Pray – **That you will have a healthy fear of the Lord that will help you to reverence Him.**

MERCY'S TWO-SIDED SWORD

Hosea 6:6 ... I desire mercy... (NIV)

Our Lord, in His ministry, had a perfect way of bringing together mercy for the soul and mercy for the body. I would say that there was never a time that He did not take care of a person's physical need, while also dealing with a person's spiritual need. We hear of radical governments threatening Christian relief organizations and warning that they are welcome to bring aid to their country's victims but they must not proselytize. I am not sure whether this can be done by Christians. How can Christians only deal with half the need? How the relief agencies deal with such a dilemma is difficult and they need our prayers.

Christ's perfect way of working out mercy for the soul and body concentrates on the most important: the mercy for a soul that will spend eternity either in heaven or hell. Jesus used His miraculous healing power to bring attention to the greater need of salvation and a focus of salvation being centered in Him. God desires that we show mercy and compassion to the physical and emotional needs of humanity even while we remember that the greatest need a person has is salvation for his sinful soul. Salvation is found in no other than Jesus Christ, our merciful Savior. Augustine, in his *Confessions*, used mercy as a proper name for God, *"I call, O God, my mercy, who made me and did not forget me when I forgot you."*

Look it up – **Proverbs 3:3; Matthew 5:7; Colossians 3:12**

This truth for me – **To whom will you show mercy both spiritually and physically?**

_____

_____

_____

Pray – That you will have eyes to see a person's spiritual and physical needs.

HIS LOVE COMES TO US IN ABUNDANCE

Psalm 27:8 When thou didst say, "Seek My face," my heart said to Thee, "Thy face, O Lord, I shall seek."

Who chooses whom? This question has been a contentious one! Is it God who chooses man unconditionally or man who chooses God? I have never heard the answer to this question more dynamically stated than in the words of John Gerstner in a short paper he wrote titled, *Divine Initiative*. Allow me to quote Brother Gerstner's response. *"When God does reveal His right arm and display His mighty strength in changing the soul, the spirit, the principle of a sinner, is then by this new nature willing and disposed and believing in Jesus Christ. Thus the man comes pressing into the Kingdom of God. He becomes a man of violence who takes the kingdom of heaven by force. He is so determined to have this Christ- whom he now sees in all His loveliness and he loves with all his heart- that he will permit nothing to stand in his way."* Do we choose God? Only if He first chooses us. Do we love God? Only if He first loves us. Do we run after Jesus? Only if we first hear His voice calling us. All initiative in the saving of a soul is in the hands of a God who has a passion to save the people He has elected to be like His Son Jesus Christ. The Christian's great privilege and duty is to be His sent ones and herald the gospel to all. This is the means by which God will call His people and give them the strength to choose Him.

*Look it up – **1 John 4:19; Colossians 3:12; Jude 1***

*This truth for me – **List how many ways you sense God's love for you.***

---

*Praise – **God for His grace in choosing you and His abounding love for you.***

ALL YOU LORD, NOT ME

John 1:13 ...born not of blood, nor of the will of the flesh, nor of the will of man, but of God.

That just about covers it...salvation, that is. *Blood* cannot accomplish salvation. It doesn't matter if our parents or family are Christians or if a person was raised in a Christian home; salvation is not accomplished by blood ties or associations. *Flesh* cannot accomplish salvation. The strongest, most gifted person is left helpless when it comes to saving oneself from eternal damnation. All human efforts of the flesh cannot bridge the gap that sin has left between mankind and God. *Will* cannot save a person. Our wills are marred just like our flesh. Sin has left us with a will that can only choose to reject Christ and is bent to sin and destruction. Our will is only free to sin and continue on in its march to death.

John reminds us in verse twelve that we must believe and receive Christ into our life in order to be saved and be called children of God. He follows this declaration immediately with verse thirteen, reminding us that believing and receiving are of God, not of man. We cannot ride another's coattails into heaven, nor work our way there through our own strength, nor will it be achieved from a depraved nature. Salvation is all and totally of God. ***PRAISE HIS GRACIOUS NAME!***

Look it up – ***Romans 9:3-33; Galatians 3:12; Hebrews 6:1***

This truth for me – ***Isn't it great to be free from sin in Christ and not in our own efforts and power? How would you describe being free in Christ?***

_____

_____

_____

Praise – ***God for the freedom He gave us through unconditional grace.***

OPEN MY EYES LORD

Luke 24:32,45 ...while He was explaining the Scriptures to us...He opened their minds to understand the Scriptures.

I once heard Dr. James Boice say, *"To have the Scriptures opened in the right way is to open the eyes to Christ. And this in turn opens our eyes in a new way to the Scriptures."* This right way begins with the calling of God to salvation, the heart being regenerated, and the mind being illuminated by the Holy Spirit. Only those who are born-again can have their mind opened to understand the Scriptures. Thus, the right way of understanding the Bible begins with salvation.

The right way then proceeds by the Christian submitting himself to the right teaching from gifted preachers and teachers (Acts 2:42; Ephesians 4:11,12). Christians can gain wisdom and understanding directly from the Scriptures, yet God gave gifted teachers and preachers to the church to help believers grow in their knowledge and understanding of Scriptures.

The right way of understanding the Scriptures also involves meditation and application. When we read the Scriptures and hear them taught and preached, we then ought to think on them in order to see how they apply to us and to living out our Christian life. The reason for following this way of understanding the Scriptures is not simply academic, but rather it helps us to see Jesus more clearly and be more like Him. The Scriptures open our eyes to Christ.

Look it up – **John 1:9; 1 Corinthians 2:14; 2 Timothy 3:16, 17**

This truth for me – **Does the Bible excite you? What is it about the Bible that is so exciting?**

Pray – **For more eagerness to study, meditate and apply the Bible's teaching.**

USELESS CHRISTIANITY

Revelation 3:16 So because you are lukewarm...

Have you ever taken a big gulp of lukewarm water when you were expecting a soothing cold drink? Have you sat in a hot tub for therapy and the water was just lukewarm? If so, you know the sensation. You literally want to spit out the water or jump out of the tub. Lukewarm is not satisfying or valued.

Christ called the Laodiceans lukewarm. They were complacent, self-satisfied and indifferent to the Lord and the things of faith. In cold hard terms—they were useless to the things of the Kingdom and to Christ. Many people who say they are religious fall into this lukewarm category. Filled up with their own sense of religiosity and self-satisfaction, they fall into the ravine of lukewarm uselessness.

Christ's illustration of cold water is a reminder of how refreshing and useful a cold drink is to someone parched and thirsty. His reference to hot water reminds us of the therapeutic elements that exist in a hot bath or whirlpool. But lukewarm, especially a lukewarm faith, is only worth being spit out. The resulting actions and attitudes of lukewarm Christianity are: a compromise of the truth, a toleration of sin, and an accommodation of so-called peace and love at any cost. This is the lukewarm current that flows through liberal Christianity and has even trickled into some pools of evangelicalism. To be a Christian means that we are to be useful to Christ and His Kingdom without compromising the truth or accommodating sin.

*Look it up – **Matthew 24:12-13; Acts 2:42-47; Romans 12:9-13***

*This truth for me – **Is your walk with the Lord lukewarm? If so, what will you do about it?***

_____

_____

_____

*Pray – **That God will help you have an exciting walk with Him.***

"OUR" ABBA FATHER

Romans 8:15 ...you have received a spirit of adoption as sons by which we cry out, "Abba! Father!"

"Theological liberalism extends the fatherhood of God to all mankind and in so doing denies the distinction between the world and the church, even the need for the Gospel. God is the Father of all in the sense that He is the creator, but in a redemptive sense, He is foremost the Father of the redeemed." This was a quote from one of my sermons. My point was to make clear the difference between the liberal understanding of the Fatherhood of God and what we recognize as the Fatherhood of God in relationship to His children who are saved and adopted into the family of God.

When we are born-again, we are granted the right to be called a child of God and with respect and affection can say *Abba Father*. We must never put any member of the Godhead in lower esteem or honor than another member. The Father should be praised and exalted for His sending of the Son; the Son should be praised for His obedience to the Father. And the Holy Spirit should be praised for His willingness to carry out the wishes of the Son and the Father. Charles Spurgeon writes: *"We are too apt to forget, that while there are distinctions as to the persons in the Trinity, there are no distinctions of honor...he who knoweth the Father, and the Son, and the Holy Ghost as he should know them, never setteth one before another..."* Praise be to *our* Father for sending His Son who sent the Holy Spirit so that we may be saved and cry, *Abba Father!*

Look it up – **Deuteronomy 32:6; Romans 8:14; Galatians 4:6**

This truth for me – **Write a note to your heavenly Father thanking Him for adopting you into His family.**

_____

_____

_____

Pray – **Thanking your Father for lavishing His love on you.**

GOD GAVE HIS BEST

John 20:22 ...Receive the Holy Spirit.

What have you given away lately? Was it something precious to you or an item that you no longer needed? Many times we are willing to give away something that has lost its luster. But how often are we willing to give away the best we have?

The Trinity is a picture of giving away the best. The Father sent the Son to be our propitiation for sin. The Father was pleased to give us His Son even to the point of seeing Him crushed so that we would have freedom from sin and death. Christ reminded His disciples that He would give another Helper after He left this earth. He would give the church the Holy Spirit. Christ gave us the Spirit to place us into a full relationship with the Lord, to seal us for His own possession, to gift us to do ministry, and to fill us so that we would enjoy a deep fellowship with God. The Son and the Spirit are two precious gifts.

What was the driving force behind such giving by the Godhead? It was divine love! God so loved that He gave. Christ died and went back to glory so that the Spirit would come. Motivated by pure and selfless love, the Father gave His Son and the Son gave us the Holy Spirit. There are no greater gifts to be given and no greater motivation than divine love. Oh redeemed sinner, rejoice in the gifts that you have been given, and let us give in a like manner.

*Look it up – **John 3:16; Luke 11:13; 2 Corinthians 1:20-22***

*This truth for me – **List what you have given up for God or will give up.***

_____

_____

_____

*Pray – **For the wisdom and courage to give up your best for Christ.***

LOVED WITH AN EVERLASTING LOVE

Ephesians 5:25 ...gave Himself up for her.

Christ's love for the Church cannot be measured. It is infinite in its depth and effect upon lost sinners. The Christian finds that such a love is incomprehensible, but we know that this divine love is real, and it is ours. This knowledge brings us comfort and assurance. Peter said in I Peter 1:8, ...*though you have not seen Him, you love Him...* Jesus loves the Church, and gave Himself for it. Why? In order to have His people *sanctified,* set apart as holy and peculiar unto Him, that we might be *cleansed* in order to be presented before the Father as children worthy of our calling. He gave Himself for us that we would be *redeemed* from the evil of sin and the curse of death and that we would be *zealous* for good works to *glorify* the Father in all we do.

Today take much time to ponder the love of Christ in giving Himself up for you, who were once a sinner, dead in your trespasses and sin. You, who were once estranged and alien to the things of God. You, who had turned from Christ and ignored His love. Remember that He chose you and gave Himself up for you to save you, free you from sin and death, and purify you so that you will be fit for presentation to the Father in glory.

*Look it up – **Psalm 100:5; Jeremiah 31:3; 1 Thessalonians 1:4***

*This truth for me – **Grab hold of all of God's love! List the ways He loves you.***

---

*Pray – **For the love of God to fill you and encourage you in all you do.***

GOD'S HIDDEN PEOPLE

Isaiah 56:7 *Even those I will bring to My holy mountain...*

Scattered throughout the Old Testament is evidence of God having His elect placed in every tongue, tribe and nation. His plan is to cause all those He has chosen to come to Him and be saved. In the midst of this prophetic section of Isaiah, concerning the admonition and restoration of Israel, there is the call to the foreigner and the eunuch to come if they hold fast to God's truth and keep His covenant. Such aliens are included in the true Israel. They are marked by faith and not nationality or ritual.

We do missions because God has His people hidden everywhere. God's people exist in our home towns and neighborhoods and in the ends of the earth. God's means for calling these scattered children is through you and me proclaiming the gospel of the cross. We can't distinguish the elect but we can be assured that they are among the people of the world. God will reveal His people when He gives them the faith to believe the gospel we present. It is such a wonderful plan, and God has given us the privilege of participating in it. Do you see it as a privilege...or do you see it as a job, challenge, or fearful responsibility? Please, see it as a privilege to serve the King and declare His glory in salvation.

*Look it up – **Deuteronomy 10:19; Hebrews 13:2; 3 John 5***

*This truth for me – **Do you have any prejudice or racial bias that keeps you from going to people with the gospel? How can you be more open to ALL people?***

_____

_____

_____

*Pray – **For an open heart to witness to all people everywhere.***

BORN-AGAIN FOR ADVERSITY

Acts 14:22 ...Through many tribulations...

The other evening I came upon a TV evangelist presenting a typical *name it and claim it* prosperity gospel ranting. I was becoming so frustrated at the profane pleas that I had to turn the TV off and pray that such a message would not be attractive to the people tuning in to the show.

There are numerous occasions in Scripture where it is clearly taught that the life of a Christian, when lived for the Lord, will be faced with tribulation, persecution, and even suffering. Jesus promised—YES, He promised—that in this world we will have tribulations. This is not a doom and gloom message but rather the reality of the two cultures: the godly and the worldly, or as Augustine put it, the two cities, *the city of God and the city of man.* God's people live for the city of God yet dwell in the city of man. Living as nomads, we aren't promised rose gardens but rather a battle with a world that hates us because it hated our Savior and His truth. Charles Spurgeon put it this way, *"But although tribulation is thus the path of God's children, they have the comfort of knowing that their Master has traversed it before them. His grace will support them."* The Christian should not be sadistic and relish suffering and trials, but we should look to the reality that we will face trials in this world, yet we also have the promise of our Savior, who declared that He has overcome all our tribulations.

*Look it up – **John 16:33; Romans 8:35; 2 Thessalonians 1:4***

*This truth for me – **Have you ever been persecuted because you were a Christian? List how you might face tribulation for your testimony at work, in school, in your home, etc.***

---

*Pray – **For the courage to be bold and face any persecution that comes your way.***

SOUND DOCTRINE FOR SOUND MINDS

1 Timothy 4:6 *...nourished on the words of the faith and of the sound doctrine...*

The trend in today's Christianity is to downplay the need for teaching sound doctrine. Fortunately the Bible doesn't minimize the importance of sound doctrine and teaching it to the Church. I counted fifteen passages in 1 and 2 Timothy, Titus, Hebrews, 2 John and Revelation where the writers tell us how important sound doctrine is and how devastating false doctrine can be.

What is doctrine? It is *teaching that reveals God, godliness and faith.* It is important because it: expresses the meaning of our faith (Titus 1:9), defines Christianity (John 2:21), defends Christianity (Titus 1:16-2:1), and gives the basis for the propagation of our faith (I Timothy 4:16). John Stott writes, *"...doctrine gives balance to your Christian life (Ephesians 1:15-19), protection from false doctrine (Ephesians 4:13-14), and equips us to reach other minds (1 Peter 1:9-11)."*

There can be pitfalls to the study of doctrine. One can make it a mind exercise only, or gravitate toward speculation, or take a wrong attitude toward differing interpretations. But good teaching of sound doctrine will always produce a mature Christian and one equipped for the battle. Let us not downplay or minimize the importance of teaching doctrine, for this may prove to be our own doom.

*Look it up – **The verses listed above in the devotional.***

*This truth for me – **Are you put off by doctrine and theology, or do you desire to search the Scriptures to learn and live? What must you do to study and learn more about your God?***

---

*Pray – **For a mind that seeks the truth from the Word.***

BE READY TO MEET THE LORD

Matthew 24:42; 25:13 ...be on the alert...

Are you ready? *Ready for what?* Ready for the return of the Lord? Christian doctrine teaches that the return of our Lord Jesus Christ could come at any moment, and will draw all things to a close here on earth. The parables of Matthew 24 and 25 that clearly point out this doctrine of imminent return are filled with warnings regarding the sudden coming of Christ. The greatest warning of all is this, *But when the Son of Man comes in His glory, and all the angels with Him, then He will sit on His glorious throne. And all nations will be gathered before Him...* This will be a solemn time of judgment. To Christian believers, He will grant entrance in the Kingdom that was prepared for them, but those who rejected Him in this life will be cast into the eternal fire.

This is a very real and sobering scene of what will occur when Christ returns. Are you ready for His return? You may be ready because you are a Christian, having been saved by God, but are you ready to meet your Savior as a faithful obedient servant? If you are not saved and still hold to anything but faith alone in the Lord Jesus Christ, you are not ready to meet Him. He is coming, and He is coming at any moment. Be ready. Be a faithful Christian prepared to meet your Lord.

Look it up – **Romans 14:10; 2 Corinthians 5:10; Revelation 1:7**

This truth for me – **Are you ready to meet the Lord? What needs to be made ready in your life?**

_____

_____

_____

Pray – **For a life prepared to meet the Lord.**

GOD GIVES GREAT FAITH

Matthew 15:28 ...*O woman, your faith is great...*

This woman from Canaan, who came to seek out Jesus, demonstrates what Jesus calls *a great faith*. What is the source of such a great faith? Some would say this type of faith is generated by that spark of goodness in each person, a goodness not affected by sin but a remnant of our original nature at creation. But such a view denies the biblical doctrine of total depravity (Ephesians 2:1-5). This doctrine teaches that sin has left all humanity dead in sin. This is both a spiritual and physical death, a death that leaves us without any capability to be holy, and please a holy God. We are not able to have a faith to believe. Faith that seeks after God and calls upon Christ to forgive can only be given by God through grace alone. Saving faith is not born out of our will or our so-called goodness, but rather is granted by God to those He seeks out and saves. *For by grace you have been saved through faith, and that not of yourselves, it is the gift of God* (Ephesians 2:8, 9). Both the grace and the faith are God's gifts. When Christ saw the great faith of this woman, He also saw the great grace of God. Our appeal to the lost is not an appeal to their ability to exercise faith or conjure up some goodness from within to respond to the gospel. We preach Christ and His gospel and look for God to work His work in a dead sinner. He gives the gift of faith to repent and believe upon Christ.

*Look it up – **Matthew 8:5-13; Romans 10:17; 1 Timothy 1:14***

*This truth for me – **Our faith to trust in God is really the faith God gives us, but we can grow in faith. How will you grow in the faith God gives?***

_____

_____

_____

*Pray – **That God would grant you His mercy and grace, and grant great faith to those you witness to, and save His people.***

OH THE GREAT GRACE OF GOD

Romans 5:15 ...*by the transgression of the one the many died...*

What are the overall effects of sin upon the human race? The book of Romans is clear in stating that death is the major effect of sin, a comprehensive death that not only kills the body but also the spirit. It sends the body to the grave and the spirit of a sinner to eternal damnation. The Bible says this is the *imputation* of Adam's sin. But there is something else. Not only was Adam's sin imputed to all mankind, but his sin nature was *transmitted* to each of us. This results in our total bent toward sin. The old Latin adage, *it is not possible not to sin,* is true. No matter how hard we try not to sin, we still sin.

Sin and its effects are powerful, but God's grace is even more powerful. Paul states in Romans 5, ...*much more did the grace of God and the gift by the grace of the one Man, Jesus Christ, abound to the many.* Sin is so powerful and human beings are so plagued by sin that we are helpless to do anything on our own to turn sin's tide. But God—yes, God!—has provided the way to be free from the chains of sin. It is through His Son, Jesus Christ, and what He did on the cross to render sin powerless. Don't let sin master you. Cry out to God, believe upon the Lord Jesus Christ, and let Him take your sin away.

Look it up – **Romans 5:12; 2 Corinthians 5:21; Hebrews 2:18**

This truth for me – **Do you have victory over sin? Christ gives you victory. How will you overcome your sin?**

_____

_____

_____

Pray – **For victory in Christ over whatever sin you might be dealing with.**

HAVING SOMETHING BETTER

Numbers 10:1 *The Lord spoke further to Moses...*

Do you know how many times Moses is mentioned in the Bible? The other day I was searching for a statement made by Moses and began reading through my concordance. The listing for Moses was extensive. What stood out the most was the statement, *...the Lord spoke to Moses.* Text after text revealed the intimacy that Moses had with God. Moses saw God, he spoke with God, and prophesied for God. He was an instrument of judgment, grace and blessing for God, and worshipped God in a closeness that none of us will experience.

Yet there are two things that stand out to me about Moses' relationship with God. The first amazing thing is Moses' sin at Meribah and God forbidding him to enter the Promised Land. This seems incomprehensible. Moses led the people out of Egypt, through the wilderness wanderings for 40 years, yet he was not allowed to enter the Promised Land. The second thing that stands out is even more incomprehensible. Even though Moses had such an intimate relationship with God and is mentioned as one of the faithful in Hebrews 11, it states at the end this chapter, *...God had provided something better for us...* We have the knowledge of God's promise of salvation fulfilled in Jesus Christ. Often Christians think they can't compare to the Moses-types of the Bible. We don't have to compare. We need to rejoice that we have something *better*—the knowledge of Christ and His righteousness completed. ***Praise be to God!***

*Look it up – **Deuteronomy 28:9; Isaiah 61:6; Hebrews 11:39,40***

*This truth for me – **Do you think of yourself as a mediocre Christian? Think on what every Christian has in Christ. List your blessings in Christ.***

_____

_____

_____

*Praise – **God for counting you as worthy as Moses or any other Christian.***

UNSELFISH PRAYING

Mark 10:35 ...we want You to do for us whatever we ask of You.

James and John, the apostles, sounded like some children when they ask their parents for things. *We want you to give us whatever we ask for.* This is selfishness at its core. When we want things on our terms without realizing the cost, it is also very naive. James and John did not realize what they were saying. Christ had just finished telling them that He had to suffer and die in order for God to honor Him by raising Him from the dead. Were James and John ready to face what Jesus was about to face on the cross? No! They only wanted to have seats of honor in heaven without having to pay the price.

How do you pray? I hope it is not like the thoughtlessness of James and John, asking the Father for things without realizing the priorities of petition. First, is what I am asking from the Father in His will? Second, is what I am asking to His glory and not mine? Third, is what I am asking a follow-up to having repented of my sins? And finally, is what I am asking going to produce more of a Christlikeness in me? When we have these priorities in mind, we can boldly come before the Father and ask to our heart's content. Our Father wants His children to come and request of Him the things they need. May we not be a presumptuous people, but rather a humble people who run to our Father with our requests.

Look it up – Psalm 10:17; Colossians 4:2; Revelation 5:8

This truth for me – Think about your prayer style and what, if anything, needs to be changed in order for your prayers to be more selfless and bring glory to God.

_____

_____

_____

Pray – For the Holy Spirit to guide you in your prayers.

PREACHING IS THE POURING OUT OF GOD'S GRACE

1 Corinthians 1:21 ...God was well-pleased through the foolishness of the message preached...

In this declaration by the Apostle Paul there is a contrast, *foolishness compared to wisdom.* The essence of the contrast is obvious when you look more closely at this passage of Scripture. The Greeks, to whom Paul was writing, held wisdom above all else. Their political power had been stripped by the Roman conquest, yet they had their wisdom with which the Romans could not compare. Now, the Apostle Paul comes along and says that it is the preaching of the crucifixion of Christ that brings true wisdom.

Why is preaching so important? Preaching is that means whereby we receive divine wisdom. It is God's means of converting the sinner to Christ and the means by which the saved are sanctified into the image of Christ.

Then why is preaching so neglected and watered down in today's church? I will offer one main reason. ***The church has placed man in front of God and no longer believes that the foolishness of preaching alone is effectual to meet the needs of man and the church.*** Are you as excited about hearing and valuing the preaching of the Word? *Preaching is God's pitcher of grace. Be a servant of the preached Word.*

Look it up – 1 Corinthians 9:16; 2 Timothy 4:2; 1 Peter 4:6

This truth for me – Are you bored or excited about the preaching of the Word? List some of the most memorable messages you heard preached.

_____

_____

_____

Pray – For God to stir in you a refreshed excitement about preaching.

HOLY AND CLEAN

Isaiah 1:18 ...Though your sins are as scarlet, They will be as white as snow...

We are unable to see the blackness of our sin silhouetted against the holiness of God. Yet sinners believe they can cleanse themselves so that they are acceptable to a holy God. The *moralist* thinks if he maintains a life free from impure acts and thoughts, he will find acceptance by whatever he calls god. The *do-gooder* is convinced that if he does enough benevolent deeds, he will surely find peace at the end of life. The *religious adherent* feels assured he will find favor and enter eternal bliss.

No matter what labels are placed on our attempts at being pleasing to a holy God, they boil down to *humanity trying to be holy by means of their own works.* But by ourselves, we can do nothing that will please a perfect, holy and pure God. No matter how good we think we are, we fall far short of God's demands for perfection. The late Dr. Donald Barnhouse illustrated this truth. *"No matter how brilliant the whitest linen shirt may seem to be, when you lay it down on a fresh layer of new fallen snow it pales a hew of yellow against the snow."* We may think that our morality and religious works will cleanse us from sin, but the reality remains—only God can make us whiter than snow. He does this through the work of Jesus. He is the only one that can purify us and make us acceptable to God. Sinner, you need Jesus. Run to Him, repent and ask Him to cleanse you. Christian, is there an area of sin in your life that needs cleansing? Run to Jesus, repent and cry out for His cleansing.

Look it up – Psalm 51:7; Titus 1:15; Revelation 7:14

This truth for me – God can make us whiter than snow. Thank Him for His cleansing work in your life.

Pray – For a holy and clean life.

A MAN'S DUTY

Genesis 4:26 ...Then men began to call upon the name of the Lord.

Men called upon the name of the Lord. With the birth of Seth, the godly line was established. God was not going to allow His covenant to be extinguished by the murderous act of Cain. God would not have men like Lamech—also a murderer—keep Him from fulfilling His promise to establish a godly line. Eventually this godly line would produce the Savior, Jesus Christ. God will always keep a remnant that will *call upon the name of the Lord.*

In a world given over to sin and death, the church is today's remnant who are to call upon the name of the Lord. *Men* are the micro-remnant that must call upon the name of the Lord. God looks to men and fathers to lead their communities and homes in calling upon the name of the Lord. You may not be a loud voice in your community, but each person that you reach with the gospel becomes another voice calling upon the name of the Lord. Each member of our family that we influence with the gospel and lead to salvation joins the choir of those calling upon the name of the Lord. Look at your home, your community, your work place, and see the need for Christ. Present the gospel and pray ...*Then men will begin calling upon the name of the Lord.*

Look it up – **Psalm 116:1,2; Luke 3:38; Romans 10:13**

This truth for me – **If you are a man, evaluate how close you are to the Lord. When is the last time you called upon the Lord to pray and praise Him? Women need to pray for men to call upon the name of the Lord.**

_____

_____

_____

Pray – **For men to call upon the name of the Lord for salvation, guidance and leadership ability.**

DELIGHT YOURSELF IN THE COMING MESSENGER

Malachi 3:1 *...and the messenger of the covenant, in whom you delight, behold, He is coming...*

This is one of the most wonderful prophetic passages of the Bible. Through the prophet Malachi, God declares that His *messenger* is coming. This messenger is coming as a refining fire who will finally and eternally bring purity and holiness to His people. The New Testament unveils for us the messenger and His charge. We see this messenger in the One who comes to His people and confronts their unrighteousness, the One who goes toe-to-toe with the priests of Israel and challenges them in all their hypocritical religious activity. Yes, the One and only One, Jesus Christ, is God's messenger who comes in the name of justice and righteousness. He is coming again to refine and bring an end to the evil and false religion of the world. What great comfort and assurance it is to know that God's messenger of holiness and justice is coming and will deal with the injustice of the world.

Don't worry about what you may perceive as unbridled evil in our days. Justice will come ultimately and eternally. Jesus Christ the appointed Judge will be victorious, and all evil, injustice and religious heresy will be judged by Him who reigns forever and ever. *Who can endure the day of His coming? And who can stand when He appears?* The answer to this is: those who have been cleansed and refined by the mercy of God and have been born-again by His grace. *Delight yourself in the Lord, for He has given salvation to His people through the Lord Jesus Christ!*

Look it up – **Joel 3:16-18; 1 Thessalonians 4:16; Titus 2:13**

This truth for me - **How does today's evil affect you? List the ways that the Lord's coming brings comfort to you.**

_____

_____

_____

Pray – **For the Lord to come quickly and bring His peace.**

UNITED IN PURPOSE

Judges 5:2 ...That the people volunteered, Bless the Lord!

I am so encouraged when I read, and even try to sing, the *Song of Deborah and Barak.* Uniting together to achieve a task for God's glory is very encouraging and something to sing about. It is difficult to unite the church today for action. In one sense, we are and will remain united in Christ. That union will never diminish or fade. But I am addressing the church uniting in purpose. Our purpose is to worship God, preach the gospel to all nations through evangelistic church planting, and build up the saints to do ministry and be prepared for His coming. Christians are busy in their allegiances and responsibilities. Too many children of God do not take time to study God through His Word or evangelize their families, not to mention their neighborhoods and America as a whole. The answer to the dilemma of uniting the church is a difficult one. It may take powerful leaders in our churches and denominations, like Deborah who called upon God's people and got results. It may take a national struggle or persecution to awaken the church to unite and focus on the priorities of what the church is to be and do. We do know this: it will take God, *...behold the Lord has gone out before you.* Deborah knew that God would have to go out before the Israelites in order for victory to be achieved. We should also know that the Lord must go before us if we want to be a strong church in word and deed. *"Lead on, O King eternal..."*

*Look it up – **Psalm 133:1; Ephesians 4:3-13; Philippians 1:27***

*This truth for me – **Have you joined your church and its efforts to proclaim the gospel, fight injustice and do mercy? How can you unite with the church and join hands in service with other Christians?***

_____

_____

_____

*Pray – **For unity of purpose in the church.***

ONLY ONE TO PLEASE

1 John 3:2 ...we shall see Him just as He is.

Who are you trying to please? In life we run across people who want to make us please them, or we assume that we must please others because of their position or relationship to us. This can be awfully frustrating, especially when the ones we are trying to please can never be pleased. They always want more. The fact is this: *the only One who demands our attention, wants us to please Him, and is the One that we should seek to please is God.* We should do well in our employment and please our boss, and we need to work hard at our studies and thus please our teachers. When we respect and obey our parents, they are pleased. However, when we first seek to be pleasing to God, generally we will be pleasing to others, and if not, we will have peace in knowing that the One we must ultimately face is pleased.

But, there is a dilemma here because on our own we cannot please God. He can only be pleased through His Son Jesus Christ. If I am not saved, I am not pleasing to God. Only by repenting of my sin and believing in the Lord Jesus Christ will God be pleased with me. And Christian, you are pleasing to God *because Christ saved you*, so when God looks at you, He sees you in His most pleasing treasure—His Son, the Lord Jesus Christ. Trust in Christ's pleasing grace.

*Look it up – **Galatians 1:10; Colossians 1:9,10; Hebrews 13:16***

*This truth for me – **Are you still trying to please God in your own strength? List anything that is displeasing to God in your life and how you need God to help you.***

---

*Pray – **For the Holy Spirit to reveal to you, through His word, how God, in Christ, has made you pleasing to Him.***

CALLED WITH A VISION

Nehemiah 2:12 ...*what my God was putting into my mind...*

Nehemiah was one man used mightily by God, and one man that had an impact on the lives of his people and God's eternal plan. Most of all he was God's chosen leader with a vision. When God calls a person to ministry, He also gives them His vision and plan for ministry. The Lord Jesus called His disciples to follow Him. He gave them the vision for being fishers of men, and a charge to go and extend the Kingdom. When God calls men to be church planters and pastors, He puts in their hearts a vision for their pastoral or planting ministry. A person may be asked to assist in a Vacation Bible School or Sunday School class, and it will be God who places in their minds a vision for what He wants them to accomplish in these areas of ministry.

Is God calling you to ministry? Whether it is to be a pastor or church planter, part of the choir or the Sunday School, God will give you a vision for what He wants you to accomplish. Nehemiah was able to follow the plan and the vision God gave to him, and he influenced many lives for revival and righteousness. Your life can also influence lives with the gospel and help build the Kingdom of God. No matter where the Lord is calling you to minister, He will give you His vision for how to glorify Him in whatever you do.

*Look it up – **Isaiah 48:14; Acts 13:2; 1 Corinthians 7:17***

*This truth for me – **What has God called you to do for Him? Write out your calling and your vision for this calling.***

_____

_____

_____

*Pray – **For clarity of your calling and the vision that accompanies it.***

A FACE SHINING IN PRAYER

Luke 9:29 ...His face became different...

How is your prayer life? Would you describe it as routine, redundant, lackluster, stoic, or just not what it should be? When Jesus prayed on the mountain, *His face became different.* In Matthew's account of this scene, Matthew says that His face *shone like the sun.* There are times when our prayers need to bring tears of remorse to our countenance and other times when our faces need to be wrinkled with concentration and focus on things of deep concern. But our prayers always need to be entered into with faces glowing in anticipation of meeting our God and having intimate communion with Him in prayer. What may be routine and mundane needs to be brightened up with the reality of being able to enter into the great throne room of God and speak personally with the Ruler of the entire universe. Even saying this makes chills go up my back that I, a wretched sinner, was elected to commune personally with God in the name of His Son and in the power of His Spirit. WOW! Break out of the cell of a rote prayer life and into the brilliance of communion with God. May our faces shine like the sun when we speak to our God and hear Him bring His will to our minds and hearts. Now, go and pray like the Son with a face shining full of grace.

*Look it up – **Matthew 6:5,6; John 4:24; Romans 8:26***

*This truth for me – **Evaluate your prayer life. What will help you see that when praying, we are having intimate communion with GOD?***

_____

_____

_____

*Pray – **Now with the understanding you are meeting with the God of the universe.***

THE FRONT RUNNERS AT THE GATES OF HEAVEN

Hebrews 13:15 *Through Him then...*

Jesus reminds us that we can do nothing without Him. Everything we accomplish for eternity's sake is not through us but through Him. We might accomplish things through our own energies, intelligence and wit, but the things that will make a mark on eternity will be those things done through Him. In our fleshly nature, we like to praise ourselves and think highly of what we can do. Many today place great accolades on people and what they accomplish, even in Christianity. In Christian circles there is too much praise given to people and things other than the Lord. All glory and honor are to be given to Him. His children only accomplish what they do by virtue of His mercy and grace, and many times that mercy and grace is not even seen in the public's eye.

I had the privilege of pastoring an elderly brother and sister (blood brother and sister who never married) and had the pleasure of watching their simple lives. They touched so many people in a very quiet and unassuming manner. I would often find out that the two of them were there to help people and give of their time and resources long before the need was even made known. The front runners at the gates of heaven will be those who knew it was *through Him* that their efforts and accomplishments were empowered.

*Look it up – **Nehemiah 1:10; Matthew 20:28; Hebrews 9:14***

*This truth for me – **What are the qualities of a quiet, behind-the-scenes, service to God?***

_____

_____

_____

*Pray – **For eyes to see where you can serve and bring God His greatest glory.***

PREACHING THAT LIGHTS UP WITH GOD'S GLORY

Isaiah 52:7 ...Your God reigns!

In his book, <u>The Supremacy of God in Preaching</u>, John Piper quotes the Puritan Cotton Mather, *"His great design and intention of the office of the Christian preacher is to restore the throne and dominion of God in the souls of men."* Mather used Romans 10:14-15 as the justification for such a statement. In brief, the job of the preacher is to direct his hearer's thoughts to God. But even more, he is to direct their thoughts to the fact that God reigns over all and in all. The preacher is to bring his flock to understand the greatness of God. The preacher does not point to his own greatness, or the greatness of a program, or the greatness of this world.

In the passage above from Isaiah, the one coming over the mountainside to herald the good news to the captives in Babylon brought news of salvation. It was God who had delivered them from captivity. *Your God reigns!* The next time you get up from hearing a sermon, ask yourself the questions: *Do I see more of God, more of His glory, more of His supremacy, more of His love and justice? Can I rejoice that my God reigns?* We so often want to walk away from a message with a good mushy feeling or a "how-to" punch list for our troubles. May the *throne of God and His dominion* be set in your minds while you hear the Word of God preached.

Look it up – **Romans 1:15, 16; 1 Corinthians 1:17-25; Ephesians 3:7-9**

This truth for me – **How do you prepare your heart and mind for the preaching of the word? List ways that will help you focus while hearing the preaching of the word.**

_____

_____

_____

Pray – **That God will give you a glimpse of His glory as you hear the word preached.**

GOD IS WAITING TO SAVE

2 Peter 3:9 ...*not wishing for any to perish...*

What holds the world back from self-destruction? God is long-suffering and is *not willing that any should perish, but for all to come to repentance.* Before going on to answer the proposed question, one quick comment on this passage. *Any* and *all* do not refer to every person in the world, but rather to all those whom God has elected to salvation. God has chosen to save an elect people and that He will save them, *not wishing for any (of the elect) to perish.*

John Gerstner, in a great sermon on *Man the Sinner,* explains the preservatives that God placed in the world which hold back final destruction. First, there is the example of *Sodom.* It is not that God is waiting for man to become righteous on his own or that man has some sort of innate righteousness. If that were the case, surely there would have been some righteous people found in the city of Sodom. God's waiting was all due to *His* mercy and grace. Second, Christians are the *salt* of the earth. God delays because Christians are still in the world and they act as salt or preservatives to a dark world. Third, there are the *sovereigns (leaders)* that God has established in the world to rule and keep law and order. We are told in Scripture that kings, presidents and legislative bodies are established by God to keep peace. Lastly, 2 Peter tells us that God is carrying out His decree to save all His elect. At times we may want to see an end to this world and our eternal heaven become a reality. But as we wait, rejoice in what God is doing to preserve His world and call all those whom He has decreed to save.

Look it up – **Psalm 145:17; Ezekiel 33:1; Matthew 7:13, 14**

This truth for me – **Praise God that He is longsuffering and will save all His chosen ones.**

_____

_____

_____

Pray – **For the unsaved that you know to come to Christ while there is time.**

BRING A HOLY SPIRIT REVIVAL

Acts 10:45 ...*the gift of the Holy Spirit had been poured out...*

Some time ago it was reported that 9/11 had no real effect in terms of a spiritual revival for the U.S. CBS radio reported that at first people flocked to their places of worship, but after three months, attendance was back to where it had been before 9/11. Some Christian commentators said that we missed a real revival opportunity with 9/11. CBS used the theme, *The Day That Changed America*. Yes, we changed in the way we think about the future and we changed our security systems. These and other sociological changes were made, yet real and lasting spiritual revival has not taken place. Should we have expected revival to break out because of 9/11? Did we really miss a grand opportunity?

Revival does not necessarily take place on the wings of disaster. A disaster may be an attention getter, but real revival is grounded in the Holy Spirit being poured out by God through the preaching of the word. In the book, Jonathan Edwards on Revival, William Cooper writes, "*In such a time (revival time), when the Spirit shall be poured forth plentifully, surely ministers shall have their proportionate share. And when such a time as that shall come, I believe you will hear much other kinds of sermons that you are wont to do now-a-days; souls will surely be dealt with at another rate.*" The events of 9/11 did not usher in a spiritual revival and you might ask, ...*if that didn't do it, what will?* It will take an outpouring of the Holy Spirit and ministers of the gospel who take the time to study the word and preach *much other kinds of sermons.*

*Look it up – **Psalm 85:6; Isaiah 57:15; John 16:8-11***

*This truth for me – **Some have said "revival begins with me." What needs revival in your life?***

_____

_____

_____

*Pray – **That God will bring revival to the hearts and minds of individuals.***

LIFT HIM HIGH

Colossians 2:9 For in Him all the fullness of Deity dwells...

I once sent a letter to the editor of our local newspaper. The paper had been covering the Jehovah Witness convention being held in our area. The reporters kept labeling the Witnesses as Christians. It finally got to me and I had to write. I tried to be gracious, but it is hard to be gracious when a cult and its teachings are decrying the deity of our Lord and Savior. I pointed out that the reporter would not call people *Buddhists* or *Muslims* if they denied the teachings of Buddha or Mohammad. So then, why call Jehovah Witnesses *Christians* when they deny the teachings of Christ and the Scriptures? To my amazement they published the letter. What was more amazing was that I only received one letter condemning my so-called intolerance and one letter was printed in the paper to rebuke me. The real issue was, is what I said true? Indeed it was! I made it very clear that the Bible and Christ Himself declare that Jesus is God, divine and Lord of all.

As I think about the times I overlook the opportunity to witness or to take the time to care for a person in need, I am convicted and filled with a fear of having to stand on judgment day and face my Lord for my neglect. How awful it would be if I had to face the Lord having ignored the times His name and person was brought low. May we take the time to lift up Jesus as God and Lord of all.

Look it up – **John 1:1-2; Philippians 2:6; Colossians 1:17**

This truth for me – **How often have you failed to stand up for Christ? What will help you defend the deity of Christ?**

_____

_____

_____

Pray – **That the Holy Spirit will give you the courage to lift high the name of Jesus.**

THE PEACE THAT GOES BEYOND

Psalm 85:10 ...Righteousness and peace have kissed...

What a beautiful way of telling us about the effect of God's glory in the lives of His people and their affairs on earth. When God reigns in the hearts of His people and their lives show forth a testimony of His grace, there is the hope of peace. We all face misfortunes and setbacks. The psalmist refers in this Psalm to hard times in the nation of Israel. His counsel for such hard times is to look to God and seek His salvation, to put one's trust in God and fear (reverence) Him, not turning again to our own foolish ways. The result of such a repentant attitude is experiencing God's peace, even in spite of the most difficult of circumstances. Living for God and trusting Him to do what is right results in peace. This promise gives hope to those caught in the tempest of life's tragedies. The key to divine peace is to turn to God and leave the former ways of sin. Whether it is a terrorist attack or a hurricane, God is the answer! Turning from our own way to God's way of salvation is the balm needed for many who suffer and are in need of release from their burdens.

*Look it up – **Judges 6:24; Romans 5:1; Ephesians 2:14***

*This truth for me – **Describe peace. In what way do you need God's peace today?***

_____

_____

_____

*Pray – **That the God of peace will bring you His blessings of peace and comfort.***

OH, TO BE LIKE HIM!

2 Corinthians 3:18 ...transformed into the same image...

When God saves a sinner He has two supreme purposes in committing such a gracious work. First, He desires to be glorified for the mercy that He demonstrates in saving such helpless and hopeless people. Were it not for God intervening in our lives and saving us in Christ, we would be futile in our own human efforts to please a holy God. Therefore, God ultimately saves us in order to receive His due glory and honor. Second, God saves us for the purpose of glorifying His Son, Jesus Christ, and recreating the sinner into the image of Christ. I often think that God saves us in order to have a special band of little Jesus's with Him forever. The Apostle Paul writes to the Romans in chapter eight and states that God will glorify those whom He saves and conform them into the image of Christ so that they will be like Christ (Romans 8:28-30).

Another idea concerning imagery is the idea that if Christians are to be holy image bearers of God, then we must act as such. All people, saved and unsaved, bear the image of God. But when God saves you and me, sinners, and gives us Jesus, we also bear the holiness of God to the world around us. Before we were saved we had a marred image and gave a false representation of God. But once saved, we can now give a true representation of a Holy God as we live out His holiness in us. There is no greater position to be in than in the righteousness of Christ. May your image bear the holiness of God to an unholy world!

*Look it up – **Genesis 1:26-27; 1 Corinthians 11:7; James 3:9***

*This truth for me – **List the ways you can be seen as the image of God.***

---

*Praise – **God for making you in His image and then recreating you in His Son's image.***

GOING BEYOND THE BIBLE

1 Peter 4:11 *...as one speaking the very words of God...* (NIV)

In this present age there are numerous so-called Christian leaders—new prophets or leaders of a new movement or church—saying they have received new revelation from God. Some preachers gravitate to this form of manipulation and tell their listeners that God gave them a special *word*. Those who have this kind of thinking have no fear regarding the sacred and holy Scriptures. They are willing to put Scripture beneath their own revelations. This departure from the Word remains a cavernous heresy in the Roman Catholic Church. Michael Horton writes, *"At the time of the Reformation John Calvin asked: since not even the Apostles were free to roam beyond Scripture, why should popes, councils and bishops have the right to do it? Even Peter, supposedly the first pope, claimed nothing for himself or others except the duty of imparting the doctrines that had been handed down by God (in the Bible)."*

Be careful, Christian, to whom you listen and what you are hearing. Only those who preach and teach the Bible, its truths and doctrines, are worthy of our ears. Don't be dazzled by all the song and dance that presents itself as Christian, no matter how humble or impressive the presentation. Only God's Word, that was given to the writers of the sacred text we know as the Bible, are the words of life.

*Look it up – **Isaiah 55:10-11; 2 Timothy 3:16; 2 Peter 1:21***

*This truth for me – **Do you ever put your own thoughts and wisdom above the Bible? When you have done this, where has it led you?***

---

*Pray – **That the Holy Spirit will always give you a high regard for the Bible and the ability to be discerning about those who put their wisdom above the Word.***

INCOMPREHENSIBLE MERCY & GRACE

James 2:13 ...mercy triumphs over judgment.

Grace is that divine love given to free the guilty sinner. Mercy is that divine love given to lift the helpless and needy. Both grace and mercy are ultimately exemplified in the person and acts of the Father through His Son, Jesus Christ. In the aftermath of hurricanes and disasters, we normally are inundated with reports of acts of mercy and how the helpless are being assisted in their needy situations. Man's mercy is to be admired and commended but never compared to the mercy of God.

Augustine in his <u>Confessions</u> writes, *"I call, O God, my mercy, who made me and did not forget me when I forgot you..."* God's mercy toward His children is incomparable and incomprehensible. God loves us and extended His mercy to us to the degree of sending His Son, Jesus Christ, to suffer and die while we were yet sinners. God was pleased to crush His Son and see Him bruised and pierced for the sake of sinners who turn from Him. What mercy can compare to the Lord's mercy? What compassion can compare to God's compassion? What acts of mercy can compare to the cross? ***...for His mercies are great...***

Look it up – **Matthew 20:29-34; John 1:14-17; Ephesians 2:4,5**

This truth for me – **What acts of mercy are you showing toward others?**

_____

_____

_____

Pray – **For the mercy and grace of God to motivate you as you serve and live for Him.**

BEING IN CHRIST

Romans 8:1 ...those who are in Christ Jesus.

There is no more wonderful a position to find oneself in than *in Christ*. We are placed *in His blood*. Our sins are covered by the precious blood of Christ and we are now white as snow. Our guilty life is now justified *in His righteousness* and we will one day be found faultless before the throne of God. Our hopeless future is now brightened with a marvelous hope of eternal life because we are *in His glorious resurrection*. Our enmity and separation from God have been reconciled because we are *in His peace*. Our fears in life and fear of death are no longer daunting because we are *in His victory over death*. Our selfishness and pride no longer motivate us to trust in our own weak powers because we are now *in His omnipotent power*. Our lack of wisdom that kept us groping for the right way can be overcome because we are *in His omniscient wisdom*. Our despair and depression can shackle us no more because we are *in His omnipresent care and love*.

It is no wonder that we rejoice in the apostle's declarations, *...There is therefore now no condemnation...who will bring a charge against God's elect...who shall separate us...from the love of God which is in Christ Jesus our Lord.*

Look it up – **Romans 15:17; 2 Corinthians 2:14; Galatians 3:27**

This truth for me – **Think and meditate on what it means to be in full relationship with Christ and list some benefits.**

_____

_____

_____

Pray – **That you will sense what it means to be in Christ.**

SIN NO MORE

Romans 6:1 ...Are we to continue in sin...

In one of the Apostle Paul's letters to the church at Rome, he begins a section by dealing with sin and the Christian's relationship to sin. There were those in Rome who thought that because God's grace saved them from sin and grace was a good thing to receive from God, they should sin more so they could acquire more grace from God. On the surface this belief sounds ridiculous, but to the philosophical mind of Paul's day, it was logical. Paul's answer is simple and direct, *May it never be!* Sin can never be considered a means for the Christian to receive God's grace and mature as a child of God. Sin, in all its forms, is an affront to God and results in negative ramifications for the believer who sins. It is obvious from Paul's writing that sin is a regular part of the believer's life. But we are exhorted to deal with sin and not allow it to master us and become habitual in our lives.

Several things to consider: first, *evil lies close at hand.* Christians must realize that the temptation to sin is always very near. Second, *even though we sin, sinning is not to become regular or a habit in our lives.* We are not to let sin reign in our lives; it can be mastered and overcome, even eradicated. Third, *we must rely upon the Holy Spirit's power through the Word* to be our weapon against sin. Only divine power through prayer and the reading and application of God's Word will defeat sin. Lastly, *we must realize that the battle against sin is continual throughout this life.* Our ultimate freedom from sin will come when we enter glory. We have a blessed hope in Christ that one day we will sin no more, and even though we sin now, we can overcome in Christ.

*Look it up – **Mark 2:10; Colossians 3:1-3; Hebrews 4:15***

*This truth for me – **What sin needs to be dealt with in your life today? Do so!***

_____

_____

_____

*Pray – **For the Spirit to empower you to fight off sin.***

FIRST THINGS FIRST

Jeremiah 49:9 If grape gatherers came to you, Would they not leave gleanings...

I have never come across the gleanings of grape gatherers, but I have discovered real gems in the gleanings of old books I purchased at yard sales or book store sell-outs. I page through these old books and find the handwritten notes of former owners. There is a wonderful richness in what the past generations reflected upon as they studied these rare and well written books.

One such book is The Small Catechism of Martin Luther, (© 1907), in which I found two pages of written thoughts at the end of the book. The owner of the book titled his or her notes, *"The Christian's Rules."* There then followed a list of six things that were gleaned from Luther's Catechism: *Believe in Christ as the Redeemer, Pray every day, Read the Bible every day, Attend Church and Sunday School regularly, My duty to my Church (lead an honorable life for her, pray for her, give her support, attend her services, defend her), Live the Christian life." (A list of Bible references followed to reinforce the duties to the Church and to study for Christian living.)* On the surface there seemed to be nothing in this scribbling that couldn't compare to today's generation of Christians who jot down important things in the books they read. But a closer look showed that this writer produced a most important list: First God, then His word, communion with Him, and His church; then finally, a list of personal needs. In a needs-driven Christendom, it was good to come across these gleanings that put first things first.

*Look it up – **Deuteronomy 6:13; Daniel 6:10; Luke 4:8***

*This truth for me – **Is God first in your life? If not, what are the obstacles?***

---

*Pray – **For help to remove the obstacles that keep God off the throne in your life.***

BOWING LOW TO LIFT HIM HIGH

Mark 12:30 And you shall love the Lord your God with all your heart...

Where does this type of love for God begin? It begins with our theology, what we believe about God and how He saved us. **If we believe:**

— that we have some spark of goodness left in us as a fallen and depraved sinner and are able to reach God with our own energy, **then we do not love God with all our heart.**

— that we accomplish some sort of good or possess a degree of religion that God has to honor in order to elect us unto salvation, **then we do not love God with all our heart.**

— that the blood of Christ is a universal balm for all to be saved if they willed, and is made effectual by one's submission on their own to Christ, **then we do not love God with all our heart.**

— that there is a self-will to resist Christ over and over and we can finally decide on our own that it is time to ask for forgiveness and be saved, **then we do not love God with all our heart.**

— that we can lose our salvation and fall back into a state of condemnation, needing salvation all over gain, **then we do not love God with all our heart.**

To love God with all my heart, soul and mind, I must hold Him up as the Sovereign King of all and believe that it was His grace alone that elected me, saved me and keeps me. *When I bow to my lowest, then I lift God to His highest!*

*Look it up – **Deuteronomy 6:5; Joshua 22:5; Mark 12:28-34***

*This truth for me – **Self always gets in the way of loving God wholeheartedly. How do you fight off self?***

_____

_____

_____

*Pray – **For God to give you victory over selfishness.***

SOUND AND SECURE

1 John 5:13 ...*that you may know that you have eternal life.*

One of the most comforting doctrines of our Christian faith is the doctrine of eternal security or what is also referred to as *perseverance of the saints*. In short, this doctrine declares that when God saves sinners, He saves them for eternity and gives them the perseverance to endure till the end. Eternal salvation reveals the greatness of God's salvation and the grace extended to the sinner through the work of Christ on the cross. *This doctrine should never be taken lightly.* To be saved for eternity is a gift that demands our thankfulness and obedience. *This doctrine should be proclaimed from our pulpits.* It is a great doctrine to preach and to hear preached. It warms our souls to know that nothing can separate us from the love of God in Christ. *This doctrine should never be compromised.* There are those who say this doctrine is not important. Many Christians say they believe this truth and yet attend churches that hold to Arminian doctrines that deny this beautiful decree of eternal salvation, along with the other sovereign doctrines of grace. What does it do to the atoning blood of Christ when we say that we can lose our salvation if we don't maintain our sanctification? *This doctrine is founded in the work of our Savior.* Christ's death provided not 50% of salvation but rather *eternal* salvation. God saves and saves eternally!

> **"Happy am I! Jesus is mine forever, never to leave...leading me on in a life ending never..."**

Look it up – **Romans 8:1-32; Ephesians 4:30; Jude 24**

This truth for me – **Do you ever doubt your salvation? List what makes you feel secure as a Christian.**

_____

_____

_____

Pray – **For the Holy Spirit to give you His blessing of peace and security.**

WHEN PEACE LIKE A RIVER...

Romans 5:1 ...we have peace with God...

As a follow-up to our focus in yesterday's devotional on *the perseverance of the saints*, I want to mention another reward of being saved for eternity. It is eternal peace with God. His work of justifying us, declaring us not guilty, is based upon the finished work of Christ on the cross and the imputation of Christ's righteousness. This brings a great peace to the heart of the once guilty and condemned sinner. We no longer need to look over our shoulder to see when God's eternal judgment will fall. **Once saved, always peace.** God's wrath against us was satisfied by His divine Servant's sacrifice, and we are the full recipients of Christ's atonement. The tense in this passage—*having been*—is another indicator that this work of justification by faith is completed and will never again need to be applied to the forgiven sinner. When the Righteous Judge declares the sinner free from guilt, he is free indeed. Praise the Lord! May your days be filled with the peace of knowing that you are set free in Christ and guilty no more.

*Look it up – **Judges 6:24; Psalm 29:11; Philippians 4:7***

*This truth for me – **List what things cause you discomfort and then think on God's peace in Christ.***

_____

_____

_____

*Pray – **That the Lord's peace will pass from you to others around you.***

FROM TRAUMA TO TRIUMPH

Luke 22:17 And when He had taken a cup and given thanks...

The cup Christ held on the night he was betrayed and handed over to the Jews and Romans for execution was representative of the bloody suffering and death He would face the next morning. How could He be thankful when He knew something horrible was about to happen to Him? In our human estimation, how can we understand that this elicited thanks? It is only when we know that what is about to happen is good.

Christ was thankful because nothing could compare to the blessings that would follow the most heinous of acts against Him—his crucifixion. Hebrews 12:2 states that Jesus endured the cross because of the joy set before Him. That joy was seeing those who would be the benefactors of His sacrifice. As He hung on the cross, He saw the work of His death saving the elect for eternity. He endured such brutality because of what His death would mean to His Father and to us. His suffering and death meant satisfaction for a holy God and salvation to wretched sinners. Yes, we too can be thankful for the testing that we face, because in that we find grace and hope, just as Christ had found on the bloody cross of Calvary.

Look it up – **Psalm 68:18; 2 Corinthians 2:14; Hebrews 12:2**

This truth for me – **What triumphs have you experienced after some hard times?**

_____

_____

_____

Pray – **For God to shine His grace through your struggles.**

THE GRACE THAT WE KNOW

2 Corinthians 8:9 For you know the grace of our Lord Jesus Christ...

Do you know His grace? The Apostle Paul is assuming that not only the Corinthians know the grace of Christ, but everyone who has been born-again knows this grace. It is *a grace that is unmerited.* No human being ever deserves such grace, nor will ever deserve the grace of God. God's grace is a gift to undeserving sinners. It is *a grace that supplied everything needed with regard to our eternal salvation.* There are no gaps or shortages when it comes to the salvation that comes by grace through faith. It saves, seals, empowers, and will bring us home to glory. It is *a grace that is of great comfort.* When God exercised His grace, based upon the finished work of Jesus Christ on the cross, He gave us peace and hope in knowing we are no longer condemned. It is *a grace that cost the Savior.* Paul, in exhorting the Corinthians to give of their resources to help the suffering saints in Jerusalem, used the incarnation to make his case: Christ became poor so that we would be rich, ...*though He was rich, yet for your sake He became poor.*

As Paul Harvey would say, *"now you know the rest of the story."* As a Christian you *know* this grace...now *live* in keeping with such a grace. If you are not born-again, then repent and cry out to God for forgiveness of your sins and ask for this grace to be given to you.

*Look it up – **Ephesians 2:8; 2 Corinthians 9:8; 1 Peter 4:10***

*This truth for me – **Write out how thankful you are for the grace God extended to you in Jesus.***

---

*Pray – **That you will always be humbled by His great sacrifice for you.***

THE CLEANSING BLOOD OF CHRIST

Genesis 3:21 And the Lord God made garments of skin...

It must have been a horrifying experience for Adam and Eve to witness the death of the innocent animal whose skins God used to cover them. Like Adam and Eve, many people fail to realize how devastating sin and its resulting death are. While looking at the lifeless animal, Adam and Eve had to be thinking, *Oh no, this is what sin and death is all about!*

Several observations are important to mention: *God demanded a substitute and it was God who had to provide the sacrifice.* We can't overcome sin and death on our own; only God can do that for us through the perfect substitute, Jesus Christ. He died in our place. *The substitute had to be sinless.* The animal was innocent of sin just like Christ, our sinless sacrifice. *The sacrifice revealed God's mercy.* God would have been just in taking the lives of Adam and Eve, but instead demonstrated His love for them by showing mercy. God demonstrates the same mercy and love for His elect in that, *...while we were yet sinners Christ died for us.* The beautiful baby in the manger would one day hang before the world as God's bloody sacrifice so that sinners would be covered by His innocent blood and find forgiveness and reconciliation with God.

> *...Why lies He in such mean estate, Where ox and ass are feeding?*
> *Good Christian, fear, for sinners here The silent Word is pleading.*
> *Nails, spear shall pierce Him through, The cross be borne for me, for you.*
> *Hail, hail the Word made flesh...*

Look it up – **Psalm 51:10; Hebrews 9:14; 1 John 5:6**

This truth for me – **Christ sacrificed all for you. What do you need to sacrifice for Him?**

_____

_____

_____

Praise – **God for sending His Son as our sacrifice for sin.**

A HUMILITY DRIVEN BY LOVE

Philippians 2:6 ...a thing to be grasped.

Have you ever been told to do something you did not want to do, so you argued and fought about the assignment? I think that we all have found ourselves in this tension. We could keep on fighting or give up and do the assignment. In the case of the incarnation, we are told that Jesus *did not count equality with God a thing to be grasped*, literally, *a thing to fight about*. He willingly and obediently emptied Himself of His divine position and put Himself in the bonds of humanity, all this so that we might be saved from sin and death, and have life eternal. There is no greater example of humility than the incarnation of God.

In the beginning of the Apostle Paul's letter to the church in Philippi, he wants to exhort the Philippians to have a selfless and humble mindset, a mind that will direct their lives and actions. To illustrate this and emphasize the point, Paul explains the incarnation of Christ—He willingly left His heavenly throne, without argument, and became the perfect sacrifice for our sins.

What about you and me? Is there something that we know we should do, yet we argue and stubbornly hold onto our position, saying, *I have the right to feel, or act, or believe like this?* If anyone had the right to hold onto His position, it was Jesus Christ. But He gave Himself up and put aside His position as the obedient Son to go to the cross.

*Look it up – **Matthew 11:29; Luke 22:15; 1 Thessalonians 2:7***

*This truth for me – **Think today about what you might be selfishly grasping and then consider what God the Son willingly gave up for you.***

_____

_____

_____

*Pray – **For a mind like Christ, humble and willing to serve.***

THE RENEWAL THAT IS NEEDED

Luke 15:18 ...Father, I have sinned...

The story of the *Prodigal Son* is a familiar one about a lost sinner and God's amazing grace. God knows how far to take a sinner before he repents. In the case of the prodigal, God took him to eat with pigs so that he would eventually come to a spiritual awakening and say, *"Father, I have sinned against heaven, and in your sight."* There are no short-cuts to salvation. One must acknowledge personal sin, repent, and by faith trust in Christ.

In this 21st century, sin is so often ignored as archaic religious fanaticism. This is how it was in the second and third centuries, the age of Christian Gnosticism. Gnosticism, New Age, or what Peter Jones calls *Neo-Paganism*, is rampant in America. He writes, *"the acquisition of self-knowledge allows no concept of sin...Gnostic believers are 'saved' when they realize who they are...a part of the divine."* (The Gnostic Empire Strikes Back)

Our culture cannot and does not acknowledge sin. Logically, if God saves those who confess their sin, repent, and call upon the name of Christ for salvation, and many in America will not acknowledge sin, then it follows that we live in a country where not many will be saved. Here is our charge: we must not only be good evangelists but also good apologists, able to give a biblical explanation of sin and its solution in Christ. It was the church that declared Gnosticism as a heresy and stopped this cancerous false teaching. Will today's church rise up to expose the lies of neo-paganism? *Renew Us, O Lord in Thy Truth!*

Look it up – ***1 Samuel 15:22-23; 2 Chronicles 7:14; Isaiah 52:1-4***

This truth for me – ***What can you do to bring about renewal in your home, neighborhood, workplace, etc?***

_____

_____

_____

Pray – ***For our country to turn from its wicked ways.***

THE STILLNESS OF TRUSTING AND OBEYING

Psalm 46:10 Cease striving [Enough] ...

Do you ever come to the point where you say, "*Enough is enough?*" God comes to that point when His people fail to trust and obey Him. There are several translations for verse 10 of Psalm 46. The NASB says, *Cease striving*. The NIV says, *Be still*. All seem to get the main point across. God wants His children to focus on His sovereign power, presence and protection, and not continually focus on the circumstances that beset them. Worry can be a terrible experience.

In sharp contrast to worry is the Psalmist's command to *be still, cease striving and determine that enough is enough*. The cure for worry is to *be still and know that God is God*. Knowing that God is *our* God and a powerful presence in the life of the believer gives peace. Knowing that God is *a river of grace* and always sufficient for our needs and struggles gives us hope. Knowing that God is *in the midst of our circumstances* and we never need feel that we are alone gives comfort. Yes, enough!—enough of our hopeless worry. Put your confidence in a God who is an ever present help in our time of need. Let's remember this!

Look it up – **Psalm 78:7; Isaiah 26:4; Jeremiah 42:6**

This truth for me – **What are you at your wit's end about? What will you do about it?**

_____

_____

_____

Pray – **For the Lord to always make Himself known to you in lonely times.**

FREE AT LAST

Deuteronomy 34:1 *...And the Lord showed him all the land...*

I once listened to Dr. Martin Luther King's address to the striking sanitation workers in Memphis, Tennessee. The message was delivered the day before he was assassinated. Dr. King's words were mystically prophetic. In the message, Dr. King uses the backdrop of Deuteronomy 34 for his announcing that he had been to the mountain and seen the promised land but wasn't sure if he was going to enter the land of justice. He didn't enter his *promised land* and experience what he called *freedom for all.* He trusted that God would have justice and freedom roll down on this land. Over a million babies are murdered each year by abortion, women and children are pawned off into the sex industry, and drugs kill many of our young people. We may think there will never be an end to all the injustice, but there will be. God has taken us to the mountain and, through the eyes of Christ, we have seen the promised land. It is a land of eternal hope where all injustice will be settled by the great and mighty Savior, Jesus Christ. The Lord will return and He will ride into this world and settle all accounts. *Justice will be established under His rule.* We, the church of Christ, will enter the eternal Promised Land and reign with Him till everything is brought under His control. Then will be heard, "Free at last, free at last, thank God Almighty we're free at last."

Look it up – ***1 Corinthians 9:19; 2 Corinthians 3:17; Galatians 5:1***

This truth for me – ***Are there times when you feel enslaved and lose hope? Meditate on the freedom there is in Christ. Write out some thoughts on freedom.***

Praise – ***God for removing us from the slavery of sin and death.***

SPECIAL DELIVERY

Deuteronomy 32:39 ...no one who can deliver from My hand.

Only God can sovereignly control the affairs of His world. God not only delivers His authority over all things but He also particularly delivers His grace to His chosen people: a delivery that saves sinners, plucks His children out of the snares of sin, and carries them home to glory. There is no god, religion or philosophy that can deliver. Only God gives life and death, peace or turmoil, joy or sorrow.

How does the sovereign control of God effect how I live my life? It should *cause me to be thankful, humble and obedient!* The knowledge that God is the Giver of all things causes me to be totally dependent upon Him. God's sovereign grace and providence should *make me realize that He is in control of all things!* I am not in control and neither is the most powerful person on earth. I can be at peace knowing that my loving, gracious and just Heavenly Father has His hands on the wheel. If God's hands have a firm grip on all the affairs of man and this world, *I need not fret.* The tyrants of the world can threaten and the markets can crash, but our God reigns! There is nothing that can be taken from God's hands and delivered over to man for his devices. *God is in control!*

Look it up – 2 Chronicles 25:20; Psalm 18:17; Luke 20:25

*This truth for me – **What has God delivered to you in His grace? List the things God delivers to His children.***

_____

_____

_____

Pray – That God will deliver unto you opportunities to serve Him and others today.

WHAT LURKS IN THE HEART OF MAN

2 Samuel 15:12 ...Absalom sent for Ahithophel...David's counselor...

The Apostle Paul told the Corinthians that only God knows the thoughts of a man. King David had no idea what was in the heart of his closest and wisest counselor, Ahithophel. He was actually plotting with David's son, Absalom, to kill David and take over his kingdom. Not only don't we know what is stirring in the hearts of others, we can't even definitely comprehend a person's salvation. How many of us assume a person is saved because they mouth the right words or become religious? Yet there are those who present a religious mask and are not real believers. Many pastors can share their horror stories about the wolves in sheep's clothing who infiltrated their churches.

What reveals such wolves? First, there is the presence of *arrogance*. The wolf will always believe that he or she has a corner on wisdom and therefore their way is always the right way. Second, there is a lack of *submission to godly rule*. Third, wolves will be exposed by their *resistance to forgiveness and reconciliation*. Lastly, a wolf likes to *tear apart doctrine*. The wolf or pack will not place themselves too far off center in doctrine, but enough to cause division. What do we do about wolves? Several helps: guard good doctrine, be perceptive and discerning through prayer and wise counsel, and be careful when placing people in teaching or leadership positions.

Look it up – 1 Chronicles 28:9; Matthew 7:15; Acts 20-29-31

This truth for me – List what a true Christian looks and acts like and then ask yourself, do I look and act like this?

_____

_____

_____

Pray – For God to keep your heart clean and holy.

A WALK YIELDED TO GOD

3 John 9,12 ...Diotrephes, who loves to be first...Demetrius has received a good testimony...

What a contrast of characters. Diotrephes is labeled as arrogant, inhospitable, and one who draws others into sinning. Demetrius, on the other hand, is perceived as a good man by all who know him. It is even more complimentary of Demetrius when he is compared to biblical godliness. He is seen by everyone to be good, *and from the truth itself.*

Being recognized by God as His child is the greatest recognition we can have. There then comes the blessing of having a good reputation of godliness among men. Solomon wrote that a *good name is better than a good ointment.* To have a godly reputation is a valuable asset. But what is a godly reputation? According to the Apostle John, in 3 John verses 3 and 4, a godly reputation is *walking in the truth.* Enoch and Noah of Old Testament fame, and members of the Hebrews 11 Hall of Faith, are characterized as men who *walked with God.*

A good reputation is built upon a life that is close to God, living godly in all things. WOW! Can anyone do this? Evidently, but not in and of themselves. It takes the Holy Spirit in us and our yielding to His leading. If you are like me, you are still working on your walk with God and day by day seeking to walk in the truth. We must keep at it - trusting the Holy Spirit and yielding to Him through the word and prayer.

Look it up – **2 Chronicles 30:8; Micah 6:8; James 4:7-10**

This truth for me – **List how you can yield to God and what it is that keeps you from being yielded to Him.**

Pray – **For a heart and mind that is yielded to God.**

GOD IS WATCHING

Jeremiah 1:12 ...I am watching...

Most Christians are familiar with God's perfections of *omniscience and omnipresence*. They refer to God knowing all things and being in all places of His creation at the same time. In the case of God telling Jeremiah that He was watching, God refers to His eye being on the carrying out of His word. God watches to see that *His word is being spread by His people*. God not only commanded His people to be His witnesses and proclaim the gospel, He also gives the church the Spirit's power and direction to preach the gospel. God watches to see that *His Word is preached and proclaimed correctly*. Paul reminded Timothy to *rightly divide the word*.

The things of God, especially His word, are sacred and need our full attention when it comes to handling the word so that people receive the correct message. Many today make up their own interpretation of the word and fail to take the time and effort—not to mention the training necessary—to be good teachers, pastors, missionaries and evangelists. God is watching to see that *His Word is lived out by those who call themselves Christians*. God wants us to be doers of the word, not merely hearers. We are to be living models of the word, not merely mouthing God's word. Finally, God is watching to see that *His word will be fulfilled*. God made sure that His word concerning Christ was fulfilled, and Jesus declared that God will fulfill even the smallest strokes and letters in His word. We can trust the word of God to be true to everything it declares and promises, *because God is watching!*

*Look it up – **Deuteronomy 32:10; Isaiah 40:27-31; Psalm 34:15***

*This truth for me – **What does it mean to you to know that God watches over His word to see that it works in our hearts?***

_____

_____

_____

*Pray – **For the word of God to do its work in your mind and life.***

WE MUST OBEY

Joshua 1:8 ...then you will have success.

Obedience to God is the key to a profitable life! When I obey God, my life will reap the blessing of a good conscience toward God. Why, then, don't we obey God? The temptation to sin is one reason; another is temptation to doubt God. And another reason is thinking that obedience won't produce the results *I* want.

Being a pastor is a very interesting calling. We are expected to direct people to obey what the word of God tells them to do. Yet, there are times we fail to give the exhortation to obey, thinking that the person either can't or won't obey. In essence, what we are doing is putting our eyes on *people,* not on the *right behavior* before God. No matter how we think a person will react to our exhortation to obey, we must still exhort. We need to trust Him to do the convicting that leads to obedience.

God did not hesitate in giving Joshua the exhortation to obey His word. God knew that Joshua would fail to obey, but it did not cause God to say, "Joshua won't listen so I won't even tell him what is right to do." Whenever we are called upon to direct people to obey God, we must do so, not assuming the results, but rather trusting God to bring about obedience. Maybe you have been told to obey God and you are rebelling. Stop it! Obey the Lord and be successful. Is God calling you to go to a brother or sister and exhort them to obey, but you are holding back thinking it is fruitless? Go and do what is right no matter what you assume will be the person's reaction. *Trust God.*

Look it up – ***Judges 2:17; Jeremiah 3:13; Galatians 5:7***

This truth for me – ***Are you obeying God? List where or how you are disobedient and then what you will do about it.***

Pray – ***For the Holy Spirit to fill you with His power to obey.***

READY FOR THE JUDGMENT DAY

Proverbs 15:11 Sheol and Abaddon lie open before the Lord...

God is well aware of His final judgment and what it entails; are we? Are you aware that God has set apart a place of damnation for those who live their lives in rebellion to Him and deny their need for the Savior, Jesus Christ? As Christians, are we ready for that day when the Lord will judge our faithfulness to Him? Our judgment will not be a judgment of damnation but rather an examination of the *works* we have done in the name of the Lord. I am not talking here of works to gain salvation, but rather works of service to the Lord.

The judgment of our works is not a time of chastening believers, but a time of rewarding the believer (1 Corinthians 3:13-15). The results of this judgment will be rewards lost or rewards gained. Several areas in Scripture mention these rewards and they utilize the term *crown*. I am not certain what the reward or a crown might be, but if we look at the word itself, the implication may be that the rewards have something to do with honor or dignity. Judgment Day will be the day when we face Christ and are examined for our works of righteousness. I will either receive my rewards or see them cast away. That day is coming; are we ready?

*Look it up – **Zephaniah 1:7; Acts 17:31; Romans 2:2-11***

*This truth for me – **Are you ready? It's a simple question yet one that haunts us. Are we ready to meet the Lord and be judged for our work in His name? Write out how you would describe your readiness.***

---

*Pray – **For God to help you to be ready to meet Christ.***

PERFECTED YET PROGRESSING

Hebrews 10:14 ...by one sacrifice he has made perfect forever those who are being made holy. (NIV)

Have you ever been given a position or title and then found out that there was a lot more to know about the new position than just the title itself? Jesus Christ purchased two things for the believer. He first paid the price for our sin debt and made us perfect (spiritually speaking), acceptable to the Father. This is Christ's work of redemption, forgiveness, justification and positional sanctification. His second purchase was *the work of the Holy Spirit* to make us holy. This we call progressive sanctification. One author says that we cannot separate these two purchases. We must remember constantly that we are in a righteous position before God because we are fully in Christ. And, we must constantly be reminded that we are a holy work in progress.

Remembering the first helps us to be obedient and thankful. Remembering we are progressing in our holiness makes us humble and merciful. It is hard to imagine that in a real sense the Christian is seen by God as perfected in Christ. It is not so hard to see that we are a work in progress. Perfected yet progressing: both are important truths for the child of God and truths that are fully worked out by God in His care and love for His children.

*Look it up – **Romans 6:22; I Thessalonians 5:23; Hebrews 10:14***

*This truth for me – **List the work that God is doing in your life to make you more into the image of Christ.***

_____

_____

_____

*Praise – **God for the work the Holy Spirit is doing in you to make you more like Jesus.***

GIFTED TO SERVE

Ephesians 3:7 ...I was made a minister, according to the gift...

I never thought of missions as a gift until I worked on the booklet *How to Identify and Use your Spiritual Gift**. It is a small booklet that has a questionnaire designed to help a believer identify his or her spiritual gift. At the end there is an excerpted list of gifts from Rev. Ronald Steel. He lists 17 gifts with definitions. He defines the gift of missions like this: *"The gift of Missions is the special ability that God gives to certain members of the Body of Christ to minister by means of whatever other spiritual gifts they have in a second culture (Acts 8:4-5; 13:2-3; 22:21; 1 Corinthians 9:19-23; Ephesians 3:7-8)."*

It seems to me Rev. Steel is saying that the gift of missions is a facilitating gift. If I have the gift of teaching, or helps, or mercy, the gift of missions will allow me to use these other gifts where I am called to serve. I am not sure how you test for this gift, but if this gift does exist, then those seeking to confirm their call to missions will need to pray that God will give them His understanding of this special ability and gain even more confidence in Him for service.

Let's broaden this concept and apply it to all Christians. We are all called to serve, and even though we may not have the gift of *missions,* we do possess spiritual gifts. Do you know your spiritual gift(s) and are you using them to serve the Lord? Pray today for the Holy Spirit to reveal to you your spiritual gift and then go and serve.

Look it up – ***1 Corinthians 14:26; Ephesians 4:11-13; 1 Peter 4:11***

This truth for me – ***What is your gift? If you haven't discovered your gift, developed your gift and are serving with your gift, go for it!***

Pray – ***That you discover and develop your spiritual gift, then use it.***

---

* Booklet available through: Alliance of Confessing Evangelicals - www.alliancenet.org

CALLED TO FACE OPPOSITION

1 Thessalonians 3:3 ...we have been destined for this.

When believers receive their call to serve the Lord, there comes a degree of persecution and suffering. It might be to the degree of being thrown into prison and killed, or it may be ridicule and harassment. But without a doubt those called to proclaim the good news of the Gospel will have to suffer - we are *destined* for this.

The Apostle's usage of the word *destined* is unique. The word is also translated *appointed* and is a rare verb meaning *to lie stretched out*. Being a preacher here in America, I have not been physically stretched out because of my witness of the Gospel. There have been times of mocking and sneers, but no physical suffering like some preachers face in certain countries of the world. Yet, the hardness of heart and the nominal blindness of America is a great challenge to the Gospel. There may come a day when preaching the Gospel in America will mean the threat of imprisonment and execution, but not now.

Today, in America, our persecution is an intellectual and covert attack upon our witness of the Gospel and we need to be as prepared for this as we would be for prison. That preparation begins and continues with faith and prayer: *"stand firm in the Lord...night and day keep praying..." (1 Thessalonians 3:8-10).* Pray for those preaching the Gospel in dangerous places and for those of us in America facing the Devil's desire to destroy our testimonies.

Look it up – **Psalm 2:1-3; Philippians 1:12-18; 1 Thessalonians 2:2**

This truth for me – **Have you faced recent adversity for being a Christian? If not, what would you do if you did face opposition to your witness for the Gospel?**

_____

_____

_____

Pray – **For courage and times to intentionally witness the Gospel.**

GOING HOME TO GLORY

John 17:5 And now, glorify Thou Me together with Thyself...

How the Savior's heart must have been beating in anticipation of His home going to glory! His work was about to be completed: His mission would be accomplished at the cross and the Father would declare His death the sufficient payment for sin, rewarding Him with raising Him from the dead. With this completion in sight, He asks the Father to prepare His home coming.

All of us are glad when a difficult task is completed and the finished product is well done. Our Savior's death on the cross was an accomplishment like no other in human history: God dying for God and this death of deaths taking away sin and wrath. Having bore our sins on the cross, it is no wonder that Jesus desired glory with such fervor.

There are several considerations here for the Christian. *We ought to be desirous of diligently completing the work God has given us,* whether it is godly living, being a good parent or spouse, or serving Him in the Kingdom. *We ought to look forward to going home.* We often hold on too tightly to this world, not desiring to go home to glory and be with the Lord. We shouldn't be fatalistic or suicidal, but rather we should have a spiritual desire for glory. Finally, *we ought to pray for such intimacy with God* as Jesus demonstrated. Too much of today's worship is either filled with fluff or an overabundance of emotionalism. Be still and know that He is God! May we desire to be at home in glory with the Father, Son and Holy Spirit!

Look it up – **Psalm 68:6; 2 Corinthians 5:6-9; Jude 24-25**

This truth for me – **List what you look forward to about going home to glory with Christ.**

Pray – **For a glimpse of what glory will be like with Jesus.**

THE LORD OPENS OUR MINDS

Luke 24:45 *Then He opened their minds to understand the Scriptures.*

It takes the Lord to open our minds so we can understand the Bible and see that the Scriptures reveal the truth about Jesus Christ! No human's will or reason can unveil who Jesus is and what He accomplished in His death at Calvary. Only God Himself can open our minds. Even the disciples, after spending three years with the Savior, were unable to conclude that Christ was the Savior of the world and that the Savior had to suffer and die in order to atone for sin.

There have been numerous people throughout history who have tried to figure out Jesus Christ on their own and all have failed. The most intelligent unsaved scholar cannot match the wisdom of a young born-again child who knows Jesus as His Savior. When the mind of a sinner is opened to understand the Scriptures, the first thing he realizes is that he is a sinner and in need of a Savior, and that Savior is Jesus Christ.

I thank God, just as Jesus did, that God reveals Christ to those of us who are nothing and makes us a Kingdom of priests and saints. Are your eyes opened to Jesus? If not, repent of your sin, believe on the Lord Jesus Christ and be born again. Talk with a Christian about salvation in Christ. If saved, humble yourself before God and thank him for opening your mind to understand the Gospel.

*Look it up – **Isaiah 64:4; Acts 16:14; James 1:18***

*This truth for me – **Write a sentence or two describing what it was like when the Lord opened your mind to believe the Gospel of Christ.***

_____

_____

_____

*Pray – **That your mind will continually be opened up to the truth of the Bible.***

FIXED ON THE LORD

Isaiah 41:10 ...Do not anxiously look about you...

What happens when we take our eyes off of the target we desire to hit? Normally we end up focusing on a distraction and never hit our target. Christians are often tempted to take their eyes off their God and put their focus, along with their trust, in other things and people. We might set spiritual goals to be more consistent with prayer, or the reading of the Bible, or attendance at church, but then something catches our attention and before long we are regretting ever getting sidetracked and not achieving what we vowed to do.

The prophet Isaiah's words are sure and meant for times when we are looking at everything but the Lord. This is a good reminder that we should keep our eyes on the Lord and not people or the circumstances that surround us. The Lord is in control of all things and even when we *feel* anxious and all alone, remember God is there. He is able and available to help His children, and there is no need for anxiety when the Lord is on your side.

When I was learning how to ride a bicycle, I was riding along a hillside and so worried about falling into the gully that I forgot to look ahead and ran into a large thistle bush - ouch! Yes, we end up saying ouch when we take our gaze off our God! May our eyes be fixed upon Jesus, who is in total control of His children's lives.

Look it up – **Hebrews 12:2; 1 Timothy 4:10; 1 John 3:3**

This truth for me – **Is there something distracting you from putting your focus on Christ? What will it take to put your eyes on Jesus?**

_____

_____

_____

Pray – **For the Holy Spirit to help you keep your eyes on Christ.**

GOD ORDAINS MEANS AND ENDS

Psalm 113:6 ...to behold the things that are in heaven and in the earth?

Are you an Epicurean? I hope not. Epicureans said that God regards nothing, but leaves all things to chance. To say that God does not pay attention to His creation, and allows things to take their own course, ignores even obvious examples of a God of order and ordination. Even the simple glance at the beauty and order of creation will lead to logical deduction that there must be One who gave such order to our creation.

In this Psalm, David clearly gives us the understanding that God is in total control of all things in both heaven and on earth. Nothing is left to chance. God sustains and governs all things in His wise and powerful providence. With this in mind, don't jump to the false conclusion that if God is sovereign and in His providence controls all things, then all we have to do is sit back and let God do His thing. God has not only ordained all that is to come to pass, but also the means for reaching the ends that He has ordained.

In evangelism, God will save His elect, and it will be through the Church as it witnesses the Gospel. God will build His Church, through the enterprise and efforts of evangelistic church planting. In many places in Scripture, we see this truth (compare Acts 23:11 with 27:31). In our personal lives, if we are to receive God's comfort, then we need to turn to His Word and exercise faith and trust in His promises. May we praise our God who is in control of all things and gives us the privilege of being the means by which He carries out His will.

Look it up – **Genesis 50:20; Psalm 36:6; Romans 8:28**

This truth for me – **Is there something in your life you feel is out of control? How does God's providence help you with this out of control feeling?**

_____

_____

_____

Pray – **To see that God is in control of all things and your responsibility.**

THE VOICE OF GOD

Isaiah 8:19 ...should not a people consult their God...

Where do you go for advice and direction? There are plenty of how-to-books, counseling agencies, and Christian brothers and sisters to whom we can turn when we need counsel. These sources are good, but not perfect. The best of human counselors is no comparison or substitute for regular quiet moments with the perfect Counselor who counsels through the Bible and prayer.

One might say, "The Bible is so impersonal, and when I am down or need help, I want a human voice at the other end." Prayer and the Bible are neither impersonal nor void of a voice. In the quiet moments of Bible reading, meditation and prayer, God speaks to us in a very personal way. His communication is not verbal, but when the Holy Spirit takes us into the throne room with God, there exists a deep intimacy with the Lord. The other day after devotions, I was meditating upon God's Word and the beauty of creation. I asked, "Oh God, if I could only hear your voice, like rushing waters." Then, instead of the sound of rushing waters, there came an inner sensing that God was listening and I started talking to Him about the many things that were on my heart and mind.

Our Father loved us enough to elect us unto salvation and to an eternity of intimate fellowship with Himself, His Son and the Holy Spirit. *Should not a people consult their God?*

Look it up – ***1 Kings 19:12; Jeremiah 10:13; Revelation 1:10***

This truth for me – ***Read your Bible; for ten minutes, meditate on what you read, then write what God's voice told you.***

Pray – ***For ears to hear God speak to you through His Word.***

THE INCOMPARABLE GOD

John 3:8 *The wind blows where it wishes…*

As I was teaching a class on the Holy Spirit, we were discussing the superintending work of the Holy Spirit. The Holy Spirit inspired the writers of Scripture to produce the Bible. One of those incomprehensible workings of God is that He inspired (breathed into) the mind of the writer to write exactly what God wanted placed into the Bible. This occurred while the writer used his own words, style and cultural backdrop, and yet the Bible remained free of human reason or error. In the Bible, we have God-inspired, infallible, absolute truth. What human could ever imagine that this would be the process by which the Bible would be produced? This is what Christianity is about: God doing things that His creation could never imagine.

C.S. Lewis says in his book, <u>Mere Christianity</u>, *"That is why I believe Christianity. It is a religion you could not have guessed. If it offered us just the kind of universe we had always expected, I should feel we were making it up. But it is not the sort of thing anyone would have made up. It has just that queer twist about it that real things have."* Our God is mysterious, and yet He reveals Himself to us and allows us to know those things He reveals. We don't know all the mind of God, but what we do know is truly wonderful. May today be another day of discovery for us as we grow in the grace and the knowledge of our Lord and Savior and in His calling of us to serve in His Kingdom.

*Look it up – **Job 11:7; Isaiah 40:18; Romans 11:33***

*This truth for me – **Think on some of the things that you find about God to be incomprehensible and write them down.***

_____

_____

_____

*Pray – **For God to give you clarity in those things you find confusing.***

THE ONENESS OF LOVE AND JUSTICE

Psalm 107:1,12 ...For His lovingkindness is everlasting... He humbled their heart...

Throughout this great Psalm, the mixture of God's love and His justice is evident. Over and over we are comforted by the statements of God's love being everlasting and extended to His children at all times, especially in times of trouble and distress. Yet the psalmist is not hesitant to say that God also exercises His justice and discipline when His children are errant or wander from His ways into rebellion.

The epitome of this blend of love and justice is seen at the cross in Christ's atonement. In our Lord's death, we experience the love of God extended to the hopeless and helpless sinner, and the justice of God being satisfied in the sacrifice of *God dying for God,* as Martin Luther said. We might think of God's love and justice as being two dimensional, but it is not. God's love and justice work beautifully together and as one. In love and the exercise of justice, God brings the rebellious sinners to face their sin, repent and *cry out to the Lord.* Christian—you who are prone to wander—remember that God's love never fails and His justice is exercised to bring us to Him, turn us from our wandering ways and find His cleansing grace.

*Look it up – **Psalm 37:28; Psalm 89:14; Psalm 101:1***

*This truth for me – **How do you balance love and justice in your own life? Where have you seen love and justice worked out?***

_____

_____

_____

*Pray – **For the Lord to give you an understanding of His love and justice to model in your own life.***

THERE IS A RIGHT PATH TO FOLLOW

Nehemiah 5:12 ...We will give it back...we will do exactly as you say...

One of the blessings of being in ministry is when you counsel people to do the right thing, according to the Bible, and they do it. In years of pastoring and counseling, I have experienced only a few times when a person would walk away being committed to do the right thing, and then follow through and do it. This kind of response glorifies God.

The right way seems good for a moment but then our human tendencies set in. People often decide that their way is better, or manufacture a reason for not following the path that God would want them to take. The temptation to be right in our own eyes is a very real and strong temptation. If we are willing to say there is no absolute truth and each person should individually decide what is the right thing to do, then what we end up with is people doing their own thing rather than doing what is profitable and good for the society. Nehemiah confronted a group of Jews who were mistreating their fellow Jews. He called them into account. They recognized their sin and decided to do what was right, even though it would cost them financially. May God's children always see God's way as the right way, no matter what the cost.

Look it up – ***Deuteronomy 12:8; 1 Kings 11:33; Hebrews 13:16***

This truth for me – ***Have you strayed from the right path lately? If so, write out what you will do to get back on the right path securely.***

Pray – ***That when you come to a crossroad in life, you will take the right path.***

THE POWER OF PROCLAMATION

Jonah 1:2 ...preach against it... **(NIV)**

If you were to make plans to attack the corruption and immorality existing in a city, you would probably mobilize the police to do a better job with crime. Additionally, you may organize citizen action groups and ask businesses to sponsor productive programs. I am not sure that preaching to the city would be high on your strategic plan to turn a city around.

Yet, when God wanted to turn the city of Nineveh around, He sent the prophet Jonah to the city to **preach.** From this directive, we need to note several key characteristics about preaching. First, *the preaching of God's Word is powerful.* What can change people and even a society? The preaching of the Gospel of Jesus Christ. It is no wonder Paul described the preaching of the Gospel as the *power of God unto salvation.* Second, *the preaching of the Word brings conviction.* We are told that the Holy Spirit was sent to *convict the world of sin, righteousness and judgment.* The Holy Spirit does not work in a void, but rather in conjunction with the preaching of God's Word. Thirdly, *the preaching of the Bible will bring glory to God.* Whether people are saved, or a community is altered for good, or the church is strengthened, all that is accomplished will bring glory to God. John Perkins, an African-American urban missiologist, declared, *"What will change the lives of people, whatever their color, wherever they live? The preached Gospel of Jesus Christ - the power of God..."* Let's preach it!

Look it up – **Exodus 9:16; 1 Chronicles 16:13; Luke 9:60**

This truth for me – **Write down the name of a person you saw changed by the power of the preaching of the Word and how it made you feel.**

———————————————————————————

———————————————————————————

———————————————————————————

Pray – **That your lips will proclaim the goodness of the Lord.**

ANGELS FROM GOD

Genesis 24:7 ...He will send His angel...

Angels continue to be a hot topic. There are numerous books on angels, both fiction and what some call non-fiction. Items with angelic motifs—jewelry, crafts and paintings—are popular. But most of what we hear and see pertaining to angels is speculation and inconsistent with the biblical account. The Bible remains the only valid source for investigating angelology. Most likely the Bible does not tell us everything there is to know about angels, but it does give us a good understanding of angels.

One of the characteristics made clear about angels in the Scripture is that angels are sent from God to assist His people. This Genesis passage is only one of many instances of an angel or angels being sent from God to give help to the people of God. Whether you believe in *guardian angels* or not, you must agree that the Bible declares the existence of angels as being special creations of God who do His bidding. We must also agree that the Bible states one of the duties of angels is to come alongside and assist Christians. There is great comfort to be gleaned from these truths. Not only can we have the comfort of knowing we have angels assisting us in our Christian walk, but even better, God specifically sent them to help us. How great and caring a God to send His powerful and beautiful creations to assist us in times of need!

Look it up – **Genesis 24:7; Judges 13:16; Acts 5:19-20**

This truth for me – **List the ways that angels help us, as revealed in the Bible.**

_____

_____

_____

Praise – **God for sending His angels to assist us in times of need.**

TIME TO GROW

1 Corinthians 3:1 ...as to babes in Christ.

At the time we are born again, we are fully placed into Christ and all His blessings are given to us. Yet we are babes in Christ, needing to grow and mature. This is called *positional* and *progressive sanctification.* We are in Christ fully, never to be cast off, and called to work out our salvation, growing in the grace and knowledge of our Lord and Savior.

Practically, the doctrine of sanctification is both a comfort and a charge. It *comforts* us to know that we are saved and secured for eternity. All the work of Christ on the cross has been applied to our lives at the point we were saved and we *have been* justified, reconciled, redeemed, and will be glorified. It is *a charge* from God to grow in the grace He has bestowed upon us, to grow in the knowledge of our Father, our Savior, and our Holy Spirit. Along with knowledge comes the requirement to live out what we know in a loving, holy, kind and humble Christian life. Our salvation was confirmed in the eternal decrees of God and established in that time and space when we repented and received the Savior. It is now our time to live for Him in all we know and do.

Look it – **2 Corinthians 3:18; Philippians 3:12; 2 Peter 3:18**

This truth for me – **Are you in a spiritual growth spurt or stagnant in your growth? List what you might do to get growing or keep growing.**

_____

_____

_____

Pray – **For a life and mind that continues to grow in the grace and knowledge of the Lord.**

WAIT FOR THE BEST

John 7:6 ...but your time is always opportune.

In the Bible, God tells us that we are not very good at determining the perfect timing of things. He tells us His ways are not our ways. There is a vast divide between the way we design things and His perfect design. So often we want things to immediately happen our way and according to our schedule. We are not a very patient people but rather a very anxious people. The Lord's disciples were of such a nature. They wanted Jesus to reveal Himself according to their timetable. If He were to do so, they may have thought it would bring them greater attention or more comfortable circumstances. But Jesus had His own plan and timing.

Several lessons are to be learned from knowing God's timing is best. First, waiting upon God produces *a godly patience*. Second, waiting upon God *allows us to see God work out the best for us*. Third, waiting upon God *brings blessing* while being impetuous makes the road to achievement longer and harder. Fourth, waiting upon God *grows our faith, trust and dependence upon Him*. Finally, waiting upon God *in obedience brings His blessing of peace* at the end of the wait. *Be still and know that He is GOD!*

Look it up – **Psalm 25:5; Habakkuk 2:3; Hebrew 6:15**

This truth for me – **Think about how hard it is to wait for God to answer you. Now, list what will help make the wait a good and patient wait.**

_____

_____

_____

Pray – **That you will see how blessed it is to wait upon the Lord and receive His best.**

A FATHER WITH A LAVISHING LOVE

Ephesians 1:3 Blessed be the God and Father of our Lord...

Too often we think of the Father as stern and lacking the compassion that our Savior possesses, yet there is no division in the Godhead; the same love and compassion displayed by the Son is also manifested by the Father. It is the Father who sent the Son for us. It is the Father who, *while we were yet sinners,* had His Son die in our place. It is the Father who raised the Son from the dead in order to give us a living hope. Finally, it is the Father who *chose us in Him (Christ) before the foundation of the world, that we should be holy and blameless before Him, in LOVE.* Yes, the Father chose us before the world came into existence and He chose us in love.

Dr. Sinclair Ferguson tells a story of a friend who went to a Russian orphanage to select a child for adoption. In time, a young girl was adopted into the friend's family. The little girl did not realize at first the depth of her new father's love, but as the father's love was manifested, she came to know she was chosen in love and adopted with all the privileges given to her by her new father. We have been chosen by the Father in love, adopted by the Father into the family of God – *according to His grace which He LAVISHED upon us...*

Look it up – **Isaiah 43:7; John 1:12; Ephesians 2:19**

This truth for me – **List how it makes you feel to be a child of God, loved with an everlasting love.**

_____

_____

_____

Praise – **The Father for adopting you into His household through Christ.**

GOD PROVIDES HIMSELF

Judges 6:12 ...The Lord is with you...

God's name, *Jehovah Jireh,* means the Lord provides. When we think of the Lord providing, we most often think of how our gracious Father provides material things for us. Certainly it is true that, by His grace, God provides everything we have. Yet, what is His most important provision? *He provides Himself!*

In this story of Gideon, it is very clear how God promises Gideon that He will provide His presence, confirmation of His promises in the signs He sets forth for Gideon, and finally His victory over the Midianites. What stands out is that God first and foremost provides His presence to His people. There is no possession that compares to having God with us, the Holy Spirit indwelling us, Jesus Christ with us in all we do, and the Father guiding and protecting us.

The first time we come across this wonderful name, *Jehovah Jireh,* is in Genesis 22, the story of God directing Abraham to sacrifice his son Isaac. God stopped Abraham from sacrificing Isaac and provided a substitute, the ram in the thicket. God provides our substitute in Jesus Christ. He is God's provision for our sin and Jesus provides Himself as our Savior. Today, remember that God provides Himself to you. If you are not saved, look to Jesus, He is God's provision for your salvation.

*Look it up – **Psalm 109:31; Jeremiah 1:8; Philippians 4:9***

*This truth for me – **When have you felt alone? How can you always know that God is with you?***

_____

_____

_____

*Pray – **For the Lord to make His presence known to you today in a wonderful way.***

THE GOOD SIDE OF BEING A FOOL

Galatians 3:1 You foolish Galatians...

It's not nice to call someone a fool, but in the Bible, the Holy Spirit chose to use this characterization on numerous occasions. Here in Galatians, people are called *foolish (ignorant)* if they trust in their own goodness or good works for salvation, instead of trusting by faith in the work of Jesus Christ. In the wisdom literature of the Psalms and Proverbs, a person is a *fool (evil)* because he despises wisdom and is morally undesirable. In most cases when the word *fool* is used in the Bible, it refers to ignorance, stupidity, evil, and immorality.

But there is an instance where the term *fool* has a positive meaning. In 1 Corinthians 3:18, the Apostle Paul says that we should first be a *fool (emptied of all self-wisdom)* in order to become wise in our understanding of the Gospel. I would not advocate that we call each other fools—the Bible frowns on this—but we would want sinners to become as fools so they can then see the wisdom of Christ, and Christians to become as fools when they become self-sufficient. If I or any of my fellow Christians think we are wise in our own wisdom, may we become a fool and then become wise!

*Look it up – **Proverbs 8:5; 1 Corinthians 4:10; Ephesians 5:15***

*This truth for me – **Think about a foolish thing that you did in the past. How was that foolishness turned into wisdom? If it wasn't, how can it still make you wise?***

_____

_____

_____

*Pray – **For wisdom to be more like Christ.***

BETTER TO OBEY

John 14:31 ...that the world may know that I love the Father...

Where does *obedience* fall in your list of ways you want to live your Christian life? Worshiping God and obeying God should be at the top of our list of things to please God. *Obedience honors God* and demonstrates that we believe His way is best. *Obedience builds us up,* granting us the peace to know that we are in the Father's will. *Obedience brings a testimony* to the world of our love for the Father and how good it is to obey.

Here in the Gospel of John, Jesus states that obedience is the supreme way we show that we love God. Jesus was an obedient Son. Although He was equal with the Father in His divinity, He willingly submitted to obey all that the Father asked Him to do, even death on the cross. In this ultimate act of obedience, our Lord shows how great a love He has for the Father. How great is our love for the Father? Is it great enough to die in obedience to His commands? May the world know we love the Father by seeing our lives lived in obedience, even when we don't *feel* like obeying.

Look it up – 1 Samuel 15:22; Luke 11:28; 1 John 2:3

This truth for me – Write down what you need to obey God in today. What do you think it will be like to obey God in this area?

_____

_____

_____

Pray – For the Holy Spirit to give you the power to obey God even when you don't feel like obeying.

HE REIGNS OVER US

Luke 19:14 ...We do not want this man to reign over us.

This is the natural response from the heart of sinful man. No matter how we might desire to follow Christ, by nature we reject His rule and turn from following His way of righteousness. No one wants to be ruled by God. Like Adam, we all desire to be left to ourselves without any restraint. Adam had only one prohibition but could not exercise obedience. Man's heart is weak and his desire is to be his own god.

Unlike Adam and the natural man, the born-again child of God realizes everything in life, even his very own existence, is dependent on Christ. Far from being independent, we are dependent on God. The unsaved may not realize this but in reality they are totally dependent on God. No matter how they fight Christ, in the end they will face Him as their God. Christians are not immune from fighting the Lord's reign in their lives. Many times we seek our independent way through life. For a Christian, upon whom God lavishes His grace, to run from Christ's rule and seek his own way is foolishness at its best. Don't we know that being ruled by Christ is real freedom? Be free and let the precious Savior reign in your heart!

Look it up – **Psalm 47:8; Isaiah 52:7; Revelation 19:6**

This truth for me – **Is there an area of your life that you have not yielded to God? List it and what you can do to give that area over to God.**

_____

_____

_____

Pray – **That God will help you have victory over any area in your life not yielded to Him.**

GOD SEES THE SECRET THINGS

Genesis 20:6 ...Yes, I know...

God is omniscient! He knows everything! It is eerie at times to believe that God knows all the things I do and the thoughts I think. There are times, especially when we are harboring sins inside our minds and hearts that we don't want anyone to know our thoughts.

King Abimelech had no intention of having an affair with Abraham's wife Sarah. God knew this. It must have been a relief for Abimelech to realize that God knew he had a clean conscience. When my thoughts are clean, it is good to know that God sees my conscience. On the other hand, how awful it is to understand that God knows when my conscience is dirty with sin.

I read in <u>Leadership</u> magazine that 38% of pastors have a problem with online pornography. Today there are so many ways that a Christian's conscience can be seared by sin. Pornography is a major sin in the life of the church and its leaders. Do we realize that God is watching? An understanding of the omniscience of God should be a deterrent to all sins, including those that we think are secret sins. Hopefully our thoughts are clean so we can hear God saying, *"I know you did this with a clear conscience."*

*Look it up – **Job 11:7,8; Psalm 139:2,3; Romans 11:33***

*This truth for me – **How does the fact that God knows everything you do affect you? Is there anything you need to talk to God about today?***

_____

_____

_____

*Pray – **For God to help you with any hidden sin.***

STILL IN NEED OF GRACE

Romans 12:1 ...by the mercies of God...

When I was born, I was totally dependent on my parents for everything in my life. As I grew older, and at some point in my teen years, I thought that I didn't need anyone's help and could handle everything on my own. I was—like the sarcastic Dutch saying goes—*too soon smart.*

When Christians are born again, they are totally dependent on the *mercies of God:* justification, reconciliation and redemption. But as we grow in our Christian life, some of us lose sight of the fact that the same need for God's mercy to save us is a constant, ongoing need in our life. You and I need His mercy and grace every moment of our existence. It is no wonder the Apostle John states that His *grace abounds to us* over and over. Even though we are secure in His salvation, we need His grace. If there is ever a time where we lose sight of this fact and think we can go it on our own, we turn blind to the bounty of sufficient grace that sustains us and gives us hope. Such blindness can cause great pain and struggle because we miss out on knowing and experiencing our Father's love, expressed in His mercy and grace. *I, a sinner still, forgiven and secure, need every moment of His outpouring of mercy.*

Look it up – **Psalm 94:17-19; John 17:11; Hebrews 6:1**

This truth for me – **List the areas of your life you need God's mercy and grace to help you grow out of some things and into others.**

_____

_____

_____

Pray – **For God's grace to help you grow in Christ.**

THE INTIMACY OF PURE LOVE

Song of Solomon 1:15 How beautiful you are, my darling...

Our minds and lives are continually infiltrated with impure sexuality. We face blatant sexual material and sexual innuendo on our computers, on billboards, on magazine racks ... and the list goes on. Our culture is flooded with illicit sexual expressions, that we tend to connect real love and expressions of real love with our culture's impure sexual hunger.

The Song of Solomon is a great reminder that we can love and express love in a pure and wholesome manner. God created marriage to be the arena for the expression of romantic love in word, deed and sexuality. How recently have you and your spouse expressed your love for each other? God expresses His love for us continually. There is never a moment when we cannot see and hear the Lord's love poured out to us. Christ's words are filled with expressions of love for His bride, the Church. Even Solomon's words, *how beautiful you are, my darling,* are given to remind us of our Savior's love for His Bride.

Husbands and wives, take time today to express your love for one another. If you are not married, look to the Lord and the love He extended to you on the cross, and each day through His grace let Him fill you with His love.

Look it up – ***Song of Solomon 5:2; 1 Corinthians 6:16; Ephesians 5:25-27***

This truth for me – ***If you are married, write down some ways to show your love for your spouse, even if you don't feel like you want to. If you are not married, find fulfillment in Christ's love for you.***

_____

_____

_____

Pray – ***For God to fill your heart with His love and joy.***

THE STRAIGHT PATHS OF THE LORD

Mark 1:3 ...Make His paths straight.

John Mark, the writer of the Gospel of Mark, quotes from the Old Testament book of Isaiah 40:3, *make ready the way of the Lord, make straight his paths.* His reference is to God's deliverance of the Jewish captives in Babylon. A herald must be sent to prepare the way for the Lord through the vast Syrian Desert between Babylonia and Palestine. The theme is deliverance. So Mark picks up this theme and applies it to the activities of John the Baptist and the Lord Jesus Christ. John cries out, "Make a straight path for the Lord to come and deliver you from sin and death" (my paraphrase).

There are two applications here. First, we the Church are to follow in the way of John the Baptist and make the paths straight for the Lord to come and save sinners. We do this through our witness and the teaching of the gospel to a lost world. God saves, but His plan is to use our witness to reach His people. Second, to those who are not born-again, John's message was one of repentance—*confess your sin and turn to Christ for forgiveness.* One commentator writes, *repentance is not only being sorry for our sin but sorry enough to quit.* This is the straight path to salvation.

*Look it up – **Psalm 5:8; Jeremiah 31:9; Acts 13:10***

*This truth for me – **How are you preparing the way for people to come to Christ? List in what ways we make paths straight, i.e. our testimonies.***

---

*Pray – **For the deliverance of unsaved family and friends.***

A DETERMINED GOD

Job 38:4 ...when I laid the foundation of the earth...

Our God is a God of order—we call Him a *teleological (designing)* God. He designed and put His creation in perfect order. Sin brought a marring to His order, yet He is still sovereignly in control of all things and keeps all things in order according to His purpose and plan. Even when we think all things are in chaos, God is behind the scenes weaving everything into a progressive movement toward the return of the Lord.

It was about 1350AD that Martin Luther discovered a book titled, the *Theolgia (Germanica)*. He wrote an introduction to it and had the book printed and circulated. One excerpt reads, *"...One says—and rightly so—that God is above and without rules, measure, and order, yet renders to all things rules, order, measure, and moral integrity..."*

How easy it might be to think that God is not in control during these times of war, terrorism, natural disasters, disease, poverty, homelessness, divorce, drugs, crime and paganism. God's statements to Job are confirmation to all that *God has all things in control!* Remember this truth today in the midst of your chaos.

*Look it up – **Genesis 1:1, 3; Psalm 104; Acts 17:24***

*This truth for me – **How does it feel to know that God is in control of everything? List what this means to you.***

_____

_____

_____

*Praise – **God for His loving providence over all things.***

JUDGMENT AND JUSTICE

Jeremiah 12:1 Righteous art Thou, O Lord...

Where do we go when things seem unfair? Jeremiah asks, *why has the way of the wicked prospered...why are all those who deal in treachery at ease?* It often seems to us that God is unjust when He allows wickedness and disaster to occur without reason or meaning . . . or, what *we may think* is without reason or meaning. In this passage, God tells Jeremiah His purpose in allowing the wicked to prosper. His purpose is to bring judgment on His people so they turn from their wickedness. Judgment is a major theme in the book of the prophet. God uses wickedness to fall down on His people so they repent.

It is not always the case that God uses wicked things to judge His people. No matter what God uses to cause us to repent, we know that God is fair in His dealings with us. He is *righteous* and the God of *justice.* The wicked may believe they are getting away with their crimes, but not so; God in the end will exercise His justice and bring the wicked to their end.

I once heard a father tell of his daughter's rape and murder and how he came to the point where he forgave the man who was convicted of the crime. Someone asked the father, "How could you forgive this man?" The father responded, "I looked to the cross and saw the forgiveness and justice God extended to me." God is always righteous in all His dealings.

*Look it up – **Amos 5:24; John 7:24; James 4:7-12***

*This truth for me – **List a time that you thought that God was unfair. Why did you think that, and what was the truth?***

---

*Pray – **For the understanding to know that God is fair in all His ways.***

CUTTING AN UNBREAKABLE DEAL

Nehemiah 1:5 ...*who preserves the covenant...*

The idea of *covenant* in the Bible is pictured for us as God *cutting a covenant,* similar to saying *cutting a deal.* Cutting is associated with God's covenants because God established His covenants with blood sacrifices. With Noah, God cuts a covenant and declares, *I will establish my covenant.* God's covenants are unconditional. The promises aligned with God's covenants are dependent upon His promise to keep them, not our fickle attempts at being faithful. We might lose blessings attached to certain aspects of the covenants, but our disobedience will not nullify the covenants because they are dependent upon God's faithfulness. The same goes for God's covenant of grace to save a people and bring them home to glory. God predestines a chosen people to be saved and calls them through the preaching of the gospel. The convicting work of the Holy Spirit justifies and redeems them based upon the finished work of Christ on the cross. The Holy Spirit provides the faith for the sinner to believe, and will glorify them into His presence at His appointed time. God is faithful to save and keep all those He has chosen, and He will fulfill His covenant. It is a covenant guaranteed! When you doubt God's faithfulness, turn to His covenant promises to keep true to what He promised and in this, find peace.

*Look it up – **Genesis 12:1-3; Psalm 89; Hebrews 8:6-14***

*This truth for me – **List how many times God has been faithful to you. How can His faithfulness to His promises help you today?***

_____

_____

_____

*Pray – **For God to give you His peace in Christ as you trust in Him.***

THE PRICE OF FAITHFULNESS

Luke 14:28 ...first sit down and calculate the cost...

Counting the cost before embarking on a project does not necessarily mean if the cost is too high, we won't get involved in the project. This might be the case, but not always. We may not begin a project if we discover we are not fit for the project or the support for the project is not in place. But counting the cost may also mean we will embark on a project knowing the risks, challenges and work necessary to complete the project. Evaluation and analysis determines both whether or not to proceed and how to proceed in light of what lies ahead.

Following Christ has its costs. In this same section of Luke, he quotes Christ: *...whoever does not carry his own cross and come after me cannot be my disciple.* C.S. Lewis, in his book Mere Christianity, states, "*The Christian way is different: harder, and easier. Christ says, 'Give me all. I don't want so much of your time and so much of your money and so much of your work: I want you...' "* Anything done for the Lord takes our all. Our will, heart and focus is the cost demanded when it comes to following Christ. The irony, as Lewis says, is that sometimes the cost is harder, *take up the cross*, while other times following Christ is easier, *my burden is light.* Christ knows how to balance this out in our lives so even the hardships are easy with the Lord. Are we willing to give ourselves to Christ no matter what the cost?

*Look it up – **Matthew 10:37; Mark 8:34; Acts 20:24***

*This truth for me – **What has being a Christian cost you? Meditate on the cost of being His disciple and write some thoughts down.***

----

*Pray – **For the Spirit's strength as you face the costs of being a Christian.***

SELF-ESTEEM OR SELF-SACRIFICE?

Luke 14:10 ...*go and recline at the last place...*

"*Humility begins as a gift from God, but it is increased as a habit we develop...*" (Jeremy Taylor - <u>Rules & Exercises of Holy Living</u> - 1650). Developing humility is not an easy task. Our society puts up formidable barriers in our quest to be humble. From every direction, advertising, sports, entertainment, business and modern teaching all shove at us the need for self-esteem and self-achievement. Me - Me - Me! We are enticed to do whatever it takes to outdo each other.

Even the Church has its own gauge for measuring value. There seems to be little room for smallness in American Christianity. Pastors and their churches are considered successes if they reach a certain mega level. Taylor lists a number of rules for humble/holy living: "*...have a realistic opinion of yourself, do good things in secret, never be ashamed of your status - no matter how lowly, reflect praise back to God, rejoice in God who gives gifts, do not entertain any of the Devil's whispers of pride, be active in praising others, focus on others' strengths in order to see your weaknesses, confess your mistakes plainly, do not expose others' weaknesses in order to build yourself up, be willing to endure whatever the Lord's will is for you...*"

Having meditated on these thoughts, I realize how much work needs to take place in my own life. How about you?

Look it up – **Psalm 139:1-18; 2 Corinthians 10:12-18; Philippians 2:3**

This truth for me – **Where do you find your self-worth, in yourself or in your position in Christ? What does it mean to be worthy in Christ?**

_____

_____

_____

Pray – **For a humble spirit and yet recognizing your great position in Christ.**

THE PRESENCE OF GOD

Psalm 42:5 *Why are you in despair, O my soul...*

Good question. Why do our souls fall into despair and, as the psalm continues, ...*why have you become disturbed within me?* It's as if the psalmist is saying there is no earthly reason for our souls to be the prey of despair and disturbance. The psalmist goes on to give us the reason why despair and disturbance of the soul is unwarranted: *Hope in God for I shall again praise Him for the help of His presence.* Despair and disturbance of soul is no match for the presence of God. Like the Apostle Paul clearly declared in Romans 8:31, *If God is for us, who is against us?* The obvious rhetorical answer is no one and nothing can stand against us because the presence and power of God is on our side. Therefore, the psalmist can confidently attack his own soul and say, "*Hey, soul, you should not be in despair; God is here and He is on your side.*"

Only the redeemed can have this confidence and ability to fight off the worry and despair with which the devil and his demons plague us. The first step into the presence of God comes through the cross of Jesus Christ. Jesus opens the way to God, and once in His presence, He is our God and Savior forever. As a Christian, are you disturbed and in despair? Know this: *God is with you, and there is nothing and no one who can stand against God. Nothing—not one thing!* If you are without Christ in your life, run to Jesus, cry out for forgiveness, and believe by faith He is your Savior. He can handle your despair and disturbance of soul.

*Look it up – **Psalm 56:9; Ezekiel 36:9; Romans 8:1-31***

*This truth for me – **Are you under attack? What is coming against you? List how much greater your God is compared to what is attacking you.***

---

*Pray – **To always be able to know that your God is for you.***

A TOTAL TRANSFORMATION

Romans 12:2 ...be transformed by the renewing of your mind...

The Apostle Paul's connection of transformation and the renewal of the mind are significant. The mind—the seat of a person's inner being—needs renewal which leads to transformation. Why? Because our entire being is totally affected by sin. The unsaved mind is as dead as its unsaved soul, and in some cases they are referenced as the same. A non-believer can be intellectual and brilliant in his or her field of study or career, but without Christ and the regenerating work of the Holy Spirit, the mind of even the most scholarly person lies wasting in the corruption of sin.

The transformation mentioned here is not an outward or intellectual transformation, but rather an internal renewal. The human mind, heart, body and soul/spirit all need to become new. This inner renewal is accomplished by God and only God. Some translations say, ...let yourselves be transformed. The passive voice here is indication that the work of renewal and its continuing action is from the outside. It first comes from the Holy Spirit's work of regenerating us, resulting in new birth. In simple terms, you must be born again in order to be renewed and progressively transformed. Lastly, the grammar tells us two more things. First, the present tense reminds us that this transformation is continual and is not concluded till glory. Second, the imperative mood tells us we are to cooperate with the Holy Spirit transforming us. Sin caused us to need renewal, and sin can hinder transformation.

Look it up – **Zechariah 3:1-7; 2 Corinthians 3:18; 1 John 3:2**

This truth for me – **List ways that you will seek to be transformed in mind, body, soul and spirit.**

_____

_____

_____

Pray – **To be open to the transforming power of the Holy Spirit through humble obedience to the will and Word of God!**

CLIMBING THE LADDER OF PRAYER

Mark 11:22 ...Have faith in God.

In this section of the gospel, Christ connects faith and prayer. Martin Luther said, *"Prayer is a special exercise of faith. Faith makes the prayer acceptable because it believes that either the prayer will be answered, or that something better will be given instead."* Luther's statement motivates us to pray with confidence and joy.

But I am afraid that our prayers are too often lacking accompanying faith. Doubt and anxiety parallel our prayers. *Will God really answer or if He does, will it be what I want?* Prayer must be supported by faith if we are to have God's answers and blessings.

What a great joy to know by faith that God will answer my prayers, to rise up from my knees and walk away confident that the answer will come. Luther quoted an ancient definition of prayer as, *"a climbing up of the heart unto God."* May our prayers climb up the heart of God. How privileged are the children of God to be able to speak to the Sovereign of the universe at any time and in any place. We need no entry pass or identification papers. Our right to commune with God is secured in the person of His Son, Jesus Christ. It is by His righteousness that we can boldly approach God's majesty and glory. Rejoice, Christian, in the joy of prayer accompanied by faith. Exercise it without ceasing. (Excerpts from <u>The Table-Talk of Martin Luther</u>.)

Look it up – 1 Kings 18:36-37; Hebrews 11:6; James 5:16-18

This truth for me – Think about your prayers. What degree of faith do you exercise when you pray? How can your prayers be undergirded by faith?

_____

_____

_____

Pray – In faith!

REVIVAL AND ME

Habakkuk 3:2 ...O Lord, revive Thy work...

Today's American Christianity longs for a revival to sweep through the churches and then our country . . . or do we? Charles Spurgeon wrote a sermon in the 19th century entitled, *Spiritual Revival: the Want of the Church.* The sermon reminds one that revival comes from the hand of God, not from contrived programs. Revival centers on a Sovereign God who quickens the church to repentance and holiness and sinners unto salvation.

The prophet pleaded for revival. You can hear it in his words, *O Lord*. But does the church really groan for revival? Some say the days of revival are over and the next great divine event to occur will be the return of the Lord; therefore revival is not a priority. Others desire revival but fail to understand that revival begins with every Christian's personal walk with the Lord. Yes, revival comes upon groups of people and regions of the world, but only after individuals are changed by God. Lastly, there are those who do not want revival to occur if it means giving up the world, for many of us have grown content with the ways of the world. It should be at the heart of the Christian to want God to revive His Church and save sinners. We really do need to groan for revival and make the way for revival to come through our holy living and fervent evangelism.

Look it up – **2 Kings 18:1-7; Psalm 80:18; Habakkuk 3:2**

This truth for me – **Look at your life, your heart, your mind. What needs revival? Where does it start in you?**

_____

_____

_____

Pray – **For God to revive His Church and pour His spirit on us.**

HE KNOWS ME

Psalm 139:1 O Lord, Thou hast searched me and known me.

No one knows us like God knows us. He knows our thoughts because He is omniscient - all knowing. He knows our actions and where we are every moment of the day because He is omnipresent - all places at all times. He knows our needs and can respond with what is best needed because He is omnipotent - all powerful. This might be scary for some Christians because there are times they might not want God to know their thoughts or how they are acting because they like what they are doing and don't want to change things. Yet Christians who seek to live for God and be like Jesus find great comfort and assurance in knowing that God can search them and know them.

J.I. Packer writes in his classic book, <u>Knowing God,</u> *"What matters supremely, therefore, is not, in the last analysis, the fact that I know God, but a larger fact which underlies it - the fact that He knows me..."* God knows you and He wants you to respond to Him in obedience and thanksgiving.

> *Search me, O God, and know my heart today;*
> *Try me, O Savior, know my thoughts, I pray.*
> *See if there be some wicked way in me;*
> *Cleanse me from ev'ry sin and set me free.*

Look it up – **John 10:27; 1 Corinthians 8:3; Galatians 4:9**

This truth for me – **How does it feel to be known by God? List how knowing this truth helps you in your walk through life.**

_____

_____

_____

Pray – **For the day-to-day realization that God knows you.**

SUPREME, SOVEREIGN, SURPASSING

Revelation 19:6 ...for the Lord God omnipotent reigneth. (KJV)

On March 23, 1743, when "The Messiah" was first performed in London, the king was present in the great audience. It is reported that all were so deeply moved by the "Hallelujah Chorus" that with the impressive words, "For the Lord God omnipotent reigneth," the whole audience, including the king sprang to its feet, and remained standing through the entire chorus. From that time to this it has always been the custom to stand during the chorus whenever it is performed. With spontaneous joy the soul stands to salute Him who "cometh in the name of the Lord." He is "King of kings, and Lord of lords" and to Him we pledge allegiance. (Tan, P. L. (1996). Encyclopedia of 7700 Illustrations)

Knowing God reigns brings many comforts for the Christian. It is our comfort to know that God is *sovereign*. It is not that God merely knows the events in heaven and earth but rather, He *reigns* over them. He controls them, and what peace in knowing that when things seem unleashed and chaotic, God reigns and has even the unruly under His control. It is our comfort to know that God is *powerful*. He is not just powerful with total ability to conform things to His will and purpose, but a child of God has His help and protection. It is our comfort to know that *God is Lord*. We do not worship and serve stone gods or philosophical wanderings but rather the supreme, majestic *Lord* of the universe. Draw great comfort - **Your God reigns!**

*Look it up – **Exodus 3:14; Psalm 113:1-6; Psalm 150:1-6***

*This truth for me – **What does it mean to you that God is supreme, sovereign and surpassing? List how this blesses you.***

_____

_____

_____

*Praise – **Read Psalm 150 several times as a prayer of praise.***

DIVINE TIMING

Ephesians 1:10 With a view to an administration (dispensation) suitable to the fullness of the times...

The Apostle Paul likes to talk about God's *timing.* In his letter to the churches in Galatia, he stated at the *fullness of time, God sent forth His Son born of a woman.* The birth of Christ was perfectly timed. Culture, language, government and the bankrupt spiritual condition of Israel added up to a perfect setting for the Savior to come to earth.

In Paul's letter to the church in Ephesus, he says another *fullness of time* is coming. All things both in heaven and on earth are moving toward the glorious return of our Lord, when He comes to rule in power. God's timing is *purposeful.* Both the good and the bad are pointing to the return of Christ. God's timing is *personal.* God's eternal plan is providential, whereby He controls all things, yet His sovereignty over all things does not neglect nor offend His children. Rather His plan is merciful. God's timing is *glorious.* All that God does and the timing for all He accomplishes is to bring glory to Himself. What seems to be lateness on God's part is only our feeble misunderstanding of His timing, working out in your life - *be still and know that He is God!*

*Look it up – **Ecclesiastes 3:11; Psalm 90:12; John 7:1-13***

*This truth for me – **God comes always at the perfect time. Can you describe an instance in your life when God came to you at the perfect time?***

_____

_____

_____

*Pray – **For wisdom to understand God's timetable and not your own.***

ME OH MY OR MY GOD AND ME

Psalm 117:2 ...His lovingkindness is great toward us...

Paul Harvey once said, "...I have never seen a monument erected to a pessimist." There are times when pessimism can capture our thoughts and visions. If we maintain a view of life from a horizontal point of reference, we are captivated by the negativism of a society in moral decline and a world trembling in unrest. When we see the apathy of the Church, along with the slow results of Americans responding to the gospel, our desires for the Lord's return are intensified and our evangelistic energies cooled. Pessimism can invade even the most aggressive and optimistic mind.

The only cure for the pessimistic bug is given in this tiny song of the Psalms, *His loving kindness is great toward us.* Our antidote for the poison of pessimism lies in knowing how great God's loving kindness and faithfulness are toward us who are weak and at times weak-minded. He is great and His kindness bends down toward His children. What other response can be expected than the one that concludes the Psalm, *Praise the Lord!* Today give praise to the Lord for remaining faithful to redeem His people and build His Kingdom.

*Look it up – **Psalm 108:4; Psalm 138:2; Romans 15:11***

*This truth for me – **List how you have recently shown pessimism about something over which the Lord can help you have victory.***

_____

_____

_____

*Pray – **For the Lord to give you an optimistic outlook and to help you see the opportunities that lie before you as you trust in God's faithfulness.***

SYMPHONY OR CACOPHONY

John 4:22 *You worship that which you do not know...*

I read a news article in the religious section of our local paper in which a well-known, so-called religious writer tried to make a case for Jesus being a feeling rather than a real person. Our times are filled with all sorts of people and movements who claim to hold the truth and worship that which they believe to be God or their higher being. Jesus was very clear in his dealings with the Samaritan woman: *your worship is false.* He tells her that the key to worship is to do so in *spirit and truth.* My interpretation of this statement is that a person must first be born-again by the regenerating work of the Holy Spirit and then approach the true God in worship according to His Word, the Bible.

It is the Bible that the Spirit uses to lead God's people into true worship. The Spirit never works in a vacuum of emotions and ecstatic experiences, but rather through the objective truth of the Word. We often *feel* worship or *experience* worship, but unless those emotions and experiences line up with the Word, we are, as Paul states, sounding gongs making a cacophony rather than a symphony of praise and worship. You can only know worship if you are saved.

Are you born-again, and if so, how is your worship? Is it led by the Spirit because your mind is absorbing the Word of God in daily devotions and Bible reading? **Worship in spirit and truth today!**

*Look it up – **John 3:21; Romans 1:25; Hebrews 10:19-20***

*This truth for me – **Describe your worship in a sentence or two. Is your worship in substance or only form?***

_____

_____

_____

*Pray – **For your worship of the true God to be in spirit and truth.***

LOST IN GOD'S PERFECTIONS

Psalm 65:11 *Thou hast crowned the year with Thy bounty...*

Fall reminds us that the year is coming to an end. When we come to the end of a project, or the completion of an endeavor, we usually take time to review and reflect on how things went. Should I have done something differently? Are there changes to make? Did things go well and change is not needed? As we near the end of a year, we should take time to evaluate. Yet, evaluation is not left open-ended, but rather, we evaluate through the lens of what our God accomplished in our lives, our famines, our work or school. Whether we faced challenges or blessings, loss or gain, all was from the hand of God.

Charles Wesley gave us a guide for evaluation through these words in one of his hymns, *"...lost in wonder, love and praise!"* Here then lies our focus for evaluation. Our reflection and evaluation must be focused on our God and how He extended His grace to us whether in good or bad, ups or downs, joy or sorrow. As we look ahead to the end of another year, let us be the kind of children who *lose themselves in the wonder, love and praise* of our great God. Our God who is sovereign over all things, both in heaven and on earth and in each of our lives.

Look it up – **Psalm 147; 2 Thessalonians 2:13; 1 John 4:9**

This truth for me – **Try to lose yourself in how good God is to you, and list the ways He loves you and cares for you.**

_____

_____

_____

Praise – **God for His bounty and His willingness to share that bounty with sinners like us.**

HE IS MINE AND I AM HIS

Psalm 118:28 *Thou art my God...*

When we purchase something of a precious nature, we take very good care of the item. We keep it looking good and show it off to those who come and visit us. We find comfort in knowing that we possess something valuable and there is even a degree of security that comes with a valuable possession.

The psalmist says he possesses God and the one who possesses God has reason to rejoice and give thanks. The irony here is that I cannot say that God is mine unless God first makes me His possession. You see, we had to be purchased by God in order to say *Thou art my God.* Jesus paid the purchase price for our wretched sinful lives, and God accepted Christ's payment for His elect. Therefore, to those who are born-again in Christ, we say, *God, I am yours and You are mine.* Can you say today, "Thou art mine?" We can utter these words only if we recognize our sin and Jesus as our Savior; we must repent and by faith, believe in the Lord Jesus Christ. For those of us who possess God, we should show Him off in our lives and value such a possession by taking great care of our relationship with Him. Blessed be the sinner, saved by grace, who cries out, **Thou art my God!**

Look it up – **2 Samuel 7:22; Psalm 43; Jeremiah 3:22**

This truth for me – **List the ways it makes you feel to know that God is your God. What benefit is this to you?**

_____

_____

_____

Pray – **For a life that will reflect the God who is yours.**

NOW ALIVE IN HIM

Ephesians 2:1 And you were dead...

I once heard John Gerstner, scholar and theologian, ask the question, *"How dead is dead?"* His accompanying illustration was of a man out in a boat with his girlfriend when they come upon a floating dead corpse. The girl said, "Throw him the life saver." The man responded, "Do you think he will reach for it?" Well, certainly a truly dead corpse does not have any ability to reach for a life saving device. He is dead and only could reach if he were made alive.

So it is with our sin and God's salvation. The Bible is clear that in our sin, we are spiritually dead, fully and completely, unable to reach out or do anything to claim God's life saver—faith in Christ and His work on the cross. God must first love, and give faith and new life in order for dead sinners, such as we are, to claim His gift of salvation by faith. It is only in knowing the extent of our deadness that we can now give God His greatest glory. *Salvation is of the Lord,* not of me! God must save and give a dead sinner all that is necessary to be saved. Are you dead in your sin? Run to God, cry out to God for the faith to believe, repent of your sin, and trust in Jesus. Christian, rejoice in the God of your salvation.

> *...Guilty, vile and helpless we, Spotless Lamb of God was He;*
> *Full atonement! Can it be? Hallelujah what a Savior!* (P.Bliss)

Look it up – **Romans 7:4; Ephesians 2:4-6; Colossians 2:13**

This truth for me – **Think on what it was like being a dead sinner and now what it is like being made alive in Christ. Write down one great thought about being alive in Christ.**

_____

_____

_____

Pray – **For sinners that you know who are dead in their sins to be made alive in Christ.**

TO KNOW HIM IS TO SHARE HIM

Daniel 12:3 *...those who have insight (are wise)... those who lead the many to righteousness...*

What will become of those who are wise and lead many to righteousness? The answer is in this same text in Daniel, *they will shine brightly like the brightness of the expanse of heaven...like the stars forever and ever.* When we enter glory, there will be those who were wise on earth and took evangelism seriously, winning souls to Christ. These soul winners will shine brightly; literally, they will be a *splendor* to behold.

There are two things Daniel mentions that are attached to soul winning: *wisdom* and *leading.* Evangelism is never void of wisdom, and wisdom is never detached from God's word and its dogmas (theology). Evangelism is motivated by a fervent knowledge of God. The higher our view is of God and the more we know Him—not only about Him—the more fervent we should be in soul winning. Knowing God and what He did for us in salvation must produce obedience and thanksgiving, two characteristics that fuel ongoing evangelism. When we are fueled by such a high knowledge of God, we will cry out like Isaiah when he acknowledged his own depravity and then saw God high and lifted up, *...here am I send me.* Be a splendor to behold. Be a soul winner, leading many to righteousness!

*Look it up - **Acts 1:6-8; Philippians 3:12-13; Revelation 17:6***

*This truth for me – **The more we know our God, the more we will want to share Him! How is this true in your life?***

---

*Pray – **For more time to study the word and know more of your God.***

NEEDED PIETY

John 10:14 ...I know my own, and My own know Me.

Philipp Jakob Spener was the founder of the Pietist movement of the 17th and 18th century. Although the radicals of later Pietism held to beliefs that were questionable and even heretical, Spener had good motivations and his writings sought to bring Biblical reform to an apathetic German Lutheran church. Spener observed that there existed in the church, "*...the need to move beyond sterile formulas about God to more intimate experience with God...*" His idea of how this would be accomplished centered on his view that the Bible had to be taken seriously and studied with great vigor.

Today, in American Christianity, we not only have sterility in some corners of the Church, but there is a growing light-hearted approach to the word, its usage in worship and in our homes, in its study, and in application. In my travels, I notice a growing number of churches where people no longer carry their Bibles (or even electronic versions), Scripture reading is non-existent, and the sound of the pages of Scripture being turned during the sermon is absent; attention is turned to a screen. When I was saved, I appreciated the exhortation, "*...turn in your Bibles to....*" Now, when I preach at some churches, I feel like I am making people uncomfortable when I ask them to turn or look to their Bibles because there are none either in their hands or in the pews and chairs. Maybe we need a new Pietist movement that will bring us back to the Bible.

"...hold fast the faithful Word..." Titus 1:9

*Look it up – **Psalm 119:1,2; 1 Thessalonians 2:13; 2 Timothy 3:16***

*This truth for me - **List several ways you can get more from your Bible as you hear a sermon or teaching.***

_____

_____

_____

*Pray – **For a mind and heart that seeks after God's word.***

HIS WORD ABOVE ALL ELSE

Psalm 119:57 ...I have promised to keep Thy words.

Not only is Psalm 119 the longest psalm in the psaltery, it also mentions the need to obey God more than any other psalm. Tied to obedience is the word of God. This is the theme of the psalm. The word of God and obedience go hand in hand. A Christian cannot, or rather, should not (because we often do) walk away from the word without a commitment to obey what the word says. This is the fervor permeating Psalm 119. We must *...keep Thy words... turn my feet to Thy testimonies...keep Thy commandments...not forget Thy law... keep Thy precepts...teach me Thy statutes... (Psalm 119:57-64).*

The psalm is filled with these types of exhortations, but why such repetition? The answer is simple: we are all prone to wander from the word of God. Even though Christians are new creations and taken from darkness into light, we still battle sin every day till that day when we will be with our Lord. Until He comes, we must do as the psalmist begs us to do: obey the word, even when we don't feel like doing so. Psalm 119 tells us: *Thy statutes are my songs...Thy word has revived me...the law of Thy mouth is better than thousands of gold... all Thy commandments are faithful...Thy commandments make me wiser...the unfolding of Thy words gives light...Thy word is very pure...Thy law is truth...Thy law is my delight...*

Look it up - **Hosea 9:17; Joel 2:13; Luke 11:28**

This truth for me – **Write down what the Bible means to you.**

_____

_____

_____

Praise – **God for revealing His heart and mind to us through the word.**

HOW DEEP IS MY LOVE

Matthew 22:37 ...You shall love the Lord your God...

Why should we love God? In his work, <u>On the Love of God</u>, Bernard of Clairvaux, a leader in the 11th and 12th century church known for his holiness of life, writes, *"You ask me, 'Why should God be loved?' I answer: the reason for loving God is God Himself...Simply because no one could be more justly loved than God..."*

God deserves our love by virtue of who He is and what He has accomplished. All of God's perfections and attributes demand our love. His love, long-suffering, mercy, grace and justice are a mere sampling of why we should love God. We should also love God because He loved such undeserving sinners as you and me. While we were yet sinners, the Father lavished His grace on us by sending His perfect Son to die in our place and be our atonement for the sin we could do nothing about. The very thought of Jesus demands the love of the Father's children. The words of Bernard's beautiful hymn call for us to love our God:

> *O hope of every contrite heart, O joy of all the meek;*
> *To those who fall, how kind thou art! How good to those who seek!*
> *(Jesus the Very Thought of Thee)*

Look it up – **John 13:1; 2 Thessalonians 3:5; Titus 3:4,5**

This truth for me – **Do you love God? Think on this, and see if there is anything in your life keeping you from loving God the way you should.**

_____

_____

_____

Pray – That each day your love for God will grow and bear fruit.

TEACHING FOR UNDERSTANDING

Matthew 11:25 ...*Thou didst hide these things from the wise and intelligent and didst reveal them to babes.*

When I began in the ministry, a dear saint came up to me after teaching a lesson and said, *"always make sure you put the cookies on the bottom shelf so the children can reach them."* It became clear to me what she was saying. She was telling me that my lesson was up on the roof where few could be nourished from what I shared.

The wisest teachers I sat under were those who could take the great truths of Scripture and bring them to a clarity that even a new believer could grasp. Sometimes I sit in churches and hear teachers try to be like a few of my old seminary professors who presented their material in such a manner that confused rather than enlightened. The church is not a seminary, but a retreat where even the simplest of Christians should be able to come and hear God's truth presented clearly and with application. The point of teaching is to open up the word so that all God's children may learn, and see and imitate Jesus in their practical living. Whether you are teaching your children, a Sunday School class, or a congregation, remember there are those who need to be able to reach out and grab the cookies of God's truth.

Look it up – **1 Corinthians 3:1-3; 14:19; 2 Timothy 4:2**

This truth for me – **Are you a teacher? We all teach, some of us in a pulpit, others across the dinner table or backyard fence. How can you teach Jesus so He is understood by unbelievers around you?**

_____

_____

_____

Pray – **For the Holy Spirit to give you clarity in your teaching and simple ways to share the great truths of Christ.**

DOING MERCY

2 Corinthians 1:3 ...the Father of mercies...

Mercy is action that helps the helpless. There are people who possess this gift of showing mercy to the helpless. They arrive at the right time and give the right gift to meet a need. Many of us have experienced this type of person. It may have been the friend or family member who came at the right time to comfort us, or arrived just in time with a gift to help meet a need before it was too late. No matter what the occasion, if we experienced someone's mercy in action, we know what being blessed is all about.

The Apostle Paul knew what it was like to experience mercy. He knew the mercy that particular churches showed toward him in meeting his ministry and physical needs. Most of all, he knew the source of all mercy was God, through His Son, Jesus Christ. God is the God of all mercy. He is mercy's author and source. His mercy is most exemplified in the sending of His Son to die for sinners. The cross is where our helpless estate was lifted by the mercy of Christ. Our calling, as ones to whom God showed mercy, is to be agents of mercy to others in helpless situations. God shows His mercy and comforts so *that we may be able to comfort those who are in any affliction...* Let's do mercy!

Look it up – **Psalm 102; Nehemiah 9:31; 1 Peter 1:3**

This truth for me – **Write a thank-you note to God for His mercy and then think of kindness you can show today to someone.**

_____

_____

_____

Praise – **God for His mercy toward you in salvation and every day.**

PRAISE HIM, PRAISE HIM...

Hebrews 13:15 ...*the fruit of lips that give thanks...*

By nature we are people who back off from praising God and offering up thanks to His name. Hidden in man's darkened heart is disgust for God, rather than praise. But when God works in our lives, we gain a heart renewed for praise. Sadly, there are so many times that Christians neglect this wonderful exercise of praise. There is no need to review the reasons we hold back praise, we just do! Therefore, an exhortation like we find here in Hebrews is well taken and needed. J. I. Packer coupled praise with prayer and wrote, *"Prayer and praise are like a bird's two wings: with both working, you soar; with one out of action you are earthbound. But birds should not be earthbound, nor Christians praiseless."* (Growing In Grace)

If you have fallen into the pit of neglected praise, take time right now to thank and praise God for something He did for you in the last several hours. It might be praise for sustaining your life, or assisting you with a need, or a simple thing like getting you home safely from work. Whatever it is, praise Him as the writer of Hebrews encourages, *Let us continually offer up a sacrifice of praise to God...*

*Look it up – **Exodus 15:1,2; Judges 5:1-3; Luke 19:37-38***

*This truth for me – **Did you ever just praise God in your prayers without petitioning Him for something? Write some things you want to praise God for.***

_____

_____

_____

*Pray – **And praise God for what He is doing for you right now.***

THE RIGHT SIDE OUT

Ecclesiastes 12:13 ...fear God and keep His commandments...

When reading the book of Ecclesiastes, one must wonder what the Pundit (teacher) really is trying to say. The essence of this treatise on vanity, meaninglessness, disappointment and futility is caught in what the writing evokes in the reader upon careful thought and self-evaluation. The reading of Ecclesiastes makes one hunger and thirst for the Lord. We must rejoice in the incomprehensible value of our Lord coming to earth and giving us the promise of eternal hope in Him. It is Christ who will take away the futility of the world and bring meaning to life. The Pundit comes to a final summation, *fear God and keep His commandments...!* This is the divine formula for overcoming the vanity and disappointments of life. What looks so bleak to us, God has under control and will weave His plan to its completion, bringing all glory to Jesus Christ.

I once owned a sweater that was woven with a beautiful winter scene on the front of the sweater. However, when the sweater was turned inside out, all I saw was a discord of wool and thread. I could not detect the beautiful wintery panorama. This sweater was a mess on the inside, but beautiful on the outside. This is just what our lives will be when Christ glorifies us. Blessed be His name!

Look it up – ***John 16:33; Philippians 2:9-11; Revelation 5:5***

This truth for me – **List what looks chaotic in your life. How does Christ turn this chaos right-side out?**

_____

_____

_____

Pray – ***For the wisdom and strength to get through chaotic times till He returns.***

NO WHERE TO HIDE

Psalm 22:24 ...when he cried to Him for help, He heard.

A most comforting truth about God is His omnipresence - always there - everywhere! There is no place on earth that God is not aware of or does not occupy. He is everywhere all the time. There is no state of confusion or depression that God is not familiar with or is isolated from. He is in all places all the time. There are no depths or heights where God cannot climb or where His presence is barricaded. God is living in all the earth every moment of every hour.

But one might say, this is optimistic thinking; how can I know God will be there for me when I am lost? How can I be assured He is there when I struggle or face the giants and darkness of the world?

Our assurance is the same about which the psalmist writes: *...O Thou my help, hasten to my assistance...Neither has He hidden His face when he cried to Him for help.* This is the suffering and abused Christ, whom the psalmist is revealing to us. Just as Jesus cried out to the Heavenly Father who hastened to His side, so we cry out to the Father who will hasten to our side. Feeling alone, struggling, confused, depressed? God is there - cry out to Him and He will hasten to your side.

*Look it up – **Psalm 139; Jeremiah 23:23.24; Amos 9:2-3***

*This truth for me – **Have you ever tried to hide from God? List how important it is to know that God is omnipresent.***

_____

_____

_____

*Praise – **God that He is always there for you.***

TO KNOW THAT POWER

1 Corinthians 15:20 ...Christ has been raised from the dead...

There will always be scoffers who deny the validity of the resurrection of Christ. The denials began soon after Christ was risen. The Jews began rumors that He had not risen from the dead, but rather His disciples stole His body. Later someone developed the *swoon theory*, saying that Christ was not really dead in the first place. When He was placed in the coolness of the tomb, He was revived, His followers moved away the stone, and He fled the burial site.

No matter how the world attempts to write off the truth of Christ's resurrection, it will fail. The power that accompanied the resurrection of Christ is still being manifested in the lives of men and women who run to Jesus for salvation. The resurrection is the promise and hope of the believer, not only in freedom from death, but in that it gives the power and a living hope to go on here and now. The Apostle Paul said that his goal in life was to know Christ and the power that raised him from the dead (Philippians 3:10). There is no doubt in the minds of those who are born again regarding the soundness of the doctrine of the resurrection. ***We know for certain He is risen, He is risen indeed!***

Look it up – ***Job 19:25-27; John 14:19; 2 Corinthians 4:14***

This truth for me – ***What does the resurrection mean for you? How will knowing that Christ rose from the dead help you through life?***

_____

_____

_____

Pray – ***For God to help you understand what it means to have resurrection power.***

A TEST THAT MEASURES MERCY

2 Corinthians 8:13 ...*that there might be equality.* (NIV)

How do we react to someone else's need? When we hear of a person in need or when a missionary or church plant has a need, how do we respond as individuals and how does our church respond? The Apostle Paul made known the needs of the Jerusalem church to the churches in Macedonia. These churches responded generously from their own impoverishment. Paul encouraged the church in Corinth to do the same—to give generously even if it meant giving out of their own poverty.

Behind this directive was what the Apostle called a test, *... to test the sincerity of your love...* (vs. 8 NIV). The way to pass this test is to look to the actions of Christ, *... though He was rich, yet for your sakes He became poor, so that you through His poverty might become rich* (vs. 9 NIV).

There is a variety of need in the world and sometimes we are overwhelmed and don't know where and how to help. Prayer and discernment are needed when seeking to help in a godly manner. *Oh, Lord, help us to heed such exhortations that we may show mercy, not some having while others have not!*

*Look it up – **Matthew 5:7; Luke 6:36; Hebrews 13:16***

*This truth for me – **How can you give to a need today, this week, on a regular basis? Write down how you will give to a need.***

_____

_____

_____

*Pray – **For a heart that mirrors Christ's heart to show mercy.***

THE LIVING WORD

Hebrews 4:12 For the word of God is living...

I have never witnessed the Bible lift off a table and hover in the air or levitate around a room, but as the writer of Hebrews states, the Bible is **living!** What I believe is meant by this is that the Bible has a *life-giving* dynamic.

One of the tests the early church applied to its discovery of what books would be accepted as Canon and included in the Bible was: *how did the writing change people's lives—was there a life-giving and changing dynamic to the writing that other writings didn't have?* Anyone who is born again knows for certain that the Bible does have such a dynamic for changing a person's life. The Bible—read, studied, meditated upon and applied—changes our lives. The Bible is called the Word of Life, the Word of Truth, the Living Word, and the Word of God. It is this last description that is the most important. Because it is God's Word, it gives life and truth.

Maybe it's been a while since you spent time in the Bible or maybe you never really developed a disciplined Bible time. Well, the time is now to read, study and meditate on the Bible and trust God to dynamically change you.

Look it up – **Psalm 119:1,2; James 1:19-25; 2 Peter 1:19**

This truth for me – **Write out your definition of the Bible. How does what you think about the Bible line up with the truth of the Bible being God's living word?**

_____

_____

_____

Pray – **For God's help to intentionally set aside more time in the word.**

OUR BUST . . . GOD'S BLESSING

Acts 18:33 So Paul went out of their midst.

We know of no church having been planted by the Apostle Paul in the city of Athens. Even though Paul thoroughly surveyed the city, had an audience with the gatekeepers of the city, spent time diligently *reasoning* with the Jews, and networked in the marketplace *day after day*, he could not plant a church.

This reminds us that not all attempts at planting churches will succeed. Yet, the efforts put into church planting, even when a plant does not result in a church, are not without divine results. In Athens, a church was not planted, but *Dionysius, Damaris and others* were saved. Some may call Athens a failure, but God would label it a success for the sake of those who believed.

We must remember this key lesson: *God's results are not ours.* What we might call a bust, God may call a blessing, even for the sake of one soul saved for the Kingdom. We must still set goals, and be diligent and sincere with our efforts to reach our goals, but when God says, "Move on," we must also know His results were accomplished. Let us pray and work for God's results.

Look it up – **Isaiah 55:8; Hosea 14:9; Romans 11:33**

This truth for me – **Can you think of a time that you seemed to fail at something and later discovered that God had His way in what you thought was a failure? What did you learn?**

_____

_____

_____

Pray – **That the Holy Spirit will help you reach your goals and that you will trust in God's will to be accomplished, no matter what the results.**

JUDGED WITH LOVE

1 Corinthians 4:4 ...the one who examines me is the Lord.

It is a sobering truth to know that God is my judge. Friends, family, associates and employers may make attempts to judge us, but in the final analysis, only God can and will judge us. This has a number of implications:

1. God *thoroughly* examines us. We cannot hide anything from God.

2. God *ultimately* examines us. We are not to be man pleasers but a God pleaser because we are finally responsible to God for everything.

3. God *justly* examines us. We belong to God. We've been bought with the price of His Son's blood, and God has every right to examine us.

4. God *lovingly* examines us. We may not like the idea of God as our judge, but all His evaluations and examinations of us are exercised out of a deep love, with the motivation of making us more like His Son, Jesus.

Judgment is left in the hands of a righteous God so that we may not become arrogant. Let us allow God to be the Judge, knowing He will *bring to light all things that are hidden.*

Look it up – **Romans 14:11-12; 1 Corinthians 4:5; 1 Peter 1:17**

This truth for me – **What will judgment day be like for you? Yes, Christians will be judged, not regarding their salvation, but rather regarding how faithful they lived their lives as unto the Lord.**

_____

_____

_____

Pray – **For God's power to help you live each day as if it was judgment day.**

THE FERTILE GROUND OF FAITH

Mark 1:27 ...so that they debated among themselves...

Debating an issue is good, but it can be overdone when the truth is staring you right in the face. In the case of Jesus exorcising the unclean spirit here in Mark 1, it is obvious that Christ was who He claimed to be—God in the flesh. Yet, the crowd at the synagogue *debated* among themselves who this Jesus was. In the end, all their debating ended in their missing the truth about Christ and nailing Him to a cross.

The foundation of Christianity is faith. Sinners find salvation centered in faith and Christians live and die by faith. Too much debate about Christ can lead to speculation and to the missing of His essential message of the Kingdom, *I am the way, the truth, and the life...* Debate must always lead to the truth. When the truth is ascertained, it must be accepted. But when faith must be applied to our feeble reasoning, it also must be accepted. Our faith is objective and not centered in subjective emotionalism, but rather in the truth of the Bible. One of my former Bible teachers would say, "When the Bible is silent, you be silent also." This silence is the fertile ground of faith.

Look it up – ***1 Corinthians 1:20; Hebrews 11:1-3; 1 John 5:4***

This truth for me – ***Do you have a question about Christ that you cannot seem to find an answer? Is this an area you need to stop and trust the Lord with? Write your thoughts.***

_____

_____

_____

Pray – ***For God to give you peace about those things that are incomprehensible.***

THE FREEDOM OF GOD

Psalm 135:6 *The Lord does whatever pleases him...* (NIV)

If we were to hear someone say, *"I'll do as I please,"* we would think that such a statement was sheer arrogance. Chaos would reign if everyone did as they pleased—disregarding laws, acting out indecently anywhere at anytime and shunning all societal mores.

Yet the psalmist states that God does whatever He pleases. What is the difference between God doing what He wants to do and mankind doing what they want to do? The difference is in the character of God versus the character of men. The psalmist declared earlier in the psalm that *God is good*. Therein lies the difference. God is good, perfectly good. Man is sinful, thoroughly sinful. God does whatever He pleases because whatever He pleases to do is righteous and just. Regarding man, maybe we should say it this way: "I'll do whatever pleases God." We can never go wrong doing things God's way. God's freedom to do as He pleases is a blessing in that His doings are always a blessing for those He calls His children. May you do what pleases God today and praise Him for doing what pleases Him.

*Look it up – **Psalm 104:34; Ephesians 5:10; 1 Thessalonians 4:1***

*This truth for me – **List what you think pleases God in your life and what is displeasing.***

_____

_____

_____

*Pray – **For the Holy Spirit to empower you to do what pleases God.***

THE CHURCH, THE BRIDE

Acts 2:4 And they were all filled with the Holy Spirit...

There are various opinions regarding the origins of the Church and its relationship to the nation of Israel. The day of Pentecost is regarded by many as the time when the Church began. There are good biblical reasons for holding such a view. First, it was Jesus who said during His earthly ministry that the building of the Church would be a future enterprise (Matthew 16:18). Second, the foundation of the Church—Christ's death, burial, resurrection and ascension—had to be in place in order for the Church to be birthed. Thirdly, the coming of the promised Holy Spirit was necessary in order for the Church to begin and develop. Lastly, the Apostolic ministry had to be established and the preaching of the Gospel recognized as the means for calling the elect.

In Jerusalem, more than 2,000 years ago, these elements were in place and the Church began its mission to reach the world with the gospel of Christ, a mission centered in evangelism and church planting. *Pray for God to blow His Spirit through today's Church in order to see people saved and churches established, and pray that you will be part of building the Kingdom.*

*Look it up – **Matthew 16:18; Acts 2:1-4; Revelation 21:9***

*This truth for me - **The Church is God's precious Bride. Write a sentence or two about how you feel being Christ's Bride.***

_____

_____

_____

*Pray – **For the Lord to return to take His Church home to be with Him.***

GOD GIVES HIMSELF

2 Corinthians 12:9 ...*My grace is sufficient*...

Christians trust God for eternal life but many times are inclined to doubt God's sufficiency when it comes to the needs and struggles they encounter in this world. If God can handle bringing us home to glory, He certainly can give us the perseverance needed when we face the circumstances of life. His grace is an *abounding grace*. It is a grace that keeps filling our cup so that we never run dry of His attention and help. Through our life experiences God gives the grace necessary to meet each obstacle in our path. His grace is an *adjustable grace*. God's assistance meets each and every circumstance we face. God's grace is never at a loss for what to do in any situation. His grace is an *affirming grace*. God affirms that at my weakest and most uneasy moments, His grace is not only available but also fully sufficient. Yet, how do we define this sufficient special grace? Karl Barth phrased it in this manner, *"...in grace God essentially gives Himself."*

Think on this for a moment, God gives Himself. What a thought . . . the Almighty God giving all of Himself for me. As children of God we can rest in knowing that God gives Himself to us whenever we call upon Him for mercy and help.

Look it up – **John 1:16; 2 Corinthians 9:8; Romans 5:20**

This truth for me – **How has God's grace abounded to you? List some times and ways you experienced God's grace and favor.**

_____

_____

_____

Praise – **God for His abounding grace to you.**

THE GOD WHO IS DIFFERENT

Hosea 11:9 ...For I am God and not man...

We should rejoice in the truth that *God is not man*. If God were man there would be no hope, no security, no comfort, no rest and no salvation. The difference between the Creator and His creation is infinite. This is of great comfort to know that my salvation and hope rests in God, who is over and above all His creation and separated from the sin of mankind and the world.

Yet, it is this same transcendent God who elected to become a man, the God-Man, Jesus Christ. He lived among us and became like us for the purpose of completing His mission of atonement at the cross. As Hosea goes on to say, *"...the Holy One in your midst..."*

Even now God, *the Holy One*, is in our midst in the person of the Holy Spirit's indwelling presence and the person of Jesus Christ who promised never to leave us. We may not see God with us, but He is, and what is even more amazing is that we love Him having not seen Him nor heard His voice. God longs for His people to walk with Him and know Him, not only as their friend, but even more as their God, high and lifted up. *May we see God this day and every day - high and lifted up!*

Look it up – **2 Chronicles 32:8; Isaiah 43:2; 2 Timothy 4:17**

This truth for me – **How can you always know that God is with you? What are ways to be reminded of His presence with you?**

_____

_____

_____

Pray – **Thanking God for giving Himself to you and being perfectly different.**

NOT SEEING IS BELIEVING

1 Peter 1:8 ...though you have not seen Him, you love Him...

Charles Spurgeon comments, *"Love feeds from love."* Christian, are you amazed at the fact that God loves you? God's love for us is a *perplexing* and *grand* statement. Why does God love us? Is there something that lies within us that causes such a love? Did and does God see an attractive attribute we possess that would cause Him to send His Son to die for us in order to demonstrate the extent of His love? Is there, deep within us, a kindness, generosity or magnetizing merit that draws God's love to us?

No, God's omni-seeing divine examination of us only reveals a heart and nature of sin, wrath and death. There is nothing in us that God could admire or love. This is why His love is so *perplexing* - that He loves wretches like us. His love is *grand* in that it is solely centered in His own purpose, will and grace. His love purposely elected us to be conformed to the image of His Son. His love wills that we be His and brought home to glory and be with Him forever. His love is abounding with the grace of the Lord Jesus Christ and thus we are fully accepted as children of God. We love Him! Yes, we, who are wretches, love Him because He first loved us and now we feed daily off His love. Oh, how great a love that saved a wretch like me - to God be the glory!

Look it – **John 13:1; 1 Peter 1:8; 1 John 4:17-21**

This truth for me – **How did you come to love God? Write out your definition of your love for God.**

Pray – **For your love for God to be seen by those around you.**

DIGGING DEEP

Psalm 139:23 Search me, O God...

A person may be able to hide things from others, but nothing in our lives can be hidden from God! We hear about our politicians, executives and pastors who hide things in their lives, only to have God expose them in due time. There may be things that we can hide for a lifetime, but in the end they are revealed before the judgment seat of God. To ask God to search our hearts is a significant step toward repentance and holiness, and a scary one.

The Psalmist asks God to search three areas of his life. First, he asks God to search his *heart*. We should want God to dig deeply into our lives and surface any sinful attitude, anger or habit that we have covered over, and then we need to deal with such sin. Second, he asks God to search his *anxious thoughts*. Isn't it the mind—our thoughts—that turn into actions? If there are things in our minds that are sinful, it won't be long before they are manifested, unless they are confronted. Third, he asks God to *see if there be any hurtful way in me*. Hurtful ways that we harbor inside may have as their focus other people or even ourselves.

The result of such a God-investigation into our lives should result in confronting our sin, dealing with it through repentance and forgiveness, and finally, trusting God to lead us in the right ways, sensing His cleansing.

Look it up – **1 Chronicles 28:9; Jeremiah 17:10; Romans 8:27**

This truth for me – **Only you and God know what lies in your heart. Is there anything that needs to be confessed and dealt with before the Lord?**

_____

_____

_____

Pray – **For your heart to be kept clean and holy.**

DISTRUST FOR GOD

1 Samuel 15:22 ...to obey is better than sacrifice...

Too often we think that the good things we do will overcome the areas of our lives where we disobey God. Saul thought that what he did in defeating the Amalekites and capturing their king was pleasing to God. But God had commanded that all the Amalekites, including their king along with all their livestock, be destroyed. Instead Saul kept the king alive and took the best of the livestock for himself and his people. Saul's actions were a blatant disregard of the Lord's commands; he was disobedient.

Disobeying God is, in reality, a lack of trust in God. When God gives us a command or task to fulfill, He wants it done His way because His way is perfect. Over and over we face these types of challenges. Will I trust God with what He wants me to do and submit myself to His direction? Will I trust Him to be about what He desires, or will I do what I want to do? Will I think that my way will be better than God's way? Saul faced the ramifications of his disobedience. God rejected Saul from being the king and he eventually faced a violent death. When we disobey God, there are negative results. Our ways are not better than God's ways, and the more we learn this hard lesson, the more we will reap the blessings of the Lord.

Look it up – ***Psalm 18:30; Hosea 14:9; Hebrews 3:10***

This truth for me – ***List some of the times you thought it better to go your way than God's way. What happened or did not happen?***

_____

_____

_____

Pray – ***That the Lord will give you more trust in the ways of the Lord.***

A WIDE OPEN MOUTH

Isaiah 40:6 A voice says, "Call out...

The proclamation of the Gospel is the broadcasting of God's good news . . . maybe we should say God's *best* news. In <u>The All-Sufficient God</u>, D. Martyn Lloyd-Jones says it this way, *"The Gospel is wonderful good news and we must always start by realizing that. If whatever represents itself as gospel is not good news, then it is not the true Gospel."* But why is the Gospel good news, and why should it be cried out to the world?

The prophet gives the answers to these questions in the previous verse from Isaiah 40:5, *...the glory of the Lord will be revealed...* In Isaiah's day this prophecy meant that God would reveal His glory to the world through the promised Messiah. Today we know God's divine glory was revealed in the God-Man, Jesus Christ. The gospel message is the revelation of the glory of God—Jesus Christ—therefore the Gospel is the power of God unto salvation. No wonder Isaiah says in verse 9, *...get up on a high mountain...lift up your voice mightily...*

Today God calls to His Church and says, **Call Out!** With loud and fearless proclamation, the church must cry out and proclaim the gospel of power to every tongue, tribe and nation, beginning with our families, friends and neighborhoods.

*Look it up – **Matthew 4:23; Luke 8:39; Ephesians 6:20***

*This truth for me – **Are you a closed mouth with the Gospel or a proclaimer of the good news? Describe how you can be a proclaimer.***

_____

_____

_____

*Pray – **That the Holy Spirit will give you ample opportunities to proclaim.***

THE IMPOSSIBLE MADE POSSIBLE

Luke 1:37 ...*nothing will be impossible with God.*

Too many times we give up on God, thinking God cannot or will not do what we desire Him to do in our lives or the lives of others. We live in an age where we want things to be instantaneous, and when we don't see results overnight we tend to give up. Even Christians fall prey to this get-it-quick mentality.

The angel said to Mary that God can do anything and that nothing is impossible with God, even making an old woman give birth to a child, as was the case with Elizabeth. Do we really believe that nothing is impossible with God? If so, then we must realize several truths that surround such a statement. Nothing is impossible with God when it lines up with the Word! God accomplished all things that are according to His Word and His will. Nothing is impossible with God and the impossible is accomplished in God's timing! How far is God's timing from ours? It is infinitely far away, yet when He provides, it is perfect. Nothing is impossible with God when it is bathed in prayer! Finally, nothing is impossible with God when our desires and requests are under-girded with faith! Is your concern for a marriage that needs to be reconciled, a family member who needs to be saved, or someone who needs healing? Remember, *nothing will be impossible with God!*

Look it up – **Job 42:2; Jeremiah 32:17; Matthew 19:26**

This truth for me – **Is there something you think is impossible for God to accomplish? List it, pray about it, and trust!**

_____

_____

_____

Pray – **For God to work the impossible in your life today.**

THE SHEEP OF HIS PASTURE

John 10:14 ...My own know Me.

There are sheep and there are non-sheep. Only two categories of people exist in the world. Modern man separates the world into many parts. Culture, race, color, profession and possessions all give certain distinctions to people. But God only has two distinctions: those who are His sheep and those who are not. The sheep—Christians saved by grace—know God. Many people will say they know God but in reality only know *of* Him. The sheep know God intimately. Sheep hear Him, obey Him, follow Him, trust Him, and know they are His possession.

It is not enough to say, *"Sure I know God,"* and then to go about your life as if God doesn't exist. Sheep are one with God and possess this oneness because the Shepherd, Jesus Christ, laid down His life for the sheep and the sheep never forget this sacrifice. Sheep are bought with the precious blood of the Good Shepherd. Are you part of the flock, a sheep, called by the Good Shepherd, Jesus Christ? If so, then you know Him and were called to obey Him, follow Him and trust Him.

*Look it up – **Psalm 23:1; Matthew 9:6; John 10:1-6***

*This truth for me – **Write down what it means, figuratively speaking, to be God's sheep in His pasture.***

---

*Pray – **That you will see all that it means to be a sheep in His pasture.***

THE BELIEVER'S JUDGMENT

Romans 14:12 ...*each one of us shall give an account...*

Have you ever thought about what it will be like to stand before the judgment seat of God? Some Christians think about this too much and begin to question their salvation, thinking God will take from them what Christ gave freely - their salvation. No, that is not what judgment means to the Christian. The salvation God gave us in Christ is secure in Christ. Other Christians think the judgment seat will be a mere slap on the wrist and then they will merrily walk away into blissful eternity. This idea of judgment is also false.

According to Paul's letter to Rome, the judgment seat is where Christians will give an account of how well they lived for Christ. The criteria for judgment could possibly be based on our love for one another, faithfulness to Christ's example and obedience to God's Word. We cannot be certain what the results of God's judgment for His children will be. The believer's judgment won't condemn us and it won't treat our sins lightly, but it will be just. Are you ready for the judgment seat? If not, repent and seek the Lord's forgiveness now!

*Look it up – **Romans 8:1; 1 Corinthians 3:13-15; 4:5***

*This truth for me – **Think on how prepared you are to face the Lord. What do you need to work on before judgment comes to you?***

_____

_____

_____

*Pray – **That you will be prepared to meet the Lord and stand before Him.***

ON THE EDGE FOR GOD

Philippians 2:30 ...risking his life...

A good Christian would never say they gamble. Yet, serving the Lord is risky and the results are never a given. In this letter to the Philippians, the Apostle Paul encourages the Philippians to receive the church planter Epaphroditus. This man left his comfortable culture and entered into the Lord's service. Paul reports that he served to the point of death.

In the original language of the New Testament, the word *risking* is a word that can refer to gambling. No, we don't like to think of ourselves as gamblers, and properly so, because no matter what the risk we take, God already has His ends ordained. Yet, when we serve the Lord, there is that element of risky business attached to our ventures, not knowing what God will have as His result. The question for us today is this—*as a child of God, are we willing to take a risk for God in order to be the means of reaching His results?* Yes, risky and a big step of faith, but isn't that what the Christian life is all about, walking by faith? Pray and ask God what risk He wants you to take for His glory.

Look it up – Psalm 27:12-13; Ecclesiastes 11:1-4; James 2:26

This truth for me – How well do you take risks for God? Write down one area where you may want to take a risk for the Lord and see Him work.

_____

_____

_____

Pray – That the Lord will give you the courage to serve Him and step out for Him even in uncomfortable situations.

IN SPITE OF THE WAY I FEEL

1 John 4:21 ...*this commandment we have from Him...*

Sometimes when we are told to do something, the resulting action lacks motivation from the heart. We may do what we are told, but we may not be happy about it. In other words, we do what is right because we are told to do it, rather than feeling like doing what is right on our own.

In John's short epistle, he tells us that God commands us to love our brothers and sisters. Do we really need to be told to love our brothers and sisters? Shouldn't love simply ooze from our inner beings? Evidently not! There are times when we need reminders from God—in the form of a commandment—to do what is right. Being obedient to God, even when we don't feel like being obedient, is the best course to travel. Normally the heart catches up with our obedience, and obedience becomes a godly virtue in our lives. If God is commanding us to do something today and we may not feel like responding, do it anyway and trust God to bring His satisfaction to your heart and mind.

Look it up – **Judges 17:6; Psalm 125:3-5; 2 Thessalonians 3:13**

This truth for me – **What keeps you from doing what is right to do? Describe your hurdle.**

_____

_____

_____

Pray – **For the right attitude to do the right things.**

HE IS ABLE

Genesis 1:1 *In the beginning God...*

It all begins here—*in the beginning God.* When it comes to understanding all the trials and circumstances of life that come against us, we must begin with the understanding of God the Creator, the Sustainer, the Sovereign of His universe, and all that happens therein. Martyn Lloyd-Jones wrote, *"So as you get on your knees to pray, and as you think of your problems, and the difficulty of understanding...and as you are on the point of doubting God...realize that you are going to express an opinion about the eternal, almighty, everlasting Being who said, 'Let there be light,' and there was light..."*

Isn't this the core of so many of our worries and problems? We are so quick to think and speak without considering the greatness, power and majesty of God. We must remember that when we need God, He is there and He is able to do above and beyond what we can hope or imagine. We must look to God's transcendent majesty and not be caught up in the earthly way God is portrayed so much in today's world. God is high and mighty, Creator of all things. Look to the mountains, the clouds and the oceans, for they will tell you He is able. But mostly look to His Son, Jesus Christ, who is *the express image of God, the Word made flesh.* He will tell you, *in the beginning God!*

*Look it up – **Daniel 3:17; 2 Corinthians 9:8; Hebrews 7:25***

*This truth for me – **When in your life has God proven Himself to be able to help you and meet your need?***

_____

_____

_____

*Pray – **For God to give you a sense of His ability to do the impossible.***

WE BOW TO BE RASIED UP

Isaiah 66:23 ...All mankind will come to bow down before Me...

At various times in the Bible we are reminded how high and lifted up is our God and the low position we must assume as His creation. Yes, a Christian is a new creation in Christ; we are lifted up on the Rock and seated in the heavens, but we must never forget from where we were lifted and Who lifted us. God is great, majestic, glorious and the monarch over all His universe, and we are mere creatures saved by grace. This is why it is important to have a good understanding of God's sovereignty and our humanity. For in knowing God's sovereign grace and our sinful condition, we are forced to bow low and lift God to His highest. Only the doctrine of grace bends us low enough to see God high and lifted up.

It is difficult for man in this day and age to bow to anything. Our pride and self-acclaim keeps us prisoners in a false sense of self-worth, not realizing that it is in bowing to God that we find real worth and value. Our worth is centered in our relationship with Jesus Christ and nothing of this world can rob us of our position in Christ. We bow to the Lord who in turn raises us up to glory.

*Look it up – **2 Kings 17:36; Psalm 138:2; Revelation 1:17***

*This truth for me – **Is there something in your life that is keeping you from bowing to the Lord . . . a sin, some form of pride? List it and think on how you can bring your life to bow before God so He can lift you up.***

---

*Pray – **For humility so that the Lord can give you the right sense of self-worth.***

FROM THE SMALLEST TO THE BIGGEST

Acts 12:23 ...*he did not give God the glory*...

For King Herod, the consequence of failing to give God the glory and claiming glory for himself resulted in being eaten to death by worms. What an end to life! We do not hear of people being eaten by worms for failing to give God His due, but nevertheless there are many times we fail to give God the glory for the grace we receive. Whether thanking God for the forgiveness we have received, the opportunities we are afforded, and blessings of all sorts that are ours, God is to be thanked.

We have three great reminders to give God the glory He deserves. First is the incarnation. Jesus came to earth willingly to confine Himself in humanity. Because of the incarnation, our Savior is our perfect sacrifice for our sin. The second reminder is the cross of Jesus Christ. Looking at the cross reminds us that God gave His all so that we might have all we will ever need—salvation from our sins. The last reminder is the empty tomb. God raised Christ from the dead and he will also deliver us from death.

If you have neglected giving God glory for everything in your life, today is a good time to begin to thank and praise God for everything, from the smallest of things to the biggest, and from the best to the worst. Give God the glory!

Look it up – **Psalm 66:16,17; Psalm 107:8; Psalm 150:6**

This truth for me – **List the things you believe are great about God.**

_____

_____

_____

Praise – **God for who He is, what He has done, and what He will do.**

OUR TEACHERS

Hebrews 13:7 Remember those who led you...

There was a time when I was part of a group writing new curriculum for a course at a Bible College. As we discussed the objectives and goals for the course, I thought back to those in my life who taught me the Word of God while attending Bible college, seminary and particularly the local church that God led me to when I was a new Christian. The exhortation in Hebrews not only says *remember* such individuals who taught you but also *imitate their faith*. I was not only privileged to have good teachers, but teachers whose lives matched their teaching and convictions. Gifted teachers are sent from God to assist us in our trek to glory.

Teachers are special gifts to the church, and they assist us with our becoming conformed to the image of Christ. The best teachers are those that exalt the Lord and humbly take their task as a gift from God. Think back today on those who have influenced you and taught you the Word in precept and in life. In this remembrance you will again find a blessing and the challenge to go and share the Lord and your life with others who need a spiritual guide for the long road home to glory.

*Look it up – **Job 36:22; Luke 6:40; John 13:14***

*This truth for me – **List the teachers God put into your life to help conform you to the image of Christ. Pray and thank God for them today.***

_____

_____

_____

*Pray – **For the teachers of God's word that you know.***

THE ROOF OF GODLINESS

Job 29:4 ...When the friendship of God was over my tent.

What guides the affairs of our homes? Do the values of our culture counsel our homes? Does the popular approach to things—everyone is doing it—guide our homes? In the case of Job, it was the counsel of God that guided his home and the affairs of the lives that lived in his home. The result in Job's case was happiness. Job's home was a righteous home filled with love for God and appreciation for all that God had given him. Even when Job lost all his possessions and his sons and daughters, he would not curse God, but rather in the end, repented of any wrong he had done while in his suffering, and God restored him.

The world is standing ready at every turn to provide godless counsel to our marriages, our children, the way we handle our possessions and especially the way we think about God. The wisest and most profitable counsel we can ever find is the counsel of God from His Word and from His godly people. Pray and ask for the counsel of God to come over your tent and those who live in that tent, and be happy in the Lord.

Look it up – ***Hosea 14:9; Romans 15:14; 2 Peter 1:3***

This truth for me – ***How would you describe your home? What is hanging over your house: godliness or something else?***

_____

_____

_____

Pray – ***For your home and that all the people in it would be godly.***

THE IMPOSSIBLE MADE POSSIBLE

Mark 10:27 ...With men it is impossible...

What is Mark saying is impossible for men to accomplish? The previous verse gives us the answer, *then who can be saved?* It is impossible for any man or woman to do anything to merit or gain their salvation from eternal damnation and separation from God. Only God can save. The kings and prophets of the Old Testament over and over declared that salvation is of the Lord, not man. Jonah stated, *salvation is of the Lord.* Micah and Habakkuk found assurance in *the God of my salvation.* Isaiah exhorted, *behold, God is my salvation.* King David found comfort in knowing *salvation belongs to the Lord.*

The Scriptures leave no doubt that salvation is totally and finally the work of a loving and gracious God. Man cannot cooperate nor do anything that will facilitate the Lord's saving of His people. All of salvation from predestination to glorification is a work of our God and we should say, *"Yes, PRAISE THE LORD it does not depend on me but rather on HIM!"* For the Christian, this brings great comfort and demands great response. We are to repay the Lord with our thanksgiving, service and obedience. For the unsaved, it also brings great responsibility. If you are unsaved, cry out to the Father today and repent of your sin. Believe upon the Lord Jesus Christ, asking God to save you and be set free and secure in the love of Christ.

Look it up – **Job 42:2; Jeremiah 32:17; Luke 18:27**

This truth for me – **What do think is impossible at this time in your life and why do you think it is impossible?**

_____

_____

_____

Pray – **For it to be God's will to change the impossible to the possible.**

THE END OF EVIL

Psalm 5:4 ...*Thou art not a God who takes pleasure in wickedness...*

By looking at the tragic events of the world around us, people may reason, *If there is a God, then He must be a God who doesn't care too much about the wickedness that pervades our world or He would do something about the evil.* Based upon the psalmist's statement that God takes no pleasure in evil and then goes on to say, *no evil dwells in God,* we must conclude that the wickedness and evil of the world affects God more than it affects us. In us, the presence and attack of evil is a constant battle, but not so for God. God has defeated evil and wickedness, and the evidence of this defeat is the death and resurrection of Christ. God overcame the Devil, the source of all evil, with Christ's victory at Calvary and His resurrection from the dead.

It may seem that God has taken a blind eye to the world's evil, but be assured that God will have His say. In the final judgment of the devil, his demons, the evil people and nations of the world, and all who stand against His truth and His Son, Jesus Christ, God will bring all evil to the great and final judgment seat of the King of Kings, Jesus Christ. Are you ready for judgment? First, be found in Christ - be born again. Next, be found living for Jesus in truth and holiness. Then His appearing will be a blessed one.

*Look it up – **Psalm 26:5; Hebrews 2:14; James 1:13***

*This truth for me – **Have you ever thought that God was evil or the author of evil? What can keep you from thinking such things?***

---

*Pray – **For God to give you the assurance that He will deal with all evil.***

WHAT SHOULD WE REALLY SEE

John 4:35 ...open your eyes... (NIV)

Do we really understand what it means for a person to be lost and going to eternal damnation? Jesus had to state it plainly, *open your eyes!* Our eyes tend to grow scales when it comes to the devastating position people are in when they are not born again.

Toward the end of a class I once taught on the end times, we focused on the great white throne of judgment where the devil, his demons and all the unsaved throughout the ages will be judged and thrown into the eternal lake of fire. It was a solemn class and one that woke most of us up to the fact that we do not have our eyes open to the fields white for harvest. When we see, really see, the unsaved in their dire need, we will have compassion, and that compassion must then translate to evangelistic action. Many studies have determined that people are open to talking about Christ and the Gospel, but unfortunately not many Christians are wide-eyed and ready to act on this openness. Literally, it is the spiritual harvest time all around us.

*Look it up – **Genesis 3:5; Isaiah 42:20; Ephesians 1:18***

*This truth for me – **How do you see the unsaved around you? What will be their eternal destiny? Write your thoughts.***

_____

_____

_____

*Pray – **For God to grant us open eyes and mouths to witness and see the salvation of His people!***

BLESSING UPON BLESSING

Ezekiel 34:11 ...I Myself will search for My sheep and seek them out.

In Ezekiel's words lie the crux of God's mercy and grace. The holy Sovereign of the universe is willing to bend low to seek out His children and save them.

This is in many ways incomprehensible. First, there is no warrant for Him to do this, other than His own love and mercy toward those He set apart to save. Second, there is nothing in any human being that would behoove a just and holy God to come after them, seek them out, and shower them with blessings so undeserved. Third, God's justice demands payment for our sinful condition. He does not look to us to make that payment for sin, but rather He sent His only Son to die and shed His blood for the payment of the sins of His children, and we are called to believe. And finally, God does not only save, He says, *...I will be their God.* He will be our God, and *cause showers to come down in their season; they will be showers of blessings. Praise God from whom all blessings flow!* The thought of God showering us with His mercy and love is enough to have us give Him all praise, glory and honor, but He goes beyond this and gives us blessing upon blessing.

*Look it up – **Psalm 65:10; Malachi 3:10; Zechariah 10:1***

*This truth for me – **Define God's mercy and then describe a blessing God is giving you right now.***

_____

_____

_____

*Praise – **God that He came and sought you out and blesses you day by day.***

THE NAME ABOVE ALL NAMES

Matthew 1:21 ...and you shall call His name Jesus...

What is in a name? In the case of the son that was born to the Virgin Mary, everything is in His name. The name Jesus is the Greek form of the name Joshua which means *will save*. Many were given the name Jesus at the time Christ was born. Jewish parents liked naming their sons Joshua after the courageous leader of Israel in the Old Testament.

However, from the birth of Jesus Christ the name Jesus no longer was associated with Joshua but rather with God. Christ took what was a common name and made it a universal magnificent name. To the helpless, the name means mercy and healing. To the hopeless, the name means to rise up and be counted. To the voiceless, it means that they now have a thunderous tongue fighting for them. To the devil, it means the end. To the Christian, it means the Father's love. The name Jesus also means either hope or destruction. To the child of God, it means eternal peace and life. To the one who rejects this name, it means eternal destruction. Whatever the name means to mankind, to God it means His only begotten Son in whom He is well pleased.

Look it up – **Acts 4:12; Philippians 2:10; Revelation 22:16**

This truth for me – **Write down what the name of Jesus means to you.**

_____

_____

_____

Pray – **That you will have a deeper reverence for the name and person of Jesus.**

MAN, GOD, JESUS

John 1:14 And the Word became flesh...

The virgin birth is incomprehensible, and what follows from the virgin birth is even more incomprehensible: God and man in one person. Is this some sort of fanciful and mystical theological construct? Is there purpose and design in God deciding to come to earth and remain one person yet possessing two natures, human and divine?

The coming of the divine Christ to take on humanity had one ultimate purpose and it is the key to the central theme of redemption. Christ is the God-Man who atones for our sins and satisfies the Father's wrath. What does this mean for us? It means that we can know that we have a solid and firm foundation in our salvation. Christ came as God to die and satisfy God's wrath and displeasure with us as sinners. Therefore, we are now accepted by the Father as His children because God satisfied God. Second, because Jesus came as a man, He is our perfect substitute and sympathizes with our weaknesses. He perfectly stands in our place and is one with us.

Let me suggest a response to this devotional. Take these thoughts and share them with an unbeliever. Share how Christ came to take away God's judgment and the fact that He can do so because He is God. And share with them that because He is perfect man, He can stand with them and forgive their sins. All glory to the God-Man, Jesus Christ!

Look it up – Isaiah 9:6; Luke 9:20; 1 Timothy 2:5

This truth for me – Write down what comfort and joy there is for you to be saved by Jesus, the God-Man.

_____

_____

_____

Pray – For God to bless you with overwhelming joy at the thought of Jesus, the God-Man.

THE TINY TRUTH OF BETHLEHEM

Micah 5:2 ...*Too little to be among the clans of Judah...*

Here again, in the words of the Prophet Micah, is the Lord's choice of foolish things to confound the world. Rome would have been a good choice for King Jesus, or any ancient capital would have been better than Bethlehem, but God chose to send His Son to the insignificant town of Bethlehem. Micah declares that from this little town there will come forth the *ruler of Israel*. This ruler's existence and essence will be from *eternity* and He will go forth to *shepherd His flock.*

Veiled as this may seem, the New Testament makes it very clear of whom Micah is speaking: the God-Man, Jesus Christ. Micah prophesied this joyous occasion hundreds of years before the fact of Jesus' birth in the unimportant town of Bethlehem. He is the Eternal One sent to rule God's covenant people, Israel, and He is the Shepherd of the church. Christmas is the time we remember the glorious things of God, but also a time to remember the inconsequential things that God set in place to reveal His glory. From tiny Bethlehem, and a tiny manger, came forth the King of Kings and Lord of Lords.

> *O little town of Bethlehem, How still we see thee lie!*
> *Above your deep and dreamless sleep, The silent stars go by.*
> *Yet in thy dark streets shineth The everlasting Light,*
> *The hopes and fears of all the years, Are met in thee tonight.*

Look it up – **Isaiah 7:14; Matthew 3:3; Galatians 4:4**

This truth for me – **What was it that you thought to be insignificant but then it proved to be wonderful? List how Christmas blesses you.**

_____

_____

_____

Pray - **Praise the Father for His gift of the Son and the reminder of the ways God blesses us through simple means.**

THEY LEFT REJOICING

Luke 2:20 ...the shepherds went back, glorifying and praising God...

It is hard to imagine what was filling the hearts and minds of these shepherds. They were visited by angels and told to go see a baby in a manger who is God in the flesh, their long awaited Messiah. Having seen the baby and his mother and father, they left the scene. They were not disappointed but rather returned to their homes rejoicing and giving God the glory for the evening.

How did this first Christmas affect these shepherds the rest of their lives? We will never know here on earth, but when we get to heaven, let's be sure to look them up and ask what that night was like, if we can. The shepherds certainly could have been disappointed. They went to see a king's birth, but instead saw a baby wrapped in cloths and lying with the other animals. Instead of being disappointed, they were thrilled.

How will you walk away from this Christmas? Will you go right back into all your routines and right back into taking Christmas and its meaning for granted? The shepherds teach us that we are to leave Christmas praising and glorifying God. And we are to keep such praise and honor for the Lord as an ongoing celebration throughout the year or until we are called home to see the real star of Christmas standing with us face to face.

Look it up – 1 Samuel 2:1; Psalm 68:3; Isaiah 25:9

*This truth for me – **What can you do to rejoice and praise God for the gift of Christmas throughout the year?***

_____

_____

_____

*Pray – **For the light of Christmas to shine in your hearts all year long.***

LEAVING ON A GREAT NOTE

2 Corinthians 13:14 ...be with you all.

Does your church have a benediction at the end of the service? For some modern Christian movements, the benediction has been lost and replaced by a song, a quick prayer or a thank you for coming out. The Bible has a number of what Chuck Swindoll calls, "inspired expressions of praise." What better way to leave the preached Word of God than to be blessed with a scriptural reminder of God's presence accompanying us as we embark back into the world.

The Apostle Paul's blessing to the Corinthians is powerful. *The grace of the Lord Jesus Christ* begins the blessing. In reality this is all we need to tackle life and the dark world around us. The grace of Christ is sufficient for all of life. *The love of God* is affirmation of our security in our relationship with God. In Ephesians we are told that God *lavished His love* on us. When we leave church, we leave under the banner of love. *The fellowship of the Holy Spirit* reminds us that we are indwelt by God and we have the Spirit of power to overcome and be comforted. This week, listen for the benediction at the end of the service and respond in your heart with a big AMEN - *let it be!*

*Look it up – **Numbers 6:24-26; Romans 15:5; Hebrews 13:20,21***

*This truth for me – **Write out your own benediction for when you leave your daily time of worship with the Lord.***

_____

_____

_____

*Pray – **That God will bless your worship of Him and that you leave with a blessing from Him.***

KINGDOM COME

Ecclesiastes 1:3 ...under the sun?

This is not a common phrase in the Bible, but more common to the pagan literature at the time of the Old Testament. The meaning of the statement alludes to viewing life from the perspective of the world—what one can see from a finite perspective. Assume for a moment that this is all there is, the world and the finite things we can see and touch. What a gloomy picture to imagine. Even with all of the world's beautiful nature and impressive monuments, it is still the world—a decaying and increasingly immoral environment. With this limited view, one will never find purpose, peace or permanence.

Only with another world view—a view of eternity and God's heaven—does living this life make sense and have meaning. We live to know our God, worship Him, and bring others in this world to a saving knowledge of Christ and join in our worship. We look, with a living hope, to the time of His return when all things will be consummated in Christ and this world will be done away with, when the child of God enters his eternal fellowship of rest and peace with the Lord. Now, this is something to look forward to!

> *Turn your eyes upon Jesus, look full in His wonderful face*
> *And the things of earth will grow strangely dim*
> *In the light of His glory and grace!*
> *(H. Lemmel)*

Look it up – Matthew 24:14; 1 Peter 4:7; Revelation 15:1

This truth for me – How far reaching is your view of life? What can you do this week to have a Kingdom view of life?

_____

_____

_____

Pray – For a view of what the eternal Kingdom of God will be like.

WHEN THINGS LOOK BAD

Psalm 73:28 ...I have made the Sovereign Lord my refuge... (NIV)

Asaph, the writer of this psalm, was filled with envy and deep despair over what he saw as injustice and unfairness. He says he was at the edge of the cliff of despair. He was just about to give up on believing God was fair and just because of how the wicked prosper and live comfortably in their abundance compared to the distress of the poor and burdens of others.

Today it is easy to take up the cry of Asaph. We see all around us what seems to be unfair conditions, and many have turned from believing God is fair and just, even giving up on God and looking to humanistic means for equity and justice. Asaph comes to his senses at the end of the psalm and says, *it was oppressive to me till I entered the sanctuary of God; then I understood their final destiny.* Asaph altered his focus. Instead of looking at the sin and injustice filling the people around him, he turned his attention to God and a specific perfection of God—God's sovereignty. *I have made the Sovereign Lord my refuge.* It is in knowing that our God is sovereign, over all things and the end to all things, that we find reality and justice. When Asaph entered into communion with God and was refreshed in his understanding of God's sovereign justice, he could say, *then I understood their final destiny.*

*Look it up – **Leviticus 19:15; Deuteronomy 32:4; Proverbs 2:8***

*This truth for me - **Does God seem unfair to you today? Remember the end has not been revealed. When all is settled, our Sovereign God will bring final justice and peace. Trust in the Lord!***

_____

_____

_____

*Pray – **That the Lord will allow you to understand His just and righteous character even when these perfections are confusing.***

A REAL CAUSE FOR REJOICING

Acts 11:23 ...witnessed the grace of God...

Dr. Luke's description of people being saved in the city of Antioch is precise and glorious. He describes the salvation of these people as being a complete sovereign work of God. Barnabas, who was sent by the church in Jerusalem to verify what was happening in Antioch, witnessed the grace *of God*. There was no question concerning what had happened among the people who heard the gospel preached by the scattered Christians coming into the city.

These sinners were completely and totally saved by God. Luke's description also includes a focus on the glory of God, *witnessed the grace*. Barnabas did not rejoice in the results of a program or that finally these pagans had come to their senses and logically or rationally decided to be born again. They came to Christ by grace alone. Dead sinners, of which we all were, must always be saved by grace alone through faith alone, and both must be given by unconditional and unmerited grace from the Lord. Have you witnessed the grace of God recently? Begin today to witness to the lost in your frame of reference, and may God allow you to witness His grace in saving sinners.

*Look it up – **Psalm 35:9; Romans 6:14; Ephesians 2:8,9***

*This truth for me – **What is your reaction when you hear of a sinner being saved? Who do you know that recently was saved? Rejoice and praise God today for His grace that saved them.***

_____

_____

_____

*Pray – **For God to give you a time of rejoicing in someone's salvation.***

BE JOYFUL IN PRAYER

Philippians 1:4-5 *Always offering prayer with joy...*

Praying in joy is a wonderful experience. There are numerous things that should fuel our joy in prayer. Hearing of the salvation of a sinner brings great joy and praise to God when we pray for that new believer. When God heals a person from illness or provides for a person in need, we have great joy in our prayers.

Here in Paul's letter to the church in Philippi, the Apostle says that the object of his joy in prayer is knowing that the church is participating with him in the gospel. The joy expressed here is first and foremost directed toward God, for His great provision of salvation along with the security there is in being saved by God. Second, Paul is joyful in prayer for the effect of salvation upon the Philippians. The church is a partaker, along with Paul, of God's grace—a grace that abounds over and over to God's people and is sufficient for all things. Lastly, Paul is joyful in prayer because of the church's participation in his ministry of evangelism and church planting.

Be joyful in prayer this new year. Be joyful in God's granting of salvation to you and in the salvation of others. Be joyful in prayer for the opportunities you have to participate with others in the spreading of the gospel and the building of His Kingdom. **May the New Year be joyful!**

Look it up – **Psalm 67:1-4; Luke 11:9, 10; John 16:24**

This truth for me – **As this year ends, write out the three major things you can rejoice in and praise God for in this past year. Then write out three things you earnestly desire God to accomplish in your life in the New Year.**

_____

_____

_____

Praise God – **For His goodness this past year and for a blessed New Year.**

Printed in the United States
By Bookmasters